Strategic Learning Package for

Psychology

STRATEGIC LEARNING PACKAGE FOR

CARLSON, BUSKIST, ENZLE, AND HETH

Psychology

THE SCIENCE OF BEHAVIOUR

Second Canadian Edition

MARY CARLSON

NEIL R. CARLSON
University of Massachusetts, Amherst

JUDY CALDWELL
Camosun College

JANET E. REAGAN
Camosun College

DAVID E. REAGAN
Camosun College

ZOE HAYES
St. Francis Xavier University

Toronto

Copyright © 2002 Pearson Education Canada Inc., Toronto, Ontario

All rights reserved. This publication is protected by copyright,
and permission should be obtained from the publisher prior to any
prohibited reproduction, storage in a retrieval system, or transmission
in any form or by any means, electronic, mechanical, photocopying,
recording or likewise. For information regarding permission, write
to the Permissions Department.

Original edition published by Allyn & Bacon, Inc., a division of
Pearson Education, Needham Heights, MA. Copyright © 1997 by
Allyn & Bacon, Inc. This edition is authorized for sale in Canada only.

ISBN 0-205-34399-6

Acquisitions Editor: Jessica Mosher
Developmental Editor: Laura Paterson Forbes
Production Editor: Sherry Torchinsky
Production Coordinator: Wendy Moran

5 6 7   05 04 03

Printed and bound in Canada.

Table of Contents

1. The Science of Psychology 1

2. The Ways and Means of Psychology 12

3. Evolution, Heredity, and Behaviour 25

4. Biology of Behaviour 40

5. Learning and Behaviour 59

6. Sensation 78

7. Perception 97

8. Memory 111

9. Consciousness 129

10. Language 146

11. Intelligence and Thinking 164

12. Life-Span Development 181

13. Motivation and Emotion 204

14. Personality 225

15. Social Psychology 242

16. Life-Style, Stress, and Health 265

17. The Nature and Causes of Mental Disorders 284

18. The Treatment of Mental Disorders 306

To the Reader

Introductions are rarely read, so consider yourself one of the exceptional few. So as not to abuse your patience, we will keep this one short. Some of you have just started your university career and have had little or no experience with university courses. Others have had much more experience and have settled on a routine of studying that seems to work well. But before you start work on your psychology course this semester, we would like to make a few suggestions—to both groups. Studying is a behaviour that most of us just "happen" into. We begin sometime in elementary school. Year by year, more and more is expected of us, and we learn to work harder and harder. Along the way we pick up a set of study habits, but few of us ever stop to reflect about what we do. And almost none of us will try experiments, studying one way for one test and another way for another and seeing which produces the best results. So although you may be firmly committed to your approach to studying, at least consider the possibility that there may be some ways to improve it.

Your instructor will, of course, give you the assignments. He or she will ask you to read chapters from the book and will probably give lectures, which may or may not follow the outline of the book. The quizzes and exams will probably be based partly on the lectures and partly on the readings; of course, you will want to learn the relative weights given to these two sources of information as soon as you can.

We would like to offer the following advice about taking lecture notes. Don't simply be a stenographer. That is, try to understand what the instructor says and think about what you are writing. A serious mistake is to realize that you don't understand what he or she is saying and tell yourself that you will write it all down. and then figure it out later. Too often, "later" comes the night before an exam, and you find, to your chagrin, that you cannot understand your notes. If you do not understand what your instructor says, ask for clarification, either during or after the lecture (depending on the size of the class and your instructor's preferences). If you are able to ask questions in class, do not be afraid of looking stupid. Unless you really are the densest student in the class (and the fact that you are reading this proves that

you are not), you will have company in your puzzlement. Your more timid fellow-students will be relieved that you asked the question, and your instructor will know that a topic is causing difficulty and needs further explanation.

We have a second suggestion, which really works. As soon as you can (preferably, immediately after class, if you have the time), go over your notes. Read them again while your instructor's words are fresh in your mind, and elaborate on them. If you wrote down a few cryptic phrases, flesh them out with complete sentences. If your instructor gave examples of some concepts, add some more of your own. The advantages of taking the time to go over your notes this way are enormous. Now, you will have a really good set of notes, which you can review when you study for an exam. In addition, just going over them and elaborating on them will put much of that information into your long-term memory. When you study your notes for the exam you will find that you already know most of what you have written in your notebook, and you will find the task much less of a chore.

Now, what about the textbook? This study guide has several functions. For one thing, it guides you through the text and makes sure that you don't miss anything important. Even better, it makes you put things in your own words, which is extremely important for long-term retention. Just as you should not simply be a stenographer, passing the instructor's words from your ears to your pen without anything happening along the way, you should not simply read a question, find the answer in the book, and then copy it. The point in answering a question is putting the information in your own words.

Here is what we think is the best approach. Our advice is based on a combination of the results of psychological research and our own experience. Read the chapter as if you were reading an interesting story. (Actually, we hope that you will find it to be just that.) Don't worry about all the details now. Then, work with the study guide, preferably, a day or two later. In Chapter 1, you will see that the first thing you find, after the title of the chapter, is a heading, "Lesson I." Each chapter is divided into two lessons, and we recommend that you take a break between them to reward your own efforts. Talk to a friend, have a snack (if that won't violate your diet), or do something else that you enjoy: You might even want to work on the two lessons on different days. The second thing you will see is the following statement: "Read the interim summary on pages 7-8 to re-acquaint yourself with the material in this section." Each chapter of the text has several interim summaries that do just what their name implies—sum up what has been said in that section. Having read the chapter a day or two earlier, you will find the interim summary helpful in reminding you about what that section discusses. So, read the interim summary.

Each lesson is divided into learning objectives, which are enclosed in a box. After each learning objective is presented, you will be asked to read a few pages from the book and then answer the questions. Read these pages, and then start answering the questions. As much as you can, answer them from memory. If you find that you don't remember enough details to answer a question, read the book, then prepare your answer and write it. Do not simply copy an answer from the text into your study guide. Put the answer in your own words. If you have to copy the information, you do not know it yet. If you cannot remember the information long enough to look away from the book, phrase it in your own words, and then write it down, you certainly will not remember the information long enough to do well on an exam. Often, students think of a study guide as a good place to put useful items of information that they can study later on the eve of an examination. That is true, of course. But a much more important use of the study guide is having to put the information into you own words; once you do so, it is yours forever. (Well, some of it, anyway.)

At the end of each lesson you will find a self test, which presents ten multiple-choice questions, the answers to which are found at the end of the chapter. So obviously, the next step is to take the self test. These questions will help you see how well you are doing, and will give you a bit of practice for the exams—if they contain multiple-choice questions, that is. If they contain essay questions, the answers you have given to the questions in the study guide will have given you plenty of practice. If you get some questions on the self test

wrong, go back and find out why. The number of the relevant learning objective is indicated along with the answer, and this information will make it easy for you to find the information in the study guide or in the text.

At the end of the study guide you will find a set of *concept cards*. In the text, important terms are indicated in boldface type and are defined in a box at the bottom of the page. The concept cards list the terms on one side and the definitions on the other. To use them, cut them apart, put them in order, and divide them into piles for the two lessons. You can work with the cards at any time, of course, but you will probably get the most out of them if you review them before you begin work on a lesson in the study guide. Practice saying the definitions. You may find that rehearsing them is more productive and enjoyable if you work with a friend. Whether you work alone or with someone else, start by going through the cards in the order in which they appear in the text. Look at the term and give its definition. If you are working alone, still say your responses aloud—even if you just whisper them.

Compare your response with the definition printed on the back of the card. If the wording of your response is different, be sure that your words mean the same as the definition on the card. If your response is correct, put the card in a separate pile and go on to the next one. If it is not, put that card on the bottom of the pile you are working on. Repeat this process until you can go through the deck for that lesson without making any serious errors.

We wish you the best of luck this semester. We think that you will find that psychology is an interesting topic. There is a lot to learn, and what you do learn will serve you well—in other courses, and in the world outside of the classroom. Some of you are taking this course to see whether you would like to pursue a career in psychology, and we hope that the course will help you make an informed decision.

CHAPTER 1

The Science of Psychology

LESSON I

Read the interim summary on page 9 of your text to re-acquaint yourself with the material in this section.

1-1 Describe the goal of psychological research, the different types of psychologists, and the problems they study.

Read pages 4-9 and answer the following questions.

1. a. State the ultimate goal of psychological research and the first two steps of this search.

   b. Explain what causal events are and why they are important to the study of behaviour.

   c. Describe the three major types of causal events that psychologists study.

2. What types of causal events (physiological, mental, and environmental) are depicted in the following examples?

   a. _____ Professor Lukins administered a test of anxiety to a group of subjects and compared the behaviour in a mock interview situation of those who received high and low scores.

   b. _____ Professor Chen explained that differences in child rearing practices accounted for the 10-point difference in the average IQ scores of infants raised in the two orphanages.

   c. _____ Marcia, a graduate student, was able to predict how much food a rat would eat by analyzing certain nutrients in the animal's blood just before it started its meal.

3. Briefly outline some of the problems caused by human behaviour that psychologists are working to solve.

4. Name and explain the two ways that research psychologists differ from one another.

5. Briefly describe the work of the following groups of psychologists, paying special attention to the typical subjects and research questions each group studies.

   a. Physiological psychologists

b. Psychophysiologists

c. Comparative psychologists

d. Behaviour analysts

e. Behaviour geneticists

f. Cognitive psychologists

g. Experimental neuropsychologists

h. Developmental psychologists

i. Social psychologists

j. Personality psychologists

k. Cross-cultural psychologists

l. Clinical psychologists

6. Most clinical psychologists provide a service. Describe what they do.

7. Complete each sentence to describe a group of psychologists.

_____ study behavioural phenomena in nonhuman subjects.

_____ usually study childhood development but sometimes study adolescents and adults.

_____ attempt to help people solve their problems.

_____ study the effects of environment on behaviour.

_____ are interested in the general principles of learning, perception, motivation, and memory and usually study human behaviour.

_____ look at a person's heredity, environment, and past behaviour in order to explain personality differences.

8. Briefly describe the work of these applied psychologists paying special attention to where they find employment.

a. Clinical neuropsychologists

b. Health psychologists

c. School psychologists

d. Consumer psychologists

e. Community psychologists

f. Organizational psychologists

g. Engineering psychologists

9. Which group of applied psychologists is likely to work on the following projects or problems?

_____ help develop programs to reduce the number of high-school dropouts

_____ assist in the design of vehicle control panels to improve safety

_____ develop strategies to help older people to live independently as long as possible

_____ advise businesses on how best to motivate their employees to improve productivity

Read the interim summary on page 14 of your text to re-acquaint yourself with the material in this section.

1-2 Outline the philosophical roots of psychology.

Read pages 9-12 and answer the following questions.

1. a. Explain why animism made intuitive sense to our ancestors.

b. Try to think of an animistic explanation for the fact that flowers wilt after they are picked.

c. Now think of an example to illustrate the fact that subjective explanations of natural phenomena have not disappeared with the rise of science.

2. The _____ _____ is the best means to ensure objectivity in trying to understand natural phenomena.

3. a. Briefly summarize Descartes's approach to understanding the world, and explain how it challenged traditional religious doctrine.

b. How, according to Descartes, were humans and animals similar and different?

c. How did Descartes explain automatic responses, which he named *reflexes*? (Study Figure 1.1 in your text.)

d. Dualism divided all _____ into either _____ or _____ .

e. How did Descartes identify and distinguish between "extended things" and "thinking things"?

f. What interaction was he the first to propose and what was its importance?

g. What early experience guided Descartes as he thought about the human body?

h. When Descartes thought about the body in terms of a relatively simple mechanical system, he was using a
_____ .

4. Explain the concepts of rationalism and empiricism, paying special attention to how they differ.

5. a. According to Locke, what was the source of knowledge?

b. How did Locke's belief about the acquisition of knowledge differ from that of Berkeley?

6. a. Explain the concept of materialism proposed by James Mill.

b. How did Mill explain the behaviour of humans and animals?

c. In what ways did he agree and disagree with Descartes?

7. Identify the philosophy represented by the following explanation of behaviour.

_____ He picked up the stick because his mind tilted the pineal body and forced fluid into the muscles in his shoulder and arm.

_____ The woman was acting crazy because the storm spirit had entered her body.

_____ The man saw that the woman was approaching him because the image of her on the back of his eyes was getting bigger.

_____ An explanation of the man's behaviour can be found through reflection and reason.

1-3 Describe the biological roots of psychology.

Read pages 12-14 and answer the following questions.

1. What did Galvani, in an early instance of scientific research on physiology, discover about Descartes's model?

2. Müller advocated what method in studying physiology?

3. a. One of Müller's most important contribution to science was the doctrine of _____ _____ _____.

   b. By what means does the brain distinguish between sources of information from the environment?

   c. What is the implication of this fact for specialization of brain function?

4. Explain how Pierre Flourens tested the implications of Müller's doctrine of specific nerve energies.

   a. After Flourens removed specific parts of an animal's nervous system, what general results did he observe?

   b. What did he conclude from his observations?

   c. Name this experimental method.

5. a. Describe the observations and conclusions of Paul Broca, who applied the logic of Flourens's method to the study of humans with brain damage.

   b. What research technique did Broca use that still remains an important means of studying the human brain?

6. Describe the procedure of electrical brain stimulation used by Fritsch and Hitzig. (See Figure 1.2 in your text.)

7. a. What belief of Müller did Hermann von Helmholtz reject?

   b. What did the successful measurement of the speed of the nerve impulse by Helmholtz suggest to later scientists?

   c. Why did Helmholtz abandon his attempt to measure the speed of a person's reaction to a physical stimulus?

   d. How did his failed attempt contribute to the emergence of the science of psychology?

8. a. What observation did Weber make about the ability of people to distinguish between perceptual stimuli?

   b. What field of study later developed?

9. Review the historical progress of the study of the human mind presented in the interim summary by completing this chart. Identify Comte's three stages and indicate the dominant explanations of the human intellectual development during each stage.

Comte's Stages   Explanations of Intellectual Development

1.   1.

2.   2.

3.   3.

LESSON I SELF TEST

1. In general, psychologists try to explain behaviour by studying its
   a. causes.
   b. consequences.
   c. implications.
   d. meaning.

2. Experimental neuropsychologists frequently study
   a. insightful behaviour.
   b. physiological reactions such as heart rate.
   c. the role of genetics in behaviour.
   d. the behaviour of people with brain damage.

3. The best means we have for ensuring scientific objectivity is
   a. the mathematical model.
   b. the scientific method.
   c. historical precedent.
   d. logic.

4. Descartes reasoned that
   a. all reality could be divided into good and evil.
   b. the body's master gland was the pituitary.
   c. the mind and body interacted.
   d. to understand the mind one had to understand God's will.

5. Empiricism is the belief that knowledge comes through
   a. the study of consciousness.
   b. introspection and self-report.
   c. contemplation.
   d. observation and experience.

6. Materialism is the belief that reality
   a. can be interpreted as responses to perceptual stimuli.
   b. is revealed through an understanding of the physical world of which the mind is a part.
   c. is the harmonious interaction between mind, body, and environment.
   d. is an individual experience arising from consciousness.

7. Johannes Müller is most closely associated with
   a. the doctrine of specific nerve energies.
   b. the doctrine of verification through replication.
   c. introspection.
   d. materialism.

8. Pierre Flourens developed the method of experimental ablation
   a. to stimulate the cerebral cortex.

b. to test the doctrine of specific nerve energies.

c. and began the field of psychophysics.

d. to study the functions of different parts of the brain.

9. Fritsch and Hitzig discovered that the body appeared to be "mapped" on the surface of the brain. They used

a. the psychophysical method.

b. the doctrine of specific nerve energies.

c. the method of electrical brain stimulation.

d. the method of experimental ablation.

10. Helmholtz abandoned his attempt to measure the speed of a person's reaction to physical stimuli because

a. there was too much individual variability.

b. ethical considerations were posed by the testing procedure.

c. the Church objected to the study of the human mind.

d. self-reports proved more reliable.

LESSON II

Read the interim summary on page 21 of your text to re-acquaint yourself with the material in this section.

1-4 Discuss the major trends in the early development of psychology: structuralism, functionalism, and the influence of Freud.

Read pages 14-17 and answer the following questions.

1. Psychology began in _____ (country) in the late _____ century, with the work of _____ _____ , who was the first to call himself a psychologist. His book _____ of _____ _____ was the first psychology text.

2. List three reasons that encouraged intellectual development in Germany, paying special attention to the influence of the scientific method.

   1.

   2.

   3.

3. a. Wundt called his approach to the study of psychology _____.

   b. Briefly explain this approach. Be sure to use the term *introspection* in your answer.

   c. List two reasons why structuralism was replaced.

   1.   2.

   d. Although structuralism was abandoned, Wundt made other important contributions to psychology. List two.

   1.   2.

4. a. Functionalism developed in the United States largely as a protest against what method?

   b. Briefly explain functionalism, paying special attention to the influence of Darwin and the principle of natural selection and the evolution of behaviours.

5. a. Name the psychologist who was the most important advocate of functionalism.

   b. What were his major contributions to psychology?

   c. Summarize the three basic principles of functionalism.

     1.

     2.

     3.

6. Describe some of the similarities and differences in the approaches of Freud and Wundt.

7. a. What created the first psychological laboratory in the British Dominion?

   b. What was the laboratory designed to study experimentally?

8. What new emphasis in psychology was being reflected in the classroom?

9. What question vexed Decartes and was returned to by James and Baldwin at the beginning of the twentieth century?

1-5 Outline the development of behaviourism, Gestalt psychology, and humanistic psychology.

Read pages 17-19 and answer the following questions.

1. Briefly explain behaviourism, paying special attention to the importance of observable behaviours and mental events.

2. a. What did Thorndike observe about animal behaviour?

   b. Name the principle he discovered and define it.

   c. What modern names are applied to the two phenomena that the principle describes?

   d. Explain how Thorndike's principle is similar to the process of natural selection.

3. Describe the discovery that Ivan Pavlov made while he was working with hungry dogs.

4. Explain the significance of the work of Thorndike and Pavlov to psychology.

   a. Thorndike

   b. Pavlov

5. Summarize John B. Watson's view of psychology, paying special attention to the role of

   a. observable behaviour.

   b. mental events.

6. Name the influential modern advocate of behaviourism who followed Watson.

7. List three practical applications based on the behaviourist approach.

   1.

   2.

   3.

8. a. Why did some psychologists react against the behaviourism of Watson?

   b. What enduring contribution to psychology did Watson make?

9. a. How did Gestalt psychologists, led by Wertheimer and his colleagues, approach the study of cognitive processes and profoundly influence the development of modern psychology?

   b. What eventually happened to the school of Gestalt psychology?

10. a. Name the father of humanistic psychology.

    b. This approach to the study of human behaviour developed as a reaction against which two schools of thought. Why?

    c. What aspects of human nature do humanistic psychologists emphasize?

    d. Why has this approach failed to influence the development of psychology as a science?

    e. What influence has humanistic psychology had?

1-6 Describe the newer trends in psychology: the cognitive revolution and the biological revolution.

Read pages 19-21 and answer the following questions.

1. a. Describe how cognitive psychologists use the information-processing approach to study mental events.

   b. Among cognitive psychologists, what is the prevalent model of the human brain?

   c. What newer model is beginning to replace it?

2. Explain how behaviour based on mental images can be measured by describing research by Kosslyn (1973, 1975).

   a. What did he first ask subjects to do? (See Figure 1.3 in your text.)

   b. When he later questioned subjects about these drawings what did he observe?

   c. What do the results suggest about objective research on private mental events?

3. a. Why did the early behaviourists reject theories about the way the brain functioned?

   b. Together with cognitive psychologists, how did they influence the study of the biology of behaviour?

   c. What developments have led to the biological revolution?

4. a. Hebb was inspired by which approach to psychology?

   b. He believed behavioural and mental phenomena could be directly related to _____?

LESSON II SELF TEST

1. Germany was the birthplace of psychology in part because
   a. German tradition emphasized the humanities over the sciences.
   b. German scientists believed the mind could be studied scientifically.
   c. national rivalry encouraged them to compete with scientists in other countries.

   d. German scientists were exceptionally well trained in philosophical approaches to the study of the mind.

2. Wundt's structuralism
   a. used the methods of experimental ablation and electrical stimulation developed a few years earlier.

b. asserted that the proper subject matter of psychology was behaviour, not the mind.

c. was inspired by Darwin's functionalism.

d. died out when the emphasis of psychological research turned toward a study of behaviour.

3. William James
   a. was a brilliant research scientist.
   b. formulated an influential and enduring theory of emotion.
   c. pioneered the field of behaviourism.
   d. based his theories on observations of patients.

4. Thorndike is most closely associated with the
   a. concept of variable errors.
   b. first journal of psychology.
   c. law of effect.
   d. concept of multiple experiments.

5. Pavlov's research on digestion demonstrated
   a. the utility of electric shock as a stimulus.
   b. that animals can learn to respond to a previously neutral stimulus.
   c. that hunger is a more powerful drive than thirst.
   d. that digestion begins in the mouth when the food is mixed with saliva.

6. Behaviourists differed from functionalists in their belief that
   a. all mental events are available through introspection.
   b. behaviour can be shaped more successfully through punishment than through reinforcement.
   c. evolution affected only the body, not behaviours.

d. mental events were beyond the scope of psychology.

7. Washburn suggested that introspection
   a. be regarded as not useful.
   b. does not help us understand the process of mental life.
   c. could be useful in certain situations.
   d. be regarded as a form of behaviour.

8. Humanistic psychology stresses
   a. the powerful influence of the unconscious on human behaviour.
   b. the positive sides of human nature and potential for growth.
   c. the co-dependence of man and nature.
   d. the validity of self-report.

9. Modern cognitive psychologists have demonstrated that
   a. behaviour that is based upon mental images can be objectively measured.
   b. the experience of imagery can be shared.
   c. the ability to recognize images cannot be studied objectively.
   d. dualism is the most useful approach to the mind-body problem.

10. The biological revolution
   a. resulted from the behaviourists' insistence on the value of biology in explaining behaviour.
   b. follows in the tradition of structuralism.
   c. began with extraordinary advances in neurobiology.
   d. has left the implications of neurological advances to the social sciences.

Answers for Self Tests

Lesson I

| 1. a | Obj. 1–1 | 2. d | Obj. 1–1 | 3. b | Obj. 1–2 | 4. c | Obj. 1–2 | 5. d | Obj. 1–2 |
| 6. b | Obj. 1–2 | 7. a | Obj. 1–3 | 8. d | Obj. 1–3 | 9. c | Obj. 1–3 | 10. a | Obj. 1–3 |

Lesson II

| 1. b | Obj. 1–4 | 2. d | Obj. 1–4 | 3. b | Obj. 1–4 | 4. c | Obj. 1–5 | 5. b | Obj. 1–5 |
| 6. d | Obj. 1–5 | 7. d | Obj. 1–5 | 8. b | Obj. 1–5 | 9. a | Obj. 1–6 | 10. c | Obj. 1–6 |

CHAPTER 2

The Ways and Means of Psychology

LESSON I

Read the interim summary on page 41 of your text to re-acquaint yourself with the material in this section.

2-1 Identify the three major types of scientific research, explain the five principal steps of the scientific method, and explain hypotheses and theories.

Read pages 26-30 and answer the following questions.

1. Why is the scientific method the predominant method of scientific investigation?

2. Restate the goal of psychological research.

3. a. List and briefly describe the three types of studies that scientists perform.

   1.   3.

   2.

   b. Circle the type that will accurately identify cause- and- effect relationships.

4. List the five major steps of the scientific method.

   1.

   2.

   3.

   4.

   5.

5. Explain the importance of replication.

6. a. What is a hypothesis?

b.   Where do hypotheses come from?

7. a.   What is a theory?

    b.   Compare theories and hypotheses.

    c.   List two ways theories are useful to scientists.

        1.   2.

    d.   Explain why not all theories suggest testable hypotheses.

8. Briefly explain the role of naturalistic observations in scientific method.

2-2 Discuss the principles of good experimental design.

Read pages 30-32 and answer the following questions.

1. What is a variable?

2. Explain the difference between an

    a.   experimental group and a control group. (See new Figure 2.2 in your text.)

    b.   independent variable and a dependent variable.(See Figure 2.3 in your text.)

3. Why are variables stated in general terms rather than specific ones?

4. a.   What is the nominal fallacy, and why is it an error?

    b.   Give your own example of a nominal fallacy.

2-3 Discuss the importance of operational definitions, explain the meaning of validity, and discuss the control of independent variables.

Read pages 32-34 and answer the following questions.

1. a.   What is an operational definition? (See Figure 2.4 in your text.)

b. Why is it important to operationally define the dependent and independent variables?

c. Your town has decided to support a project to encourage voluntary recycling of plastic and will evaluate the success of the project in six months. Write an operational definition of "success."

d. Is your operational definition of success the only one that could have been devised? What does this answer say about the importance of making such a definition explicit and communicating it to others?

2. a. Explain the concept of validity and its importance to research.

b. How is the validity of an operational definition increased by repeated experimentation?

3. a. State the general purpose of an experiment, using the terms dependent and independent variable.

b. Define the word *confound*, as it applies to experimental design.

c. Explain the expression *confounding of variables*.

4. If the independent variables of an experiment are confounded, what will the effects be on the interpretation of the results?

5. Briefly describe the experimental procedure used by the zoology department's guest speaker.

a. In what order did the speaker show the cardboard models to the restrained birds? (See Figure 2.5 in your text.)

b. What were the results?

c. What potential problem did the speaker fail to anticipate and why did this flaw make the study useless?

d. Study Figure 2.6 in your text and explain what he should have done and why he should have done it.

e. What is the name of the procedure he should have followed?

6. Examine the experimental procedure used in the hypothetical study of the effects of an oil extracted from a tropical bean on aggression to explain how the confounding of variables can occur. Begin by identifying the

a. hypothesis.

b. experimental group of subjects.

c. control group of subjects.

d. presumed independent variable.

e. dependent variable.

f. operational definition of aggression.

g. experimental procedure.

h. results.

i. presumed conclusion.

7. Carefully explain why the results do not support the hypothesis.

8. a. Now identify all the variables that did not remain constant throughout testing.

b. What modifications should the experimenter have made to prevent the confounding of variables?

2-4 Explain the meaning of reliability, describe the selection of subjects for an experiment, and discuss the problem of subject expectations and controls for this.

Read pages 34-38 and answer the following questions.

1. a. Explain the concept of reliability and its importance to research.

b. If an operational definition is reliable, can we then assume it is also valid? Explain.

2. a. Why is it more difficult to make reliable measurements of children's friendly behaviour than their reading speed? Be sure to use the terms *objective* and *subjective* in your answer.

b. Explain the concept of interrater reliability and the importance of high interrater reliability to an experiment.

c. What steps may be taken to correct low interrater reliability?

3. Describe several methods for the random assignment of subjects to the various groups participating in an experiment and explain why it is important to do so.

4. Study Figure 2.6 in your text and explain what the consequences will be if some subjects become angry and leave.

5. a. What was the explanation for the short-lived increase in productivity at the Hawthorne Plant of the Western Electric Plant?

   b. What is the name of this effect?

   c. Describe three ways in which a subject's knowledge of participating in an experiment can influence their behaviour.
      1.
      2.
      3.

6. In the hypothetical experiment testing the effects of a stimulant drug on fine manual dexterity, one group of subjects is given amphetamine and a second group of subjects is given nothing, and then all subjects are tested for dexterity.

   a. What is the problem with this experimental procedure?

   b. How can the procedure be improved to overcome this problem? Be sure to use the term *placebo* in your answer.

   c. What is the name of this procedure?

7. a. In the hypothetical experiment studying the effects of a drug on the communicative behaviour of patients with mental disorders, how might the ratings of researchers be affected by their knowing which patients received the drug?

   b. How can the procedure be improved to overcome this problem?

   c. What is the name of this procedure?

8. In the hypothetical experiment studying the effects of a particular kind of psychotherapy on therapist-patient communication, why should the ratings be done by someone other than the person who performs the psychotherapy?

9. To demonstrate the importance of following procedures to prevent the confounding of subject variables, describe the experimental procedure and how it contributed to the confounding of subject variables and what safeguards could have been used in the following studies.

a. the hypothetical experiment to test the effects of a drug on task learning

b. the hypothetical experiment to test the effect of a drug on mental patients' willingness to engage in conversation

2-5 Describe correlational studies, and how this relates to the issue of generality.

Read pages 38-40 and answer the following questions.

1. a. Under what conditions is a correlational study the most appropriate type of research?

b. In your own words, state the basic principle underlying correlational studies.

c. If we observe a correlation between two variables that we are studying, can we conclude that a cause-and-effect relationship exists between them? Use the example shown in Figure 2.8 in your text in your answer.

2. a. Describe the matching procedure.

b. Explain its rationale.

c. List several weaknesses of the matching procedure even when it is carefully followed.

3. Explain what it means to generalize experimental results and why it is important to be able to do so. Be sure to use the term *sample* in your answer.

4. Match the following situations with the name of the appropriate concept.

_____ "Attractive people are more likely to have their requests fulfilled."

_____ "Attractiveness is defined by ratings of photographs made by a group of university students."

_____ number of people who agree to give the person money for the parking meter

_____ The researcher thought that the definition of *attractiveness* was an appropriate one.

_____ Unfortunately, all of the attractive people in the experiment were under the age of twenty, and all of the unattractive people were over the age of forty-five.

_____ the mean rating received by a person's photograph

_____ Based on the results obtained from the study, the researcher concluded that an attractive person would have a better chance of getting other people to comply with a request.

a. dependent variable

b. hypothesis

c. generalization

d. validity

e. independent variable

f. operational definition

g. confounding of variables

LESSON I SELF TEST

1. A theory
   a. is the starting point of any study.
   b. is a way of organizing related hypotheses.
   c. can always be tested following the scientific method.
   d. is the culmination of a lifetime of research.

2. The addition of a control group
   a. permits a contrast between manipulating the independent variable and no treatment.
   b. increases the validity of the operational definition.
   c. works best with human subjects.
   d. assures a random sample of subjects.

3. The independent variable is
   a. manipulated by the experimenter.
   b. measured by the experimenter.
   c. manipulated by the subject.
   d. found only in observational studies.

4. An operational definition
   a. applies only to the independent variable.
   b. may be modified during the experiment.
   c. emerges from the results of the experiment.
   d. must remain constant throughout the experiment.

5. The Zoology Department's guest speaker should have counterbalanced his experiment. That is, he should have presented the models of predators
   a. at the same speed to all birds.
   b. in different orders to different birds.
   c. in the same order to all birds.
   d. only once to each bird.

6. If a researcher assigns subjects randomly to the various groups used in an experiment,
   a. retrospective studies will be impossible.
   b. confounding of subject variables is less likely.
   c. confounding of independent variables is less likely.
   d. a control group will be unnecessary.

7. A single-blind study means that
   a. subject expectations will not affect the results.
   b. researcher expectations will not affect the results.
   c. only one independent variable will be manipulated.
   d. drugs will be used.

8. In a correlational study
   a. only the independent variable is manipulated.
   b. only the dependent variable is manipulated.
   c. no variables can be manipulated.

d. there are no dependent or independent variables.

9. Researchers turn to correlational studies when
    a. large groups of subjects are involved.
    b. they are certain that subjects can remember accurately what happened to them earlier.
    c. variables of interest cannot be altered by the researchers.
    d. communication may be a problem.

10. Generalization involves
    a. matching our experimental and control groups so they are generally the same.
    b. carefully selecting our samples.
    c. using a correlational study
    d. applying our specific results to the population as a whole.

L E S S O N   I I

Read the interim summary on page 45 of your text to re-acquaint yourself with the material in this section.

2-6 Discuss ethical issues involved in psychological research and describe the guidelines to promote the humane and ethical treatment of living subjects.

Read pages 42-44 and answer the following questions.

1. Before research using human subjects is conducted in a psychology department in Canada that receives federal research funds, what review takes place?

2. Give two historical examples of unethical experiments conducted with human subjects.

3. List the seven widely accepted values that most people follow in their everyday lives.

4. List the seven principles for research ethics that are derived from interpersonal values.

5. a. Why is it sometimes necessary to deceive subjects about the purpose of the research?

    b. If deception is necessary, what two conditions must be met?
        1.
        2.

    c. What is the purpose of a debriefing?

6. What steps must researchers take to ensure the confidentiality of subjects?

7. Compare the regulation of scientists who use animal subjects in their research with the regulation of pet owners. (Miller, 1983)

8. Briefly explain why there are no substitutes for laboratory animals in research.

2-7 Discuss the value of cross-cultural research.

Read pages 44-45 and answer the following questions.

1. In general, what is the research interest of cross-cultural psychologists?

2. Define *culture* in your own words.

3. What can we conclude if the results of similar studies with people of different cultures produce similar results? different results?

4. List the two major types of variables that differ among cultures and give several examples of each.

   1. Variable   Examples

   2. Variable   Examples

5. Carefully explain why cross-cultural studies and correlational studies share the same limitations.

6. Describe some of the topics of cross-cultural research.

Read the interim summary on pages 51-52 of your text to re-acquaint yourself with the materials in this section.

2-8 Explain the use of descriptive statistics, and the calculation and use of measures of central tendency, measures of variability, and the measurement of relations.

Read pages 45-48 and answer the following questions.

1. a. Define *descriptive statistics* in your own words.

   b. Cite two reasons why they are used in scientific experiments.

2. a. Define *measure of central tendency* in your own words.

   b. The most common measure of central tendency is the _____, but the most representative measure of central tendency is the _____.

c. According to Suzanne's attendance record, she was absent 3 days in September, 1 day in October, 4 days in November and 2 days in December. Calculate the mean number of absences per month for that semester.

3. a. Explain how the median is calculated.

   b. Follow the income calculations in the "small town" example in your text to explain why the median is a more representative measure of central tendency than the mean.

   c. Cite two reasons why the mean is still used.

4. a. When researchers analyze experimental data, they frequently compare the scores of two groups of subjects. Name these groups.

   b. Why and how do researchers compare these scores? Be sure to mention *measure of variability* in your answer.

5. a. Study Table 2.1 in your text and explain how to calculate the range.

   b. Briefly explain what the range indicates and why it is not used very often.

6. Follow the calculations in Table 2.2 in your text and explain how the standard deviation is computed.

7. Study the data presented in Table 2.3 and Figures 2.9 and 2.10 in your text.

   a. The test scores and average grades of students can be graphed to make a _____.

   b. Define *correlation coefficient* in your own words.

   c. What is the range of possible values of the correlation coefficient?

   d. What does a correlation coefficient of +.5 mean?

   e. What does a negative correlation indicate about the relationship of two measures?

8. a. Points on a scatterplot that fall along a line indicate a _____ relation.

   b. Briefly explain why a correlation coefficient does not accurately represent a nonlinear relation. (See Figure 2.11 in your text.)

   c. How, then, are nonlinear relations usually presented?

2-9 Explain the concept of statistical significance and its use in determining the difference between two group means.

Read pages 48-51 and answer the following questions.

1. Why do researchers want to know whether the results of their experiments will be statistically significant?

2. How do researchers use descriptive statistics? inferential statistics?

3. If the size of the difference between the performance of two groups of subjects is large, relative to the variability, the results of the experiment are probably _____ _____ , but if the difference is small the results are probably due to _____ .

4. Study the data presented in Tables 2.4, 2.5, and 2.6 and Figure 2.12 in your text and describe the in-class experiment.

    a. Why was the mean height calculated so many times?

    b. Explain what a frequency distribution is and say why it is useful for organizing data.

    c. Explain how the distribution of mean differences in heights from 1000 random divisions supported the original hypothesis that the last letter of the first name is related to height.

5. a. Researchers do not usually determine statistical significance this way. Explain why the special mathematical properties of the standard deviation are useful in assessing the significance of results.

    b. What does a researcher mean when he or she reports that experimental results were statistically significant at the 1 percent level?

    c. Explain why statistically significant results need not be important.

LESSON II SELF TEST

1. The formal codes of ethics for the Canadian and American Psychological Associations, cited in the text
   a. have grown from formal governmental legislation.
   b. express very different values.
   c. are primarily derived from philosophical considerations.
   d. are primarily derived from the values and concerns of psychologists.

2. Which of the following pairs of cultural variables includes a biological and an ecological variable?
   a. high incidence of malaria; high incidence of illiteracy
   b. nomadic lifestyle; wealth measured by animal ownership
   c. temperate climate; high population density
   d. little consumption of meat; short stature

3. The median is calculated by
   a. adding the individual values of the sample and dividing by the number of observations.
   b. arranging all scores in numerical order and finding the midpoint.
   c. subtracting the lowest score from the highest score.
   d. adding the differences between each score and the measures of central tendency and then dividing by the number of scores.

4. The mean
   a. is the most common measure of central tendency, but the median is more representative.
   b. and the median of two sets of numbers are always different.
   c. is easier to calculate than the median, but the median is more useful because it has special mathematical properties.
   d. and the median are most accurate when the sample is small.

5. The standard deviation
   a. and the correlation coefficient of a sample are close in value.
   b. is inversely related to the range.
   c. measures the degree to which scores in two samples are correlated.
   d. is the square root of the variance.

6. A scatterplot
   a. with points distributed along a line running from the lower left to the upper right represents a negative correlation.
   b. with points distributed along a horizontal line represents a correlation of +1.0.
   c. indicates the relation between two variables.
   d. indicates the statistical significance of differences between means.

7. The correlation coefficient is more convenient than
   a. the range because standard tables to determine its value have already been developed.
   b. showing scatterplots of the scores.
   c. calculating the average deviations of scores from both the median and the mean.
   d. the range because it makes calculating the standard deviation unnecessary.

8. If the results of an experiment are statistically significant, we may conclude that the
   a. operational definitions were reliable.
   b. experiment was important.
   c. dependent variable had an effect on the independent variable.
   d. results were probably not due to chance.

9. When an experimenter determines whether results are statistically significant, he or she
   a. repeats the experiment.
   b. constructs a scatterplot.
   c. examines the performance of the control group.
   d. calculates the likelihood that the difference in mean scores was caused by chance.

10. A small difference in the performance of a control group and an experimental group can be statistically significant if
    a. the number of subjects is very large.
    b. the variability within the groups is very large.
    c. a single-blind experimental design is used.
    d. the correlation is positive.

Answers for Self Tests

Lesson I

1. b Obj. 2–1	2. a Obj. 2–2	3. a Obj. 2–2	4. d Obj. 2–3	5. b Obj. 2–3
6. b Obj. 2–4	7. a Obj. 2–4	8. d Obj. 2–5	9. c Obj. 2–5	10. d Obj. 2–5

Lesson II

1. d Obj. 2–6	2. a Obj. 2–7	3. b Obj. 2–8	4. a Obj. 2–8	5. d Obj. 2–8
6. c Obj. 2–8	7. b Obj. 2–8	8. d Obj. 2–9	9. d Obj. 2–9	10. a Obj. 2–9

CHAPTER 3

Evolution, Heredity, and Behaviour

LESSON I

Read the interim summary on pages 63-64 of your text to re-acquaint yourself with the material in this section.

3-1 Explain how evolution and genetic variables influence behaviour and how Darwin developed his theory of natural selection.

Read pages 56-59 and answer the following questions.

1. Define *biological evolution* and *adaptive significance* in your own words.

2. Explain how these concepts guide psychologists in their efforts to understand behaviours such as gregariousness by examining the

   a. past environmental conditions.

   b. immediate environmental influences.

   c. ultimate causes.

   d. proximate causes.

3. What is the benefit of understanding how adaptive behaviour evolved? (Skinner, 1987)

4. In general, what do evolutionary psychologists study? (Leger, 1991)

5. Define *culture* in your own words and go on to explain how an understanding of evolutionary processes may contribute to an understanding of culture as well as cultural change.

6. A second British naturalist by the name of _____ devised the theory of natural selection at approximately the same time as Darwin.

7. Explain how Darwin's observations during the voyage of the *Beagle* and his study of artificial selection eventually led to his theory of natural selection. (See Figure 3.1 in your text.)

8. Define *natural selection* in your own words.

3-2 Explain the concepts of reproductive success, variation, and competition and how they enter into natural selection.

Read pages 59-61 and answer the following questions.

1. Carefully state the four basic premises of the theory of evolution.

   1.

   2.

2. a. Define *reproductive success* in your own words.

   b. Explain how a particular trait, such as a wolf's running speed, may influence an animal's reproductive success. (See Figure 3.2 in your text.)

   c. Now explain why reproductive success is the real measure of survival of the fittest.

   d. List the two factors that determine an animal's reproductive success.

   1.   2.

3. a. Define *genotype* and *phenotype* in your own words.

   b. An organism's _____ results from the interaction between its _____ and the environment. The _____ determines how much the environment can influence an organism's _____ and _____ .

4. Using the example of identical twins reared apart, explain how a common genotype can result in two different phenotypes through the influence of environmental variables.

5. a. What did Grant (1986) observe about the effects of rainfall and food size on the survival of finches with small, thin beaks and bigger, thicker beaks?

b. What do his observations indicate about

    1. the length of time before changes due to natural selection are apparent?

    2. selective advantages conferred by particular phenotypic variations and survival of a particular organism?

c. Why did both finches with small, thin beaks and bigger, thicker ones continue to survive?

6. Explain how natural selection is influenced by competition between members of

    a. the same species for food and mates.

    b. different species for food and territory.

3-3 Discuss how bipedalism and encephalization contributed to the success of human evolution.

Read pages 61-63 and answer the following questions.

1. Trace the evolution of humans from Homo habilis to Homo neanderthalensis and Homo sapiens. Be sure to include a discussion of tool-use in your answer.

2. a. Define *bipedalism* and *encephalization* in your own words.

    b. Discuss some advantages conferred on the human species by

        1. bipedalism.

        2. an increased life span.

        3. language. (Skinner, 1986)

        4. encephalization.

3. a. Discuss Dunbar's (1993) theory of why humans developed a larger brain.

    b. What are some other advantages conferred on the human species by encephalization?

4. a. Now define *cultural evolution* in your own words.

b. What human capacities permitted our species to make adaptive changes to the environment?

c. How did Harris (1991) account for the evolution of learning ability?

d. What are some of the social problems that have resulted from cultural evolution?

Read the interim summary on page 75 of your text to re-acquaint yourself with the material in this section.

3-4 Explain the basic principles of genetics and the role of genes, chromosomes, meiosis, dominant and recessive alleles, genetic diversity, and the influence of gender on heredity.

Read pages 64-68 and answer the following questions.

1. Define these terms in your own words.

   a. genetics

   b. heredity

   c. gene

   d. DNA

2. a. What part of his theory of natural selection was Darwin unable to explain?

   b. Who did detail the basic principles of heredity?

3. Genes, which direct the synthesis of _____ and _____, are segments of genetic material called _____ (DNA). The _____ and _____ strands of DNA are joined together by the four _____ molecules _____, _____, _____, and _____ in a shape that resembles a _____ _____. (See Figure 3.4 in your text.)

4. a. What are proteins composed of?

   b. How is the synthesis of a particular protein designated?

   c. Although there are no genes for behaviour, how do genes ultimately affect behaviour?

5. What is the function of enzymes?

6. a. Where are genes located? chromosomes?

   b. Like the genes, chromosomes are composed of _____ .

   c. How many pairs of chromosomes do cells other than the sex chromosomes contain?

   d. Explain how new body cells are created.

7. a. Explain how the sex chromosomes are created, paying special attention to the number of chromosomes in the sperm and ova.

   b. What is this form of cell division called?

   c. Explain why sexual reproduction always results in individuals (except identical twins) with unique genetic combinations·

   d. How many types of sex chromosomes are there? What is the sex chromosome pattern for a male? a female?

   e. Study Figure 3.5 in your text and briefly explain how the sex of an individual is determined.

   f. At what point does this occur?

8. Each pair of _____ contains pairs of _____ which may be either _____ or _____ . If these alternate forms of genes, or _____ , are identical the gene combination is called _____ , but if they are different the gene combination is called _____ .

9. Study Figure 3.6 in your text and, using the example of eye color, explain how the phenotype of a homozygous and a heterozygous gene combination is determined. Be sure to use the terms *dominant allele* and *recessive allele*.

10. Offer one reason why it is difficult to determine how personal development and behaviour are influenced by genetics.

11. Explain why natural selection favours species that reproduce sexually.

12. Discuss how raising many generations of fruit flies in high- versus low-density conditions can influence the frequency of certain phenotypes (Sokolowski, et al., 1997).

13. a. If hemophilia, a serious blood disorder, is caused by a recessive gene carried on the X chromosome, why do females who have inherited this gene fail to develop the condition, but males with this gene do?

b. Explain the difference between a sex-linked gene and a sex-influenced gene.

3-5 Describe how changes in genetic material occur and describe the following genetic disorders: Down syndrome, Huntington's chorea, and phenylketonuria.

Read pages 69-70 and answer the following questions.

1. Identify the two mechanisms that produce changes in genetic material. Define them in your own words.

   1.

   2.

2. How do mutations occur and what is usually the result? occasionally the result?

3. What two ways can chromosomal aberration affect the chromosomes of a cell?

4. What is the effect of inheriting recessive lethal genes? dominant lethal genes?

5. a. Explain the genetic cause of Down syndrome.

   b. Who is most likely to give birth to an afflicted child? (Risher and Easton, 1992)

   c. What are some of the physical and mental characteristics of people with Down syndrome?

6. a. Explain the genetic cause of Huntington's chorea.

   b. When does the condition first appear and how does it affect the person?

7. a. Explain the genetic cause of phenylketonuria (PKU).

   b. What metabolic change results from synthesis of a faulty enzyme in people with PKU?

   c. When is PKU detected and how is it treated?

8. Why do individuals or couples seek genetic counselling?

LESSON I SELF TEST

1. Natural selection
   a. is a consequence of the fact that organisms reproduce differentially.
   b. prevents the extinction of species.
   c. may lead to a decrease in genetic diversity between related organisms.
   d. suggests that physical characteristics rather than behavioural traits have a greater effect on survival.

2. Darwin
   a. was the first to propose a theory of evolution.
   b. searched for an explanation for living things because he had never accepted the creationist point of view.
   c. formulated his theory during the voyage of the *Beagle*.
   d. waited twenty years to publish his theory.

3. Genotype is an individual's_____ and _____.
   a. genetic endowment; is unique to each individual
   b. physical appearance and behaviour; is the outward expression of its phenotype
   c. cognitive strategies; reveals how genes influence behaviour
   d. intellectual ability; is influenced by interaction with a changing environment

4. The study of the relationship between rainfall, food supply, and the island finch population reaffirms that
   a. changes resulting from natural selection occur slowly.
   b. phenotypic variation affects survival rate.
   c. competition influences survival, and variation does not.
   d. extinction is not a result of competition.

5. The most important function of language may have been
   a. to provide a means of preserving accumulated knowledge.
   b. to permit warning others of danger.
   c. to reinforce social ties.
   d. to facilitate problem solving by small groups.

6. _____ are located on the _____ and direct the synthesis of _____ .
   a. genes; chromosomes; proteins
   b. chromosomes; genes; DNA
   c. genes; strands of DNA; nucleotide molecules
   d. chromosomes; nuclei of cells; genes

7. Most human cells contain _____ pairs of _____.
   a. 46; genes
   b. 46; chromosomes
   c. 23; genes
   d. 23; chromosomes

8. A person who has a homozygous gene combination for a particular trait or condition received
   a. either a recessive or dominant gene from each parent.
   b. only dominant genes from each parent.
   c. a recessive gene from the mother and a dominant gene from the father.
   d. a dominant gene from the mother and a recessive gene from the father.

9. The gene for hemophilia, a serious blood-clotting disorder, is an example of a
   a. sex-limited gene.
   b. sex-linked gene.
   c. sex-related gene.
   d. sex-influenced gene.

10. Changes in genetic material result from either
    a. mutation or chromosomal aberration.
    b. radiation or poisoning.
    c. homozygous or heterozygous alleles.
    d. variation or competition.

LESSON II

3-6 Discuss the role of heredity in population differences and how genetic influences are studied.

Read pages 70–74 and answer the following questions.

1. Define *heritability* and *inheritance* in your own words, paying special attention to how they differ.

2. The more the variability of a trait within a given population is influenced by _____ factors, the _____ is its heritability.

3. What do behaviour geneticists study?

4. Define mandelian and nonmendelian traits.

   1.   2.   3.

5. List the primary tools of behaviour genetics.

6. a. In a classic study, what kind of subjects did Tyron (1940) use and what did he train them to do?

   b. What criterion did he use to select his breeding pairs?

   c. How did he rule out the possibility that young rats somehow learned the maze from their mothers?

   d. Study Figure 3.7 in your text and describe the results of selective breeding over many generations.

7. a. In later studies, how was maze learning affected when both bright and dull rats were raised in enriched environments? (Cooper and Zubek, 1968)

   b. How did environmental change affect genetic differences between subject rats?

8. What kind of research will be possible when the mapping of the nucleotide bases of human chromosomes is completed?

9. Define knockout mutation and genetic markers.

10.a. Discuss three barriers to studying the effects of heredity on human behaviours.

   b. Now explain how such limitations can be overcome by studying multiple births. Be sure to use the terms *monozygotic* and *dizygotic* twins in your answer.

11. Monozygotic twins are _____ for a trait if both or _____ expresses it; and they are _____ for a trait if only one of them expresses it.

12. If there is a high concordance for a trait in monozygotic twins and a low concordance rate for dizygotic twins, what can we conclude about the role of heredity? (Study Table 3.1 in your text.)

13. What are some of the traits that twin studies indicate are affected by genetic factors? (Bouchard and Propping, 1993; Bouchard and McGue, 1981)

3-7 Describe how the genetic factors that may influence alcohol addiction are studied and state the conclusions of research on this topic.

Read pages 74-75 and answer the following questions.

1. a. Why has alcoholism been studied extensively?

   b. What three kinds of research have been used to study this social problem?

2. a. Compare the concordance rates for alcoholism for

      1. nearly 4,000 monozygotic and dizygotic Australian twins. (Heath et al., 1990)

      2. male and female monozygotic and dizygotic American twins. (Pickens et al., 1991; McGue et al., 1992)

   b. Who do these results suggest has the greater genetic predisposition for alcoholism?

3. a. In a study of 1000 adopted males in Sweden, which males were most likely to become alcoholics? (Cloninger et al., 1981)

   b. What were the results of a similar study of females? (Bohman et al., 1981)

   c. How do the drinking patterns of alcoholic males and females differ? (Cloninger, 1987)

4. a. Compare the behaviour of rats with a preference for alcohol with the behaviour of rats who have no preference for alcohol. (Lumeng et al., 1995)

   b. What did an examination of the brains of rats from these two strains suggest about brain mechanisms and alcoholism?

5. a. The results of the three kinds of research on alcoholism provide an example of _____ evidence.

   b. Why are results like these important in science?

6. a. Approximately what percentage of the male relatives of alcoholics are also alcoholics?

   b. Compare this number to the males in the general population. (Cotton, 1979; Plomin, 1990)

   c. Explain why a greater number of the male relatives of alcoholics do not become alcoholic.

7. What factors that may influence eventual alcoholism are not completely accounted for by twin and adoption studies? artificial selection studies?

8. Finally, what can we conclude from all three approaches to research about a genetic basis for alcoholism?

   To review: Match the terms on the left with the correct definition on the right.

   _____ heritability   a. changes in the genetic or physical characteristics of a population over time

   _____ concordance rate   b. the consequence of the fact that organisms reproduce differentially

   _____ genotype   c. an organism's physical appearance and behaviour

   _____ alleles   d. the ability to move on two feet

   _____ monozygotic twins   e. tendency of a trait to be passed on from parent to offspring

   _____ biological evolution   f. the phenotype appears more frequently in one sex than the other

   _____ natural selection   g. alternate forms of a gene

   _____ inheritance   h. develop from a single fertilized ovum

   _____ phenotype   i. a DNA sequence that occurs at a particular place in a chromosome

   _____ bipedalism   j. amount of variability in a trait in a population due to genetic differences

   _____ sex-limited gene   k. the degree to which a trait is expressed

   _____ sex-linked gene   l. an organism's genetic endowment

   _____ genetic marker   m. resides on the sex chromosome

Read the interim summary on pages 82-83 of your text to re-acquaint yourself with the material in this section.

3-8 Define sociobiology and explain how it uses the concept of reproductive strategies to explain different mating patterns.

Read pages 75-78 and answer the following questions.

1. a. Define *sociobiology* in your own words.

   b. What are some general research topics in sociobiology and what kind of subjects are usually employed?

2. a. Now define *reproductive strategy* in your own words.

b. Explain these major classes of reproductive strategy. (See Figure 3.8 in your text.)

   1. monogamy

   2. polygyny

   3. polyandry

   4. polygynandry

c. List these strategies according to their prevalence in human society. (Badcock, 1991)

d. Why did these different strategies evolve? (Trivers, 1972)

3. a. Define *parental investment* and *sexual selection* in your own words.

  b. Explain why these factors can play a critical role in mate selection.

4. a. According to sociobiological theory, what determines the nature of an individual's parental investment?

  b. Which parent makes the greater parental investment?

5. Summarize some of the reasons for this unequal division of parental investment.

  a. Why do females have fewer opportunities to reproduce than males?

  b. In what ways does gestation or pregnancy and birth affect a female?

  c. How much of the care of the dependent newborn is accepted by each parent?

  d. How does the more limited reproductive potential of the female affect her investment in her offspring?

6. a. In a polygynous society, how do males determine mating rights?

  b. In what situations is the physical size of a male adaptive? maladaptive?

  c. How does the unequal investment required of females affect their choice of mates?

7. a. Why may monogamous relationships have evolved in some species?

  b. Although two parents share responsibility for the offspring, why does the parental investment of the female continue to be greater than that of the male?

c. What evidence suggests that monogamous societies are not exclusively so? (For example: Kinsey et al., 1948)

d. How have western cultural influences affected reproductive strategies that developed in the evolutionary past?

8. a. Which nonhuman species are most likely to exhibit polyandry?

b. Explain why some of the people in remote Himalayan villages practice polyandry.

9. a. Why is group parental investment adaptive for a polygynandrous group such as chimpanzees?

b. Sometimes in a polygynandrous group a consortship develops. Explain this relationship and an accompanying benefit and risk.

3-9 Describe how sociobiologists study altruism and discuss criticism of the sociobiological explanation of social behaviour.

Read pages 78-80 and answer the following questions.

1. a. Define *altruism* in your own words and give several examples of altruistic behaviour you may have read about or observed.

b. For each of your examples of altruistic behaviour, identify the parties whose chances of survival—and thus reproductive success—are decreased? increased?

c. Why does altruistic behaviour, which reduces the odds of individual survival, pose a dilemma for sociobiologists?

2. a. Outline Hamilton's (1964, 1970) explanation of the evolution of altruistic behaviour through natural selection. Be sure to use the terms *inclusive fitness* and *kin selection* in your answer. (Maynard Smith, 1964)

b. How does this perspective help us understand the altruistic acts of a parent? (Barash, 1982)

c. What, then, was Hamilton's contribution to understanding altruistic behaviour?

3. a. What is the relationship between people involved in an act of reciprocal altruism?

b. What may be the reason people put themselves at risk for nonrelatives?

4. List the three conditions that increase the likelihood that a person will act altruistically toward a nonrelative.

1.

2.

3.

5. When acts of reciprocal altruism do not meet these conditions, what may explain them?

6. a. Why do some critics of sociobiology argue that cultural evolution, rather than biological evolution, shapes human behaviour?

   b. How do sociobiologists respond?

7. Why do sociobiologists and their critics differ on generalizing results from research with nonhuman animals to humans?

8. How do sociobiologists refute the criticism that they have ignored the influence of environmental factors on human social behaviour?

9. a. Outline the political criticism of sociobiology.

   b. What do sociobiologists say in their defense? (Wilson in Barash, 1982)

3-10 Discuss evolutionary and environmental origins of ethnocentrism.

Read pages 81-82 and answer the following questions.

1. Define *ethnocentrism* in your own words.

2. a. What hypothetical choice did Silverman (1987) give to subjects and what did about 70 percent of these subjects choose?

   b. What does their choice suggest about the prevalence of ethnocentrism in human society?

3. Explain why we should seek the ways that genetics *and* learning influence ethnocentrism.

4. How have some people sought to justify ethnocentrism rather than understand it?

5. Explain the false assumptions of the universality fallacy and the naturalistic fallacy and say how they affect research.

6. a. What research tools did Irwin (1987) use to study ethnocentrism among Netsilingmiut Inuits, neigbouring Inuits, and Native Americans?

   b. What did he discover about the altruistic acts among members of the Netsilingmiut Inuits and between them and members of other tribes?

   c. But if historical patterns of social interaction between general populations of these tribes are examined, how does the tendency toward ethnocentrism change?

7. In general, how does our ability to recognize our degree of relationship with others affect our behaviour toward them?

8. What can we conclude about the biological origins of ethnocentrism? (Durham, 1991) the social origins?

LESSON II SELF TEST

1. Heritability is the
   a. tendency of a trait to be passed from parent to offspring.
   b. sum of inherited traits and tendencies.
   c. estimate of the potential for successful reproduction by a member of a given population.
   d. amount of variability in a particular trait in a particular population at a particular time due to genetic factors.

2. By selectively breeding pairs of maze "bright" and maze "dull" rats, Tyron demonstrated
   a. the importance of parenting in trait expression.
   b. that the expression of a trait through selective breeding cannot be maintained indefinitely.
   c. that a trait can be manipulated to appear more or less often across succeeding generations.
   d. how to determine all the variables that affect the expression of a trait.

3. Dizygotic twins
   a. are genetically identical.
   b. are, on average, as genetically alike as any two siblings.
   c. are always of the same sex.
   d. are never of the same sex.

4. A child whose natural parents are alcoholics has
   a. an increased risk of alcoholism.
   b. an increased risk of alcoholism only if raised by the natural parents.
   c. no increased risk of alcoholism if raised by nonalcoholic adoptive parents.
   d. no increased risk of alcoholism regardless of the home environment.

5. Polygyny is
   a. one male mating with one female.
   b. one male mating with more than one female.
   c. one female mating with more than one male.
   d. several males mating with several females.

6. High male and low female parental investment describes a
   a. polygynandrous relationship.
   b. polyandrous relationship.
   c. polygynous relationship.
   d. monogamous relationship.

7. Altruistic acts
   a. have a genetically selfish basis.
   b. are of recent evolutionary origin.
   c. have not been observed in nonhuman species.
   d. usually result in the death of the altruist or recipient.

8. Acts of reciprocal altruism are most likely to occur if
   a. witnesses are present.
   b. the anonymity of the altruist is assured.
   c. the risk to the altruist is low.
   d. the altruist ignores the likelihood of success.

9. Critics assert that sociobiologists overemphasize the
   a. effect of cultural practices on behaviour.
   b. importance of atypical behaviour such as acts of altruism.
   c. role of environmental factors.
   d. relevance of research with nonhuman animals.

10. A large majority of subjects who were given a choice of escaping imminent danger by taking one of two boats
    a. chose to deprive a person of a different ethnic background a seat.
    b. chose to deprive a person of a different ethnic background a seat only if that person was male.
    c. refused to deprive a child of a seat regardless of ethnic background.
    d. refused to make a choice.

Answers for Self Tests

Lesson I
1. a Obj. 3–1	2. d Obj. 3–1	3. a Obj. 3–2	4. b Obj. 3–2	5. c Obj. 3–3
6. a Obj. 3–4	7. d Obj. 3–5	8. a Obj. 3–5	9. b Obj. 3–5	10. a Obj. 3–5

Lesson II
1. d Obj. 3–6	2. c Obj. 3–6	3. b Obj. 3–6	4. a Obj. 3–7	5. b Obj. 3–8
6. b Obj. 3–8	7. a Obj. 3–9	8. c Obj. 3–9	9. d Obj. 3–9	10. a Obj. 3–10

CHAPTER 4

Biology of Behaviour

LESSON I

Read the interim summary on page 99 of your text to re-acquaint yourself with the material in this section.

4-1 Outline the basic structure of the nervous system.

Read pages 88-92 and answer the following questions.

1. Hebb showed how brain functioning could be understood in terms of both individual _____ and larger _____. Since his work, neuroscientists have learned that the nerve cells of the brain are organized into clusters called _____ which are connected to other _____.

2. List the two primary functions of the brain.

   1.   2.

3. Study Figure 4.2 in your text and list the two divisions of the nervous system and identify the major structures within each of them.

   1.   Structures

   2.   Structures

4. Study Figure 4.3 in your text and then add labels to the leader lines of Figure 1.

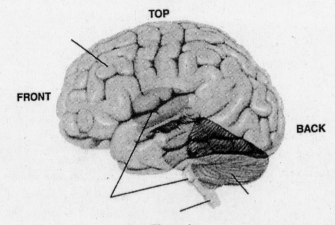

Figure 1

5. a. The _____ _____ is believed to be the most primitive region and controls _____ _____ and _____ _____.

   b. The _____ _____ are believed to be the most recently evolved parts of the brain.

c. The _____ looks like a set of miniature _____ _____ and is involved in the control of _____.

6. Explain how the vertebrae, the meninges, and the cerebrospinal fluid protect the brain and the spinal cord from injury. (Refer to Figure 4.2.)

7. a. The _____ _____ of the cerebral hemispheres is a thin layer of tissue consisting of billions of _____ _____, which are connected to the rest of the brain by the nerve _____ called the _____ _____. (See Figure 4.4 in your text.)

   b. Bulges or _____ and large grooves or _____ greatly increase the _____ of the cerebral cortex.

8. Describe the function of the nerves of the peripheral nervous system.

9. What is the difference between spinal nerves and cranial nerves? (Refer to Figure 4.2 in your text.)

4-2 Describe the structures of the neuron and the action potential.

Read pages 92-94 and answer the following questions.

1. List four functions that neurons perform.

   1.   3.

   2.   4.

2. List five functions that glia perform.

   1.   4.

   2.   5.

   3.

3. Now list the four major parts of a neuron shown in Figure 4.5 in your text and identify their primary functions.

   1.

   2.

   3.

   4.

4. Refer to Figure 4.5 and add labels to the leader lines in Figure 2.

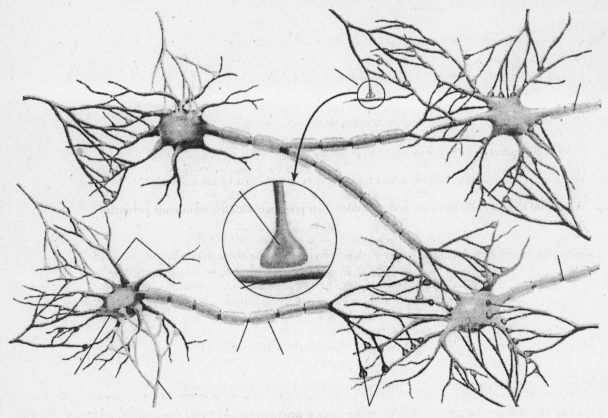

Figure 2

5. Use one word to describe how messages are transmitted between neurons.

6. a. Name the insulating substance that covers many axons.

   b. Where is it produced and what is it made of?

   c. Describe how the myelin sheath surrounds the axon. (Refer to Figure 4.5.)

   d. In addition to insulating the axon, what is another function of myelin?

7. Briefly explain the cause of the sensory and motor impairments characteristic of multiple sclerosis.

8. An axon carries messages _____ from the soma. When an _____ _____ is sent down the axon, the _____ _____ secretes a chemical called a _____ _____, which affects the activity of the cell with which it communicates.

9. Study Figures 4.6 and 4.7 in your text for a closer look at how an action potential is transmitted.

   a. What is the electrical charge of the membrane of a resting axon with respect to the interior?

b. Why does the electrical charge occur?

c. How are ions produced?

d. Explain how ions move between the inside and outside of the axon.

e. What is the position of the ion channels when the axon is resting?

f. At what place on the axon does the action potential begin?

g. When an action potential begins, what change occurs in some nearby ion channels?

h. What kind of ions enter the axon and how does their presence alter the membrane potential?

i. When the membrane potential reverses, what two changes then occur in nearby ion channels?

j. What kind of ions can now leave the axon and how does their absence alter the membrane potential?

k. Finally, how do the ion transporters help to terminate the action potential?

4-3 Describe a synapse and the effects of synaptic transmission, and explain how a simple neural circuit transmits messages and the effects of neuromodulators on this process.

Read pages 94-99 and answer the following questions.

1. Define *synapse* in your own words.

2. a. Study Figure 4.8 in your text and describe a motor neuron and its relation to a muscle.

   b. What happens when the motor neuron fires?

   c. Explain the relationship between rate of firing and strength of muscular contraction.

3. Explain the following terms.

   a. presynaptic neuron

   b. postsynaptic neuron

   c. excitatory synapse

   d. inhibitory synapse

4. Now use these terms to explain how the rate of firing of a particular axon is determined. (Study Figure 4.9 in your text.)

5. Study Figures 4.10, 4.11, and 4.12 in your text and describe the release and effects of the transmitter substance.

   a. What triggers the release of a transmitter substance?

   b. Name the space into which the terminal button releases transmitter substance and describe its location.

   c. To which structures does the just–released transmitter substance attach and where are they located?

   d. When activated, what effects can receptor molecules produce in the postsynaptic neuron?

   e. By what means do receptor molecules produce their effect?

   f. What kind of ions enter a neuron at excitatory synapses? leave a neuron at inhibitory synapses?

   g. Name and describe the process that usually stops the effects of a transmitter substance at most synapses.

   h. Explain the relationship between rate of reuptake and duration of the effect of the transmitter substance.

6. Now label the following structures in Figure 3: terminal button, presynaptic membrane, synaptic cleft, postsynaptic membrane, and receptor molecules. Then draw and label some molecules of transmitter substance. Finally, draw arrows to indicate the release and reuptake of transmitter substance.

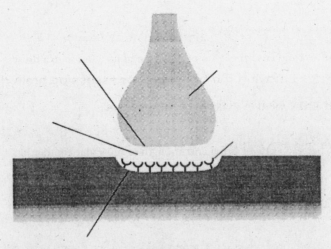

Figure 3

7. Study Figure 4.13 in your text and describe a simple withdrawal reflex in response to an unpleasant stimulus.

   a. Name the neurons that first detect the stimulus.

   b. What is the location of the terminal buttons of the axons of these neurons?

c. Name the neurons they excite.

d. Where are they found?

e. Interneurons stimulate another set of neurons. Name them.

f. What change now takes place in the muscle?

g. What was the overall effect of this sequence of events?

8. The casserole was so hot that you felt it burning your fingers through the potholders. Somehow you managed to put it down without dropping it. Explain how the simple withdrawal reflex that you have just described was inhibited. (Study Figure 4.14 in your text.)

9. a. Compare the range of action of transmitter substances and neuromodulators.

b. The best-known neuromodulator is a category of chemicals called _____ or _____.

c. List two of their behavioural effects.

   1.   2.

d. When are these chemicals released?

e. What is their general effect and why is it significant?

f. How do opiates produce their effects? (Pert et al., 1974) What chemicals do they mimic? (Terenius and Wahlstrom, 1975)

g. List some of the behavioural effects of other neuromodulators produced by the brain.

Read the interim summary on page 106 of your text to re-acquaint yourself with the material in this section.

4-4 Describe methods for studying the brain and for assessing brain damage.

Read pages 100-105 and answer the following questions.

1. a. Define brain plasticity in your own words.

b. What method is used to trace the effects of plasticity? What kind of changes in neurons can this method highlight?

2. a. What do the letters CT stand for? How is a CT scan produced? (See figures 4.16 and 4.17 in your text.)

b. Give an example of the kind of information that can be obtained by using a CT scanner.

3. What does the acronym PET stand for? How are PET scans produced? (See Figure 4.21 in your text.)

4. a. What do the letters MRI stand for? How are MRI scans produced? (See Figure 4.18 in your text.)

   b. Give an example of the kind of information that can be obtained by using an MRI.

5. Return to Figures 4.17, 4.18, and 4.21 an describe and compare the kinds of images these machines produce.

6. Physiological psychologists frequently study the brain by producing brain lesions in experimental animals.

   a. What is a brain lesion?

   b. Explain the underlying logic of research that employs brain lesions.

7. Study Figure 4.19 in your text and explain how brain lesions are produce in the laboratory.

   a. Carefully describe a stereotaxic apparatus and describe the position of the animal. Be sure to explain why this equipment is used.

   b. How does the researcher actually produce the brain lesion?

8 a. Explain the logic of electrical recording studies.

   b. Study Figure 4.20 in your text and describe the apparatus and procedure used in an electrical stimulation experiment.

   c. Explain the logic of brain stimulation studies.

9. Give two examples of using stereotaxic apparatuses to operate on humans.

10. Describe some uses of chemicals in brain research.

11. a. What do the letters fMRI stand for? How does the fMRI work?

   b. Provide examples of when a psychologist would use this technique.

c. What are some of the limitations of an MRI?

4-5 Discuss the evidence for the interaction of hereditary and environmental factors on brain development.

Read pages 105-106 and answer the following questions.

1. a. Why do most modern psychologists find the nature/nurture distinction irrelevant?

   b. What kind of questions are more relevant to the study of the physiology of behaviour?

2. Outline evidence that environmental factors influence normal brain development.

   a. Describe the enriched and impoverished environments of rat litters studied by Rosenzweig and his colleagues. (Rosenzweig, 1984)

   b. List some physical differences they found in the brains of rats reared in the enriched environment.

   c. Describe the results of subsequent studies that revealed changes in

      1. neurons. (Greenough and Volkman, 1973)

      2. synapses. (Turner and Greenough, 1985)

      3. the adult rat brain. (Sirevaag et al., 1988)

3. Now outline evidence that environmental factors influence the development of specific parts of the brain.

   a. How is the vision of a young animal affected if one eye is closed during a critical period of brain development? (Wiesel, 1982)

   b. What changes occurred in the brains of young animals trained to move a foreleg when they saw a particular visual stimulus? (Spinelli and Jensen, 1979; Spinelli et al., 1980)

   c. What observation led Moore and her colleagues to study maternal licking?

   d. Briefly summarize their findings. (Moore, 1992)

4. What does the evidence suggest is the role and importance of heredity and environment on the brain and behaviour?

LESSON I SELF TEST

1. Most of the brain tissue is found in the
   a. cerebral cortex.
   b. cerebral hemispheres.
   c. ventricles.
   d. cerebellum.

2. Fissures and gyri
   a. increase the surface area of the brain.
   b. separate the brain from the skull.
   c. are pathways for cerebrospinal fluid.
   d. line the ventricles.

3. The principal function of myelin is
   a. to carry messages away from the soma.
   b. to insulate axons from each other, preventing the scrambling of messages.
   c. to regulate the rate at which an axon fires.
   d. to control the metabolism of the neuron.

4. The action potential begins in the _____ and is transmitted to the _____.
   a. terminal buttons; end of the axon attached to the soma
   b. end of the axon attached to the soma; terminal buttons
   c. dendrites; terminal buttons
   d. soma; axon

5. Transmitter substances exert their effects by
   a. producing action potentials.
   b. inhibiting action potentials.
   c. attaching to postsynaptic receptor molecules.
   d. causing reactions in the presynaptic membrane.

6. In a simple withdrawal reflex, the noxious stimulus is detected by
   a. sensory neurons.
   b. interneurons.
   c. motor neurons.
   d. association neurons.

7. CT scanners use _____ and MRI scanners use _____ to produce images of the living brain.
   a. magnetic fields and radio waves; X-rays
   b. X-rays; magnetic fields and radio waves
   c. a radioactive substance; magnetic fields and radio waves
   d. X-rays; a radioactive substance

8. Which of the following is used to produce a brain lesion?
   a. functional MRI
   b. PET scanner
   c. X-ray machine
   d. stereotaxic apparatus

9. The nature–nurture controversy is now over because most people believe that
   a. almost all behaviour is affected by both factors.
   b. heredity is the sole influence on normal development.
   c. environmental factors do not influence normal development.
   d. unbiased cross-cultural assessments of nurture are impossible.

10. If female rats did not lick the genital region of their male offspring, in adulthood these males would
    a. be sterile.
    b. attempt to mount other males.
    c. show decreased sexual behaviour.
    d. require less tactile stimulation to become sexually aroused.

LESSON II

Read the interim summary on pages 113-114 of your text to re-acquaint yourself with the material in this section.

4-6 Describe the primary sensory cortex, primary motor cortex, and association cortex and discuss the concept of lateralization of function.

Read pages 107-110 and answer the following questions.

1. List again the two basic functions of the brain.

   1.   2.

2. Now list the five major senses.

   1.   4.

   2.   5.

   3.

3. Finally, list the three areas of the cerebral cortex that receive information from the sensory organs.

   1.   3.

   2.

4. Study Figure 4.22 in your text and then add labels to the leader lines in Figure 4. Label the appropriate arrows as "anterior" and "posterior."

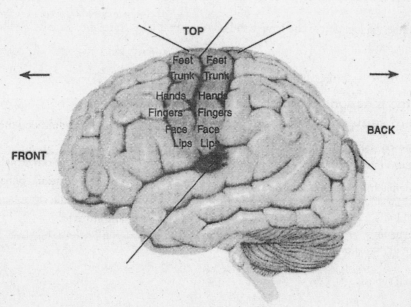

Figure 4

5. Each cerebral hemisphere receives information from the contralateral side of the body. Explain what that statement means.

6. a. The portion of the cerebral cortex not occupied by the primary sensory or motor areas is known as the

        _____ _____.

    b. What do these areas do?

7. a. Identify the landmark on the surface of cerebral cortex that divides the anterior and posterior regions. (See Figure 4.22 in your text.)

    b. Identify the general activities of each of these two regions.

8. a. Study Figures 4.22 and 4.23 in your text and then go back to Figure 4 and label the four lobes.

    b. Briefly explain the general function of sensory and motor association cortex, especially the relationship between function and the proximity, of sensory association cortex to primary sensory cortex.

    c. Finally, study Figure 4.24 in your text and then go back to Figure 4 and label the sensory association cortex and the motor association cortex.

    d. Which region sends information about the environment to motor association cortex?.

9. Describe the functions of the right and left hemisphere using these terms: *lateralization, analysis,* and *synthesis.*

10. Identify and describe the location of the large band of axons that joins the right and left cerebral hemispheres. (See Figure 4.25 in your text.)

4-7 Describe the functions of the four lobes of the cerebral cortex and the surgical treatment of seizure disorders.

Read pages 110-113 and answer the following questions.

1. a. State the principal function of the occipital lobe.

    b. A small lesion to _____ _____ cortex caused a "hole" in the visual field, whereas damage to _____ _____ cortex does not cause blindness, but the individual will not be able to _____ objects.

    c. Describe visual agnosia.

2. a. State the principal function of the temporal lobe.

b. What happens after damage to the

    1. primary auditory cortex?

    2. left auditory, association cortex?

    3. right auditory association cortex?

3. a. State the principal function of the parietal lobe.

    b. What happens after damage to the association cortex of the right parietal lobe? the left parietal lobe? Examples of the kinds of deficits resulting from damage to the left and right parietal lobes are shown in Figure 4.26 in your text.

    c. Review the experiences of the patients described in the opening vignette to be sure you understand the concept of unilateral neglect.

    d. List some tasks that are difficult for patients who have damage to the parietal lobe of the

        1. left hemisphere.

        2. right hemisphere.

4. a. State the principal function of the frontal lobe.

    b. Damage to right primary motor cortex results in paralysis of which side of the body?

    c. List the four categories of deficits that result from damage to prefrontal cortex.

        1.   3.

        2.   4.

    d. What happens after damage to Broca's area? (See Figure 4.27 in your text.)

5. a. What is happening to the neurons in the brain during a seizure?

    b. What is the general name for regions in the brain that can irritate surrounding brain tissue, causing a seizure?

6. a. How did Penfield, one of the pioneers of seizure surgery, determine the brain tissue he could safely remove? (See Figure 4.28 in your text.)

   b. How did he use seizure surgery to study brain function?

7. a. Explain how the brain attempts to limit the excitatory activity of the seizure focus. Be sure to use the term *interictal inhibition* in your answer.

   b. How does this inhibition affect nearby healthy tissue?

   c. Now refer to this mechanism to explain why seizure surgery often leads to an improvement in the patient's neuropsychological abilities.

Read the interim summary on pages 118-119 of your text to re-acquaint yourself with the material in this section.

4-8 Describe the control of internal functions and automatic behaviours by the brain stem, the cerebellum, the thalamus, the hypothalamus, and the limbic system.

Read pages 114-118 and answer the following questions.

1. In your own words, define

   a. *homeostasis.*

   b. *species-typical behaviour.*

2. List the three structures of the brain stem and their principal functions. (See Figure 4.29 in your text.)

   1.

   2.

   3.

3. a. What are some of the functions of the cerebellum?

   b. What kind of deficit results from damage to the cerebellum?

4. Briefly describe how researchers discovered a possible additional function of the cerebellum.

5. Study Figure 4.29 in your text and describe the location and appearance of the thalamus.

6. a. Describe the two basic functions of the thalamus.

   b. Underline the more primitive function.

   c. What is the only kind of sensory information that does not go directly to the thalamus?

7. a. Describe two ways that the hypothalamus receives sensory information.

   b. Name the gland directly controlled by the hypothalamus.

8. _____ _____ such as the pituitary gland secrete hormones directly into the _____ _____ which carries them throughout the body. Hormones travel _____ distances than transmitter substances or neuromodulators but exert their effect in the same way by stimulating _____ _____ on the _____ cells.

9. Explain why the pituitary gland is considered the "master gland." (See Figure 4.30 in your text.)

10. The autonomic nervous system is also largely controlled by the hypothalamus. List its two branches and their functions. (Study Figure 4.31 in your text.)

    Branch   General Function   Activities

    1.

    2.

11. Briefly explain one of the homeostatic functions of the hypothalamus—the regulation of body temperature.

12. List the three most important structures of the limbic system. (See Figure 4.32 in your text.)

    1.   3.

    2.

13. List several effects of damage to the following structures.

    1. amygdala

    2. hippocampus

Read the interim summary on pages 124-125 on your text to re-acquaint yourself with the material in this section.

4-9 Explain the effects of drugs that cause changes in synaptic transmission or cause sedation.

Read pages 119-122 and then answer the following questions.

1. List some of the means by which drugs can influence the effects of transmitter substances.

    1.   4.

    2.   5.

    3.

2. a.   What do the letters NMDA stand for? What makes this receptor special? Be sure to discuss the process shown in Figure 4.33 of your text.

    b.   What kind of changes in the brain is this process thought to underlie?

    c.   What happens when a genetic knockout of NMDA is used in mice?

3. Let's look at these more closely. Study Figure 4.34 in your text and name a specific drug that

    a.   facilitates the release of the transmitter substance acetylcholine.

    b.   prevents the release of this transmitter substance.

4. a.   Now study Figure 4.35 in your text and name a specific drug that

        1. stimulates acetylcholine receptor molecules.

        2. blocks these receptor molecules.

    b.   What are the behavioural effects of these drugs?

    c.   Briefly explain how antipsychotic drugs used to treat schizophrenia produce their effects.

    d.   Study Figure 4.36 in your text and explain how cocaine and amphetamine produce their effects.

5. a.   Name the principal effect of barbiturates.

    b.   What is the effect of barbiturates in low doses? high doses?

    c.   Why are barbiturates poor sleeping medications?

6. a.   Name an important class of antianxiety drugs and give a specific example.

b. How do these drugs exert their effect on neurons in the brain?

c. What are some of the conditions for which benzodiazepines are an effective treatment?

7. a. Name the most commonly used depressant drug.

b. The effects of a moderate dose of alcohol plus a moderate dose of barbiturates is _____ and can be _____.

c. How does alcohol appear to affect neurons in the brain?

8. a. Explain the different appearance of the two rats shown in Figure 4.37 in your text that had been given enough alcohol by injection to make them pass out. (Suzdak et al., 1986)

b. Explain why this drug will probably not be widely used.

4–10 Describe the effects of drugs that cause excitation, modify perceptions or produce hallucinations, and psychotherapeutic drugs.

Read pages 122-123 and answer the following questions.

1. a. Briefly explain how amphetamine and cocaine mimic the effects of reinforcing stimuli.

b. Name and describe the serious symptoms that occur after heavy use of these drugs.

c. What are the implications of drug-induced psychosis for research on schizophrenia?

2. a. Briefly explain how opiate drugs affect neurons in the brain.

b. List the inhibitory and excitatory, behavioural effects of opiate drugs.

c. Circle the effects above that contribute to their abuse.

3. a. Explain why drugs that suppress serotonin-secreting neurons produce hallucinations.

b. Compare the hallucinations produced by cocaine and LSD and say what we may conclude from this comparison.

4. a. How does THC, the active ingredient in marijuana, exert its behavioural effects?

   b. List some of the beneficial and detrimental behavioural effects of this drug. (Howlett, 1990)

5. Psychotherapeutic drugs often affect synapses using particular types of transmitter substances.

   a. Symptoms of schizophrenia can be induced by drugs such as _____ and _____ that _____ synapses that use _____. These symptoms can be reduced or eliminated by using drugs such as _____ which _____ these receptors.

   b. Antidepressant drugs such as _____ tend to _____ synapses that use serotonin.

   c. _____ _____ is an effective treatment for severe mood swings between depression and _____. The reason for its therapeutic effect is _____.

4-11 Evaluate the importance of the distinction between "physiological" and "psychological" addiction.

Read pages 123-124 and answer the following questions.

1. How do Eddy et al. (1965) define the following terms?

   a. physical dependence

   b. psychic dependence

2. Now define these terms in your own words.

   a. tolerance

   b. withdrawal symptoms

3. Carefully explain how the body's compensatory mechanisms to re-establish homeostasis may account for both drug tolerance and the accompanying withdrawal symptoms.

4. Explain why withdrawal symptoms are not the reason why a person becomes a drug addict but do contribute to continued addiction.

5. Cite two additional findings that support this explanation of the nature of addiction. (Jaffe, 1983)

6. Evaluate the importance of both physiological and psychological factors in understanding the causes of drug addiction.

LESSON II SELF TEST

1. The central fissure divides the cerebral cortex into
   a. hemispheres.
   b. occipital and temporal lobes.
   c. anterior and posterior regions.
   d. primary and association cortex.

2. Lateralization of function refers to the fact that the two sides of the brain
   a. perform identical functions.
   b. do not perform identical functions.
   c. receive information from the opposite side of the body.
   d. operate independently.

3. Although he is not deaf, Mr. R. can no longer understand what people say to him. He has most likely suffered damage to the
   a. occipital lobe.
   b. temporal lobe.
   c. parietal lobe.
   d. frontal lobe.

4. People who exhibit unilateral neglect, like Miss S. in the opening vignette, ignore the left half of their environment. They have most likely suffered damage to the
   a. right occipital lobe.
   b. left temporal lobe.
   c. right parietal lobe.
   d. frontal lobe.

5. The _____ consists of three structures: _____, _____ and _____.

   a. limbic system: the thalamus, the hypothalamus, the pituitary gland
   b. brain stem: the medulla, the pons, the midbrain
   c. endocrine system: the hypothalamus, the pituitary gland, the target cells
   d. parietal lobe: the cerebellum, the brain stem, the spinal column

6. The limbic system plays an important role in
   a. digestion.
   b. movement.
   c. respiration.
   d. emotional behaviour.

7. Antipsychotic drugs that are effective against schizophrenia
   a. stimulate the reuptake of dopamine.
   b. inhibit the reuptake of dopamine.
   c. duplicate the effects of dopamine.
   d. block dopamine receptors.

8. The effects of alcohol and _____ are additive, that is, moderate doses of each taken together
   a. barbiturates; can be fatal.
   b. benzodiazepines; produce agitation and excitation.
   c. amphetamines; can be highly addictive.
   d. antidepressants; produce a feeling of serenity and well-being.

9. Drugs such as LSD suppress the activity of _____-secreting neurons permitting _____.

a. serotonin; hallucinations to occur
b. dopamine; a deep feeling of euphoria
c. acetylcholine: a reduced sensitivity to pain to develop
d. dopamine; symptoms of schizophrenia to develop

10. A person becomes a drug addict because
a. fear of withdrawal symptoms.
b. of the breakdown of the body's compensatory mechanisms.
c. of the reinforcing effects of the drug.
d. tolerance, a decreased sensitivity to the drug, requires higher and higher doses.

Answers for Self Tests

Lesson I

1. b	Obj. 4-1	2. a	Obj. 4-1	3. b	Obj. 4-2	4. b	Obj. 4-2	5. c	Obj. 4-3
6. a	Obj. 4-3	7. b	Obj. 4-4	8. d	Obj. 4-4	9. a	Obj. 4-5	10. c	Obi. 4-5

Lesson II

1. c	Obj. 4-6	2. b	Obj. 4-6	3. b	Obj. 4-7	4. c	Obj. 4-7	5. b	Obj. 4-8
6. d	Obj. 4-8	7. d	Obj. 4-9	8. a	Obj. 4-9	9. a	Obj. 4-10	10. c	Obj. 4-11

CHAPTER 5

Learning and Behaviour

LESSON I

Read the interim summary on page 138 of your text to re-acquaint yourself with the material in this section.

5-1 Define learning and describe short-term and long-term habituation.

Read pages 131-132 and answer the following questions.

1. a. Define *learning* in your own words. Your definition should state what changes occur and why.

   b. Learning cannot be _____ directly; it can only be inferred from changes in _____.

   c. Define *performance* in your own words.

   d. Describe two circumstances that influence the performance of a behaviour.

2. a. Mark was reading when he first heard the deep hum. Immediately he turned his head toward the source of the sound which, he realized, was simply his neighbour working out on her new treadmill. What name do psychologists give to Mark's response?

   b. Now, when Mark's neighbor works out on her treadmill, Mark no longer notices the noise. What name do psychologists give to the change in Mark's response?

3. Compare short-term and long-term habituation.

4. Why is habituation beneficial?

5-2 Discuss the key concepts of classical conditioning, explaining the terms unconditional stimulus, unconditional response, conditional stimulus, and conditional response.

Read pages 132-134 and answer the following questions.

1. a. Study Figures 5.1 and 5.2 in your text and explain why the child in Figure 5.2 is grimacing even before the balloon bursts.

b. Now explain the child's behaviour using these terms: defensive reaction, neutral stimulus, important stimulus, classically conditioned.

2. a. Briefly retell how Pavlov's original research interests led to his classic work in conditioning. Be sure to note what event suggested that salivation was not an automatic reflexive response.

b. Study Figure 5.3 in your text and describe Pavlov's apparatus.

c. Describe the original conditioning procedure. Be sure you mention the time interval between hearing the sound and receiving the food.

d. How did the dog respond if there was a long delay between hearing the sound and receiving the food? if the sound occurred after the dog received the food?

e. What is this kind of learning called?

3. Psychologists have given formal names to the stimuli and the responses. Study Figure 5.4 in your text and name the

a. original eliciting stimulus (such as the taste of food).

b. salivation caused by the taste of food.

c. neutral stimulus (such as a bell).

d. salivation caused by the sound of a bell.

4. a. John, a house painter, is often stung by wasps. Last week, just after setting his ladder against a house, he heard a buzzing noise and ducked his head. His response is a(n) _____. The buzzing noise is a(n) _____.

b. John does not remember the first time he was stung by a wasp. Describe what must have happened, using the correct terms for the stimuli and responses that occurred then.

5-3 Explain the two functions of classical conditioning and basic principles of acquisition, extinction, and stimulus generalization. Read pages 134-137 and answer the following questions.

1. a. List the two important functions of classical conditioning.

1.   2.

b. Cite research on the aggressive and mating behaviour of tropical fish that underscores the importance of classical conditioning. (Hollis, 1982; Hollis et al., 1989)

c. Cite research on nematode worms (Wen et al., 1997) that underscores the importance of classical conditioning in survival.

2. a. Let's examine some of the characteristics of classical conditioning beginning with acquisition of the response. Identify and explain how researchers paired stimuli and responses to teach two human subjects a conditional eyeblink response.

   1. UCS   3. CS

   2. UCR   4. CR

   b. Study the results of this research shown in Figure 5.5 in your text and describe both subjects' progress during the first 100 trials.

   c. After 100 trials, the intensity of the puff of air, or _____, delivered to Subject 1 _____, while the _____ for Subject 2 remained the same.

   d. How did the change in procedure for Subject 1 affect performance? Why?

   e. Discuss another factor that influences the acquisition of the CR. (Study Figure 5.6 in your text.)

3. a. Carefully explain how the pairing of the UCS and the CS is changed to gradually eliminate the CR.

   b. Name this procedure.

   c. Compare the extinction rates for both subjects shown in Figure 5.5. Why did extinction occur more rapidly for Subject 1?

4. What did Pavlov observe when he

   a. placed the dog in the experimental apparatus after successfully extinguishing the CR? Name this phenomenon.

   b. again paired the UCS and the CS?

5. a. Explain why other stimuli that resemble the CS may also evoke the CR.

   b. Name this phenomenon.

6. a. Explain how an animal can be trained to distinguish between similar but different stimuli using these terms: CS+ and CS-. (Study Figure 5.7 in your text.)

   b. Name this phenomenon.

   c. Why is the ability to discriminate among stimuli beneficial to an animal?

5-4 Discuss conditional emotional responses and the essential characteristics of the conditional stimulus.

Read pages 137-138 and answer the following questions.

1. a. Suppose that seeing some fossils in a museum reminds you of the times you went fossil hunting with your grandfather, and you have a feeling of nostalgia. How would you explain this event in terms of classical conditioning?

   b. Describe the conditioning procedure to establish a conditional emotional response used by Todrank et al. (1995).

2. Define *phobia* in your own words and explain how a phobia may result from either direct or indirect experience with the UCS and CS.

3. Review once again the procedure for classically conditioning a blinking response to a puff of air. Explain why only the tone eventually elicited a blinking response and not the other stimuli that were present in the classroom at the same time the tone sounded.

4. List the two conditions that must be met if a neutral stimulus is to become a CS.

   1.

   2.

Read the interim summary on page 150 of your text to re-acquaint yourself with the material in this section.

5-5   Describe Thorndike's discovery of the law of effect and Skinner's contributions to the study of operant conditioning.

Read pages 138-140 and answer the following questions.

1. a.   What kind of relationships do we learn about through habituation and classical conditioning? through operant conditioning?

   b.   Explain the relationship between an animal's behaviour and the types of events that immediately follow that behaviour.

2. a.   Briefly retell Thorndike's experience with the cat in the "puzzle box." How did he explain the cat's improved performance on successive trials?

   b.   What did Thorndike call this relationship?

   c.   Explain why the law of effect, like natural selection, contributes to an organism's survival. (Skinner, 1981, 1990)

   d.   How did Thorndike's discovery affect the development of psychology?

   e.   Name the new area of research that resulted.

3. Summarize some of the important scientific contributions of B.F. Skinner.

4. See Figure 5.8 in your text and describe an operant chamber used for rats.

5. During operant conditioning, the responses of subjects are recorded as they occur by a _____ _____. The number of responses made during a given amount of time is called the _____ _____. Events that strengthen responding _____ response rates and events that weaken responding _____ response rates.

6. In what two ways did the invention of the operant chamber and cumulative recorder advance research?

7. Recall the explanations of teaching a dog to bark on the command "Speak" and answering the telephone found in your text. Fill in the blanks in the table below.

	Dog Learning to "Speak"	Answering the Telephone
preceding event		
response		
following event		

8. a. By which more formal names do we refer to these three events?

   b. What more formal name did Skinner use to describe the relationship between these three events? (See Figure 5.9 in your text.)

9. What do we mean when we say that consequences are contingent upon behaviour?

10. Carefully explain the circumstances in which the operant behaviour will

    a. produce a consequence.

    b. have no effect.

11. How may motivational factors affect a response?

5-6 Describe the nature of reinforcement and punishment and the phenomenon of extinction.

Read pages 140-143 and answer the following questions.

1. a. Which element in the three-term contingency is the most frequently manipulated variable in experiments?

   b. List the five different kinds of consequences that can follow operant behaviours.

   1.   4.

   2.   5.

   3.

2. Let's look at each of these more closely. Begin by defining

   a. positive reinforcement.

   b. appetitive stimulus.

   c. positive reinforcer.

d. negative reinforcement.

e. aversive stimulus.

f. negative reinforcer.

3. What is the effect of both positive and negative reinforcement on the likelihood a particular response will occur again?

4. Positive reinforcement is the _____ in the frequency of the response that is reliably followed by the _____ of a(n) _____ stimulus and negative reinforcement is the _____ in the frequency of the response that is reliably followed by the _____ of a(n) _____ stimulus. Punishment is the _____ in the frequency of the response that is reliably followed by a(n) _____ stimulus.

5. Carefully explain the difference between negative reinforcement and punishment. Be sure to discuss the changes in the frequency of the behaviour in your answer.

6. Summarize some of the negative side effects of the use of punishment.

7. a. Why is immediacy of reinforcement or punishment essential for learning?

   b. What is the exception to this rule?

8. Define *response cost* punishment in your own words.

9. Punishment causes a behaviour to _____ and negative reinforcement causes a behaviour to _____.

10. a. Define *extinction* in your own words.

    b. Explain the difference between extinction and forgetting.

    c. Explain the utility of extinction for an animal.

11. Complete the figure below after studying Figure 5.10 in your text. Fill in the five blanks at the left of the figure and the five boxes at the right.

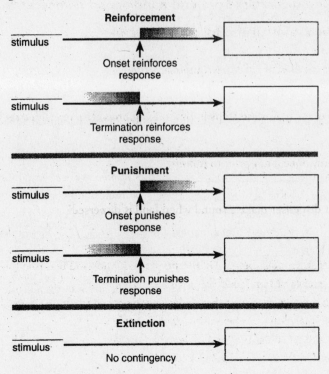

12. Complete these sentences to review some definitions and concepts of operant conditioning.

a. A stimulus that an organism seeks out is called a(n) _____ stimulus and an unpleasant or painful stimulus is called a(n) _____ stimulus.

b. The occurrence of an appetitive stimulus immediately after a behaviour will _____ the probability that the behaviour will be repeated. This phenomenon is called _____ _____.

c. The occurrence of an aversive stimulus immediately after a behaviour will _____ the probability that the behaviour will be repeated. This phenomenon is called _____.

d. The termination of an appetitive stimulus immediately after a behaviour will _____ the probability that the behaviour will be repeated. This phenomenon is called _____ _____.

e. The termination of an aversive stimulus immediately after a behaviour will _____ the probability that the behaviour will be repeated. This phenomenon is called _____ _____.

f. _____, when it occurs, requires the simple passage of time. _____ takes places only when an organism makes a response that is _____ reinforced.

5-7 Describe some other operant procedures: shaping, intermittent reinforcement, generalization and discrimination, and conditioned reinforcement and punishment.

Read pages 143–147 and answer the following questions.

1. Explain why shaping is a method of successive approximations.

2. Explain the importance of each of these steps in the training procedure to teach a rat how to press a lever when a red light goes on.

   a. Why is the rat fed only once a day prior to training?

   b. Why must the pellet dispenser make a sound when food is dispersed?

3. Number these steps so that they can be read in the proper sequence and describe the solution to the problem of training a rat to press a lever to obtain food.
   _____ equipped with a pellet dispenser that makes a noise when food is dispensed
   _____ at feeding time place rat in an operant chamber
   _____ by waiting for the rat to eat the food pellet, then delivering a few more while the rat is near the dispenser so the noise will become an appetitive stimulus
   _____ train the rat to eat from the dispenser
   _____ wait until the rat touches the lever with any part of its body before activating dispenser
   _____ make the rat hungry by feeding once a day
   _____ wait until the rat leaves the dispenser and then turns back in the direction of the lever before activating the dispenser
   _____ wait until the rat presses the lever hard enough to operate the switch by itself before activating dispenser
   _____ activate pellet dispenser for the first time

4. Define *intermittent reinforcement* in your own words.

5. Identify the factor that determines the rate at which a reinforcer is delivered in probability-based patterns of reinforcement? interval-based patterns of reinforcement?

6. Study Figure 5.11 in your text and explain the pattern of intermittent reinforcement and the pattern of response if a researcher uses a

   a. fixed-ratio schedule.

   b. variable ratio schedule.

   c. fixed-interval schedule.

d. variable-interval schedule.

7. Explain the difference between and importance of fixed and variable schedules by describing the likely work habits of a sales associate whose sales manner is evaluated

   a. every six months by the department manager.

   b. twice a year by a team of anonymous professional shoppers who make surprise visits to each department.

8. The two pigeons described in your text were trained to peck at a disk in order to receive food. The responding of one is reinforced on a one-to-one ratio, while the other receives, on the average, one reinforcer after every fifty responses.

   a. When pecking is no longer reinforced, how will each bird respond?

   b. State the rule that describes the pigeons' behaviour.

9. What personality variable may be related to experience with different schedules of reinforcement?

10. a. Carefully explain what generalization means in classical conditioning and in operant conditioning.

    b. Now explain what discrimination means in classical conditioning and in operant conditioning.

    c. What kind of discriminative stimuli do not elicit a response in operant conditioning?

11. a. What did Herrnstein and Loveland (1964) want to teach pigeons through discrimination training involving learning to peck at a translucent disk (a procedure you are already familiar with)?

    b. How did they then present the concept of a human to the pigeons?

    c. Which trials were reinforced and which were not?

    d. What was the discriminative stimulus?

    e. What were the results?

12. List some practical uses of the ability to generalize and discriminate between stimuli.

13. What did Jitsumori and Yoshihara (1997) train pigeons to categorize? What were the pigeons using to form their categories?

14. Njegoran and Weisman (1997) trained two groups of chickadees to discriminate pairs of songs.
    a. How did the pairs of songs differ? Which group of chickadees learned faster?

    b. What did they find when comparing birds raised in the wild with birds raised in the laboratory?

15. a. State the essential difference between primary reinforcers and punishers and conditioned reinforcers and punishers. Define and give an example of each of these stimuli.

    b. Give an example of each of these stimuli that is meaningful to you.

16. a. A neutral stimulus that regularly occurs just before an appetitive stimulus will become a conditioned
    _____.

    b. A neutral stimulus that regularly occurs before an aversive stimulus will become a conditioned
    _____.

    c. List two reasons why it is important that neutral stimuli can become classically conditioned reinforcers or punishers.

LESSON I SELF TEST

1. Angela noticed that her infant, who used to cry every time the phone rang, no longer does. The absence of a response is an example of
   a. species-typical behaviour.
   b. habituation.
   c. extinction.
   d. classical conditioning.

2. A child who has a balloon burst in his or her face squints whenever he or she blows up a balloon. The first time the child saw an expanding balloon it served as a(n) and the second time it was a(n)
   a. CS; UCS
   b. UCR; neutral stimulus
   c. neutral stimulus; CS
   d. UCR; CR

3. Extinction will eventually occur if
   a. neither the CS or the UCS are presented.
   b. the animal forgets the association between the neutral stimulus and the CS.
   c. the CS continues to be presented, but is no longer followed by the UCS.
   d. the CS and the UCS are not presented simultaneously.

4. Through classical conditioning
   a. learning becomes permanent.
   b. neutral stimuli take on some of the properties of important stimuli and can shape and modify behaviour.
   c. the relation between the UCS and UCR is strengthened.
   d. responses of the autonomic nervous system are protected from becoming CRs.

5. The law of effect describes the relationship between behaviour and
   a. its consequences.
   b. its persistence.
   c. neutral stimuli.
   d. resistance to extinction.

6. The _____ of an aversive stimulus is _____ and the _____ of an appetitive stimulus is _____.
   a. termination; reinforcing; termination; punishing
   b. termination; punishing; termination; reinforcing
   c. onset; reinforcing; continuation; punishing
   d. onset; punishing; termination; reinforcing

7. _____ causes a behaviour to _____ and _____ causes a behaviour to _____.
   a. Primary reinforcement; increase; conditioned reinforcement; decrease
   b. Punishment; decrease; negative reinforcement; increase
   c. Negative reinforcement; decrease; punishment; decrease
   d. Response cost; increase; negative reinforcement; decrease

8. Which one of these statements about shaping is correct?
   a. Experience indicates that food is the best reinforcer to use when shaping a behaviour.
   b. Shaping is the reinforcement of successive approximations at regular time intervals.
   c. Shaping is a formal training procedure, but something like it occurs in the outside world.
   d. The criteria for a successful response remain constant throughout the shaping procedure.

9. An animal that has been reinforced on a variable-interval schedule of reinforcement will respond
   a. rapidly, receive the reinforcer, pause a little, and respond again.
   b. more rapidly with each succeeding reinforcement.
   c. at a slow, steady rate.
   d. faster than it would on a variable-ratio schedule.

10. Njegovan and Weisman (1997) trained chickadees to discriminate pairs of songs and found that chickadees
    a. raised in the lab learned to discriminate faster
    b. learned to discriminate unrelated songs faster
    c. could not learn to discriminate pairs of songs
    d. discriminated faster when one note was always higher than the other

LESSON II

Read the interim summary on page 150 of your text to re-acquaint yourself with the material in this section.

5-8 Discuss how the capacity to learn is affected by an organism's genetic program and the development of superstitious and ritualistic behaviour.

Read pages 147-150 and answer the following questions.

1. According to Mayr (1974), what is a genetic program and how does it affects an organism's behaviour?

2. Complete the chart below.

	Closed Genetic Programs	*Open Genetic Programs*
Species		
Life Span		
Maturation Rate		
Parental Care		
Learning Capacity		

3. Review the courtship ritual of the three-spined stickleback (see Figure 5.12 in your text) and the Sandula bachelor ritual of the Laiapu Enga (Schwab, 1995) and compare the likely origins of this behaviour.

4. Explain why the customs and rituals of any culture endure. (Guerin, 1992, 1995)

5. a. What does a psychologist mean by the term *superstitious behaviour*?

   b. Briefly describe the demonstration based on Skinner's research. (Skinner, 1948)

   c. How does Skinner explain the acquisition of this behaviour?

   d. And how may humans also acquire superstitious behaviours?

6. What is the value of ritualistic behaviours such as the Sandula bachelor ritual to a culture?

7. What human characteristic permits us to adapt our behaviour to changing environmental conditions?

Read the interim summary on pages 159-160 of your text to re-acquaint yourself with the material in this section.

5-9 Discuss the learning of complex behaviours and conditioned flavour aversions, the aversive control of behaviour, and the learning that occurs through observation and imitation.

Read pages 151-155 and answer the following questions.

1. Explain why we are willing to work hard to master a difficult task.

2. For each of the following situations, suggest the conditioned reinforcer(s) which shape and maintain this behaviour.

   a. practicing a musical instrument

   b. learning to knit

   c. writing a computer program

3. Discuss two reasons why control of behaviour through aversive means is widespread.

4. Punishment can be explained as a form of classical conditioning. Briefly review the first encounter of the dog with the porcupine and study Figure 5.13 in your text and identify the

   a. species-specific defense reaction of the dog and the porcupine

   b. the UCS and UCR

5. At the next encounter with the porcupine the dog quickly ran off. Identify the

   a. CS   b.   CR

6. What is a feedback stimulus? Discuss this concept in terms of the dog and porcupine example.

7. Explain the difference between an escape response and an avoidance response.

8. a. What information must the organism have to successfully make an avoidance response?

   b. Review the encounter with a boring party guest at the buffet table and identify the external discriminative stimulus that causes you to turn away from the buffet table at a subsequent party.

9. Explain why phobias

   a. often involve avoidance responses.

   b. are especially resistant to extinction. (Study Figure 5.14 in your text.)

10. Explain how conditioned flavour aversions are acquired through classical conditioning.

11. List two reasons why psychologists study conditioned flavour aversions.

    1.   2.

12. In research by Garcia and Koelling (1966), illustrated in Figures 5.15 and 5.16 in your text, how successful were the following attempts to form conditioned aversions?

   a. taste stimulus followed by illness

   b. taste stimulus followed by shock

   c. auditory stimulus followed by illness

   d. auditory stimulus followed by shock

13. What do the results of this experiment suggest about

   a. the kind of information rats are capable of learning?

   b. the neural circuits involved in this kind of learning?

14. a. What is the evolutionary significance of the ability to learn conditioned flavour aversions?

   b. What do the different ways rats and some birds (Wilcoxon et al., 1971) form conditioned flavour aversions suggest about the adaptability of this response?

15. Describe how a young woman developed a conditioned flavour aversion to spearmint gum.

16. Indicate how the role of the same stimulus—food that causes illness—can be interpreted in two different ways.

   a. If food aversion results through operant conditioning, what is the role of flavour?

   b. If food aversion results from classical conditioning, then what is the role of flavour?

17. a. Why do some cancer patients undergoing chemotherapy develop conditioned flavour aversions? Why can these aversions have serious consequences (Bernstein, 1978, 1991)?

   b. Describe the procedure that can reduce the likelihood of such aversions. (Broberg and Bernstein, 1987)

18. Discuss a useful application of conditional flavour aversions with wildlife.

19. Describe some examples of learning through observation and imitation without external reinforcement.

   a. birds learning a song (Marler, 1961)

b. developing a fear of dogs (Bandura and Menlove, 1968)

5-10 Discuss how human behaviour is influenced by instructions, the use of symbols, and drug use and abuse.

Read pages 155-156 and answer the following questions.

1. Briefly explain why researchers study the interaction between reinforcement and rules.

2. a. Summarize how students in a study by Buskist and Miller (1986) responded when the information they were given about the reinforcement schedule in effect for the experiment was

   1. true.

   2. false.

   3. ambiguous.

   b. What do the results suggest about the kinds of rules that influence behaviour?

2. a. What do behavioural pharmacologists study?

   b. What are the origins of this discipline?

   c. What is the corresponding terminology for

      1. *discriminative stimuli*

      2. *responding*

      3. *consequences*

3. Most psychoactive drugs function as _____ in both _____ and _____. When administered, these drugs induce _____ _____ of _____.

4. Now state the conclusions of supporting research on the effect of

   a. drugs on response rates (Griffiths et al., 1980).

   b. cocaine on the behaviour of rhesus monkeys (Johnson et al., 1976).

   c. reinforcement for nondrug-taking behaviour (Higgins et al., 1994).

5. People become more sociable under the effects of alcohol. These effects do not necessarily arise from the drug itself. Discuss.

6. Explain how the reaction to the effects of a drug may be conditioned. Also explain how a change of environment from where one typically takes the drug can lead to an overdose.

5-11 Discuss the nature of insightful behaviour and compare the approaches of behaviour analysts and cognitive psychologists to the study of learning.

Read pages 156-159 and answer the following questions.

1. Summarize some common beliefs about insight.

2. Describe and discuss studies that examined problem-solving behaviour.

    a. Briefly retell how

        1. Sultan succeeded in reaching some bananas that hung in his cage. (Köhler 1927/1973; see Figure 5.17 in your text.)

        2. some cats learned to escape from a latch box. (You may wish to review this research discussed earlier in this chapter.)

    b. When Köhler compared the problem-solving behaviour of the chimpanzee and the cats, what did he conclude?

3. a. Describe the two tasks experimenters taught to a pigeon. (Epstein et al., 1984)

    b. Once the pigeon learned the tasks, how did they test the pigeon's insightful behaviour and how did the pigeon respond?

    c. What four separate tasks did they later teach another pigeon? How did the pigeon use this experience to reach a banana hanging overhead? (Epstein, 1985; See Figure 5.18 in your text.)

4. What, then, must precede an instance of insightful behaviour?

5. In their attempt to better understand learning and behaviour, what kind of events do behaviour analysts study? cognitive psychologists?

6. According to cognitive psychologists, what three factors influence learning?

7. Why do behaviour analysts question the existence of internal events and their influence on behaviour? (Skinner, 1978; 1990)

8. How do scientific debates such as this one advance human understanding?

LESSON II SELF TEST

1. The zig-zag dance of the three-spined stickleback
   a. is seen in a species with a closed genetic program.
   b. depends on previous experience.
   c. has no effect on fertility.
   d. indicates that this species is incapable of learning.

2. Superstitious behaviour develops when a response
   a. is inadvertently reinforced.
   b. causes the appetitive stimulus.
   c. is also a species-typical behaviour.
   d. terminates an aversive stimulus.

3. Society frequently employs aversive control of behaviour because
   a. the loss of money is a powerful reinforcer for all income levels.
   b. it produces almost immediate behavioural change.
   c. negative reinforcement is equivalent to punishment.
   d. punishment is more effective than positive reinforcement in changing behaviour.

4. Aversive stimuli
   a. have the same effects on behaviour as appetitive stimuli.
   b. elicit species-typical defensive responses.
   c. reinforce a wide-variety of responses.
   d. lead to extinction.

5. "The organism endures the effects of an aversive stimulus until its behaviour terminates the stimulus" best defines
   a. escape response
   b. punishment
   c. shaping
   d. positive reinforcement

6. Rats learn to avoid a particular taste that is followed by _____.
   a. illness
   b. shock
   c. noise
   d. cold

7. Baby birds reared apart from other birds can learn the song characteristic of their species if they hear the song over a loudspeaker. Their behaviour demonstrates learning through
   a. reinforcement.
   b. generalization.
   c. trial-and-error.
   d. imitation.

8. Human subjects in an operant conditioning study
   a. never learned that the schedule was really an FI 30-sec. schedule after being told it was FI 60-sec.
   b. responded to the contingencies of the schedule and ignored what they were told.
   c. never learned that the schedule was really an FI 30-sec. schedule after being told it was FI 15-sec.
   d. ignored only ambiguous information.

10. Learning through insight
    a. appears to be an innate tendency.
    b. requires external reinforcement.
    c. is usually reinforcing by itself.
    d. requires some experience with components of the new behaviour.

11. Cognitive psychologists disagree with the strict emphasis of behavioural analysts on
    a. the environmental determinants of learning.
    b. the mental processes that affect learning.
    c. the role of insight and imitation.
    d. genetic determinants of learning capacity.

Answers to Self Tests

Lesson I

1. b	Obj. 5-1	2. c	Obj. 5-2	3. c	Obj. 5-3	4. b	Obj. 5-3	5. a	Obj. 5-5
6. a	Obj. 5-6	7. b	Obj. 5-6	8. c	Obj. 5-7	9. c	Obj. 5-7	10. a	Obj. 5-7

Lesson II

1. a	Obj. 5-8	2. a	Obj. 5-8	3. b	Obj. 5-9	4. b	Obj. 5-9	5. a	Obj. 5-9
6. a	Obj. 5-9	7. d	Obj. 5-9	8. a	Obj. 5-10	9. d	Obj. 5-11	10. a	Obj. 5-11

CHAPTER 6

Sensation

LESSON I

Read the interim summary on pages 172-173 of your text to re-acquaint yourself with the material in this section.

6-1 Describe how sensory organs detect environmental events and convert the information into sensory codes.

Read pages 164-167 and answer the following questions.

1. Describe the difference between *sensation* and *perception*.

2. List the five "traditional" senses and the additional components of the somatosensory system.

3. a. Explain the process of transduction and describe the role of the receptor cells.

   b. Study Table 6.1 and list in the table below the characteristics of the stimuli transduced by the sense organs.

Location of Sense Organ	Environmental Stimuli	Energy Transduced
Eye		
Ear		
Vestibular system		
Tongue		
Nose		
Skin, internal organs		
Muscle		

4. a. List the two general types of sensory coding and give an example of each of them.

   b. Explain how the two methods code the location and intensity of a somatosensory stimulus.

6-2 Describe the basic principles of psychophysics, including signal detection theory.

Read pages 167-170 and answer the following questions.

1. Define *psychophysics* in your own words.

2. a. Explain the principle of the just-noticeable difference (jnd) discovered by Weber.

   b. Explain Weber fractions.

3. Study Figure 6.1 in your text and summarize research by Fechner using jnds to measure the magnitude of sensations.

   a. Describe the testing procedure. Be sure to use the terms *sample stimulus* and *comparison stimulus*.

   b. To begin, the sample stimulus is turned _____ and the comparison stimulus is gradually turned _____ until the subject can _____. The level of the comparison stimulus is one _____.

   c. Next, the sample stimulus is turned on at a level of one _____ and the intensity of the comparison stimulus is _____ until the subject can again _____ a difference. This level is equal to _____ jnds.

   d. Study Figure 6.1 and 6.2 in your text and explain how Steven's power function explains their differences.

4. Explain the concepts of difference threshold and absolute threshold. In the Fechner experiment, what did the first comparison measure? the subsequent comparisons?

5. Explain the 50 percent standard, as it applies to a threshold.

6. a. In your own words, describe the premise of signal detection theory.

   b. Describe the tone detection experiment outlined in your text.

   c. List the two events that fall under each of the following categories. (See Figure 6.3 in your text.)

      1. correct responses

      2. incorrect responses

d. When it is very difficult to determine whether a tone followed the flash, a decision is affected by a person's _____ _____.

e. Study Figure 6.4 in your text and explain why and how a researcher manipulates a person's response bias.

f. Now study Figure 6.5 in your text and carefully explain what accounts for the difference between the two ROC curves. Be sure to explain what ROC stands for.

g. Why is signal detection theory the best way to study a person's sensitivity to the occurrence of a stimulus?

6-3 Describe and evaluate the usefulness of subliminal self-help instruction.

Read pages 170-172 and answer the following questions.

1. a. List several ways subliminal self-help instruction is presented.

b. By what means is subliminal self-help purported to work?

c. How should its effectiveness be evaluated scientifically?

d. And how is its effectiveness demonstrated by the self-help manufacturers?

2. List three reasons that account for consumer product testimonials.

1.   3.

2.

3. a. Briefly describe the hoax perpetrated by an advertising expert. (Weir, 1984)

b. Now describe research on subliminal persuasion commissioned by the Canadian Broadcasting Corporation. (Pratkanis et al., 1990)

4. a. Define *subliminal perception* in your own words.

b. Outline the study by Cheesman and Merikle (1986) that showed that subliminal perception is real.

c. What is the effect of subliminal perception?

5. a. What task were volunteer subjects asked to do in the memory-improvement study by Pratkanis et al., 1990?

b. How did the experimenters change the task for some of the subjects?

c. When subjects were asked to evaluate improvement in either their memory or self-esteem, what did they report and what did objective tests indicate?

d. How did tape switching appear to affect satisfaction ratings?

6. What does scientific research suggest about the effectiveness of subliminal self-help instruction?

Read the interim summary on page 184 of your text to re-acquaint yourself with the material in this section.

6-4 Describe the structure of the eye and its functions.

Read pages 173-177 and answer the following questions·

1. Light consists of radiant energy that always travels at a speed of _____. The frequency of oscillation determines the _____ of radiant energy. (See Figure 6.6 in your text.)

2. The entire range of wavelengths is called the _____ _____ and the portion our eyes can detect is called the _____ _____. (See Figure 6.7 in your text.)

3. List the ways the eye is protected from injury.

4. a. Study Figure 6.8 in your text and then attach labels to the leader lines in Figure 1 on the next page.

b. State the function of the following parts of the eye.

1. cornea

2. iris

3. aqueous humor

4. cornea and lens together

5. retina

6. photoreceptors

5. The change in the shape of the lens to adjust for _____ is called _____.

6. Study Figure 6.9 in your text and describe the physical shape of the eye which causes a person to be either nearsighted or farsighted.

7. a. What is the name of the location where all axons leave the eye? (See Figure 6.10 in your text.)

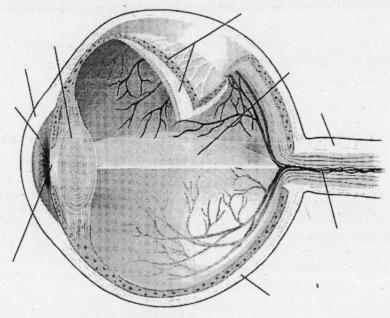

Figure 1

b. Try the demonstration illustrated in Figure 6.11 in your text and explain your reaction by referring to photoreceptors.

c. Describe how Scheiner demonstrated the function of the lens.

8. a. Name the three principal layers of the retina through which light passes. (See Figure 6.12 in your text.)

b. By what means do photoreceptor cells pass information to bipolar cell layer?

c. What is the name of the cells that receive information from bipolar cells and then transmit information to the brain?

9. Complete the following table about the photoreceptors found in the human retina.

Photoreceptor	Illumination Detected	Role in Color Vision

10. a. Where is the fovea located? (Refer back to Figure 6.8.) What is the name of the only kind of photoreceptors found there?

   b. Explain why our most detailed vision occurs in the fovea.

   c. Explain why sensitivity to light increases, but visual acuity decreases, at points farther away from the fovea.

6-5 Describe the transduction of light by photoreceptors, adaptation to light and dark, and the nature and function of eye movements.

Read pages 177-179 and answer the following questions.

   a. Name the vitamin from which a molecule that plays a key role in visual transduction is derived.

   b. In general terms, describe the two molecules that constitute a photopigment.

   c. How many kinds of photopigments are there in the human eye and where are they located?

   d. _____ is the photopigment found in the rods.

   e. What is a photon?

2. Now you are ready to describe how photoreceptors in the photoreceptor layer of the retina transduce the energy of light. (Study Figure 6.13 in your text.)

   a. When a photon strikes the photopigment of a photoreceptor cell, what happens to the photopigment?

   b. What kind of changes occur in the photoreceptor cells when the photopigment splits apart?

   c. Name the cells with which the photoreceptors synapse.

   d. Name the cells to which the bipolar cells send a message.

   e. Name the cells which transmit the message to the brain.

3. a. What happens to the characteristic colour of a photopigment when it is split apart by a photon?

b.   What is needed for the molecules to recombine and form a photopigment again?

c.   What determines how many intact molecules of photopigment are present in a photoreceptor at any one time?

4.   Explain dark adaptation by referring to levels of photopigment and the changing number of intact photoreceptors.

5.   In your own words, define

a.   *fixation point*.

b.   *stabilized image*.

6.   a.   Figure 6.14 in your text diagrams how Riggs and his colleagues (1953) were able to project stabilized images onto a subject's retina. Describe the results of this research.

b.   What do the results suggest may be the purpose of the small random movements the eye makes?

7.   Name and give examples of the three kinds of "purposive" movements the eye makes.

1.

2.

3.

6-6   Describe the physical and perceptual dimensions of colour and compare colour mixing and pigment mixing.

Read pages 179-180 and answer the following questions.

1.   What do we mean when we say: "Each of the three types of cones in our eyes contains a different type of photopigment that responds best to a particular wavelength of light"?

2.   Study Table 6.2 in your text and complete the following table.

Physical Dimension of Light	Corresponding Perceptual Dimension of Light

3. In terms of saturation and brightness, what will be the result of mixing white light with a light of a single wavelength? (See Figure 6.15 in your text.)

4. a. Explain the difference between colour mixing and paint or pigment mixing. (See Figure 6.16 in your text.)

   b. Explain why we see an object as having a particular colour.

   c. Mixing two paints together results in a _____ colour, whereas mixing two or more lights together always results in a _____ colour.

   d. To produce white light, is it necessary to recombine all the colours of the visual spectrum? Explain. (Study Figure 6.17 in your text.)

6-7 Describe colour coding by cones and ganglion cells in the retina, negative afterimages, and genetic defects in colour vision.

Read pages 180-184 and answer the following questions.

1. a. Briefly explain Young's hypothesis of colour vision, the trichromatic theory, by referring to the number and kind of colour receptors.

   b. Later research found that the human eye does contain three kinds of cones that respond to three different wavelengths of light. List the three kinds of cones by their commonly accepted names.

2. How are the three types of cones in the retina affected when a spot of white light shines on them? a spot of pure blue, green, or red light? a spot of yellow light?

3. a. List the two types of colour-coding ganglion cells.

   1.   2.

   b. Describe the firing rate of these cells when they are not being stimulated.

   c. Study Figure 6.18 in your text and carefully explain how these spots of different coloured light affect the firing rate of red/green ganglion cells.

   1. red light

   2. green light

   3. yellow light

   d. What is the name of this coding system?

4. Try the demonstration in Figure 6.19 in your text and then explain why you saw the negative afterimage. Be sure to refer to the rebound effect in your answer.

5. Why are males rather than females more frequently affected by colour blindness?

6. Summarize information about colour blindness by completing this table. (See Figure 6.20 in your text.)

Colour defect	Cause	Sex Most Frequently Affected

7. a. What is the nature of the problem for people with either protanopia or deuteranopia?
   b. What may be the reason that these two colour defects are more common than tritanopia?

LESSON I SELF TEST

1. All sensory systems use rate of firing to encode _____ of stimulation.
   a. presence
   b. type
   c. source
   d. intensity

2. A stimulus with a value of 1 jnd is just above the
   a. difference threshold.
   b. absolute threshold.
   c. receiver-operating characteristic.
   d. response bias.

3. Receiver-operating characteristic curves
   a. can be used to detect the presence of response bias.
   b. indicate the detectability of stimuli.
   c. are composed of jnds.
   d. are a comparison of the investigator's and the subject's estimate of the threshold of detection.

4. Subliminal perception _____ occur and its effects _____ produce useful changes in people's behaviour.
   a. does; do

   b. does; do not
   c. does; are unlikely to
   d. does not; cannot

5. Visual information passes to the brain according to the following sequence.
   a. cornea, retina, fovea, brain
   b. photoreceptor, bipolar cell, ganglion cell, brain
   c. lens, ganglion cell, bipolar cell, brain
   d. photoreceptor, optic nerve, optic disk, brain

6. What is the role of photopigment in the transduction of light?
   a. It reflects light onto the retina.
   b. It splits apart when struck by a photon and begins the process of transduction.
   c. It stimulates the production of a molecule derived from vitamin A.
   d. It recombines to maintain visual acuity.

7. When driving at night, it is more difficult to see if the driver of an oncoming car does not dim the high beams because
   a. bright light directed at the fovea reduces visual acuity.

b. the number of intact rods is reduced in the dark.

c. bright light bleaches many molecules of photopigments.

d. there are too many intact rhodopsin molecules for your eyes to respond immediately to bright light.

8. Wavelength is a _____ dimension of light and hue is the corresponding _____ dimension.

a. perceptual; physical

b. physical; perceptual

c. perceptual; psychological

d. psychological; perceptual

9. Thomas Young was essentially correct when he hypothesized that the eye contains _____ types of colour receptors that respond to _____.

a. three; red, green, and blue

b. three; black, white, and gray

c. six; the spectral colours

d. two; red/green and yellow/blue

10. The most important cause of negative afterimages is

a. mechanical stimulation of the eve.

b. bleaching of photopigment.

c. the absence of rods in the fovea.

d. changes in the firing rate of ganglion cells.

LESSON II

Read the interim summary on page 193 of your text to re-acquaint yourself with the material in this section.

6-8 Describe the structure and functions of the auditory, system.

Read pages 184-191 and answer the following questions.

1. What does sound consist of?

2. For the following phases of vibration, indicate the corresponding changes in air pressure and direction of movement of the eardrum. (See Figure 6.21 in your text.)

Direction of Movement of Vibrating Object	Air Pressure	Eardrum
moving toward you		
moving away from you		

3. Sound is measured in frequency units of cycles per second called _____.

4. What is the corresponding perceptual dimension of intensity? frequency? complexity? (See Figure 6.22 in your text.)

5. Study the anatomy of the ear shown in Figure 6.23 in your text and then add labels to the leader lines in Figure 2.

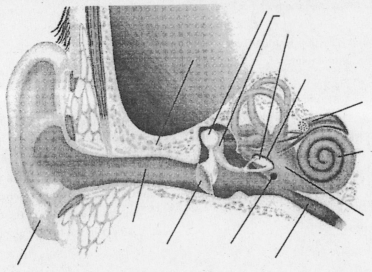

Figure 2

6. Next to each of the parts of the ear that you have labeled, indicate its function.

7. a. Refer to Figure 6.23 and describe how the liquid inside the cochlea moves in response to sound vibrations. (Be sure to note the role of the oval window.)

   b. Study Figure 6.24 in your text and indicate which regions of the basilar membrane vibrate in response to high-, middle-, and low-frequency sounds. (Now be sure to note the role of the round window.)

   c. Explain the importance of the surgical procedure called fenestration.

8. a. What is the name of the cells of the auditory system that perform the same function as the photoreceptors of the visual system?

   b. Where are they located? (See Figure 6.25 in your text.)

   c. Describe the location and appearance of the cilia.

9. a. Explain how the cilia respond when sound vibrations cross the basilar membrane. What change occurs in their membrane when a mechanical force is exerted on the cilia?

   b. Arrange these events in the correct order to explain how information about sound vibrations is transmitted to the brain.

   causing the release of transmitter substance / found in the auditory hair cells / changes the electrical charge / excites a neuron of the auditory nerve / across their membrane / and the dendrite of the auditory nerve /

which transmits messages to the brain / at a synapse between the auditory hair cell / a mechanical force exerted on the cilia / through the auditory nerve

Now let's examine how the brain distinguishes these characteristics of sound: loudness, pitch, timbre, and location.

10. a. Let's begin with pitch. Cite evidence that makes it unlikely that the brain encodes pitch through synchronous firing of axons.

b. By what means does the brain receive information about the high- and medium-frequency sounds? (Refer back to Figure 6.24.)

c. Summarize supporting research.

1. What did von Békésy (1960) observe?

2. Describe how Stebbins et al. (1969) used antibiotics to study the anatomical coding of pitch.

11. a. State the results of research by Kiang (1965) on how the brain receives information about low-frequency sounds.

b. Describe how the basilar membrane encodes low-frequency sounds.

c. Summarize supporting research with white noise by Miller and Taylor (1948).

12. By what means does the brain receive information about the loudness of high- and medium-frequency sounds? low-frequency sounds?

13. a. In your own words, define

1. complex tone.

2. overtone.

3. fundamental frequency.

4. timbre.

b. Use these terms to explain how the ear identifies a sound such as a clarinet. (See Figure 6.26 in your text.)

14. a. What is the most effective means of identifying the location of high-frequency sounds? Study Figure 6.27 in your text and explain why.

b. By what means do we identify the location of a sound frequencies below approximately 3000 Hz. (See Figure 6.28 in your text.)

c. Compare the vibrations of the eardrums when the sound is located to the side of the head and in front of the head.

15. a. Discuss the method Dong et al. (1999) used to investigate aftereffects in sound localization.

b. What did these researchers find?

16. Describe the effects of age-related hearing loss.

6-9 Explain how the use of sign language unifies the Deaf community.

Read pages 191-193 and answer the following questions.

1. Describe the Deaf community and sign language by completing these sentences.

a. Not all deaf people are members of the Deaf community because

b. The most common sign language used in North America is

c. The grammar of ASL is based on

d. Word-for-word translations from a spoken language to a sign language are impossible because

e. Because there is no single, universal sign language

2. List the three aspects of deafness that follow the "90-percent rule."

1.

2.

3.

3. Briefly explain how having hearing parents and educational "mainstreaming" affect the use of sign language and ultimately the Deaf community.

4. a. What is the oralist approach to deaf education?

b. Outline some of the difficulties that deaf children educated this way must overcome?

5. Explain why some deaf people

a. who can communicate using sign language prefer it to oral communication.

b. would not choose to hear.

c. are relieved that their offspring are also deaf.

6. a. What is a cochlear implant?

   b. List the groups most likely to benefit from this surgery.

   c. What are some of the implications of the increased use cochlear implants for the Deaf community?

Read the interim summary on page 197 of your text to re-acquaint yourself with the material in this section.

6-10 Describe receptor cells on the tongue, their role in transducing gustatory stimuli, and the four qualities of taste.

Read page 194 and answer the following questions.

1. _____ and _____ or the chemosenses help us detect _____ in our environment. We perceive only four qualities of taste: _____, _____, _____, and _____. Taste, or _____, is not the same thing as _____ which includes both _____ and _____.

2. Briefly explain why the flavor of food diminishes when you have a head cold.

3. a. What is the name of the bumps on the tongue? (See Figure 6.29 in your text.)

   b. Where are receptor cells on the tongue located?

   c. Describe the microvilli and their function.

4. Study Figure 6.30 in your text and then add labels to the leader lines in Figure 3.

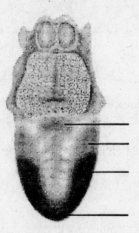

Figure 3

5. a. What characteristic of the stimulus determines the kind of taste we experience?

   b. What is the probable biological significance of our ability to detect the following tastes?

      1. salty

      2. bitter

      3. sweet

      4. sour

6-11 Describe the anatomy of the olfactory system and the dimensions of odour.

Read pages 195-196 and answer the following questions.

1. a. How does our sense of smell differ from our other senses?

   b. What is a possible explanation for the unique ability of particular odours to evoke old memories and feelings?

   c. Suggest some of the ways the ability to detect odours is important in the lives of most mammals.

2. Study Figure 6.31 in your text then add labels to the leader lines in Figure 4.

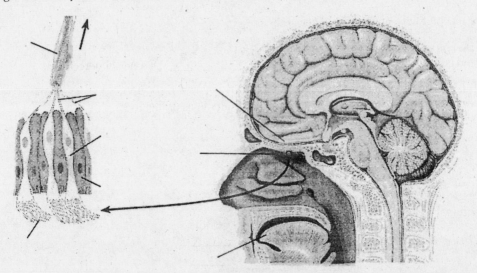

Figure 4

3. Compare the effects of odour molecules on receptors with that of transmitter substances on postsynaptic receptors of a neuron.

4. All other sense modalities send information to the _____, but the olfactory system sends information to the _____ _____.

5. a. Dalton et. al. (2000) investigated the cross modal integration of taste and olfactory stimulation. How did they investigate this phenomenon?

   b. What were their results and what did they conclude?

6. a. How many different receptor molecules may be used by the olfactory system? (Jones and Reed, 1989; Buck and Axel, 1991; Axel, 1995)

   b. How do odour molecules and receptor molecules apparently interact?

Read the interim summary on page 201 of your text to re-acquaint yourself with the material in this section.

6–12 Describe the somatosenses, the internal senses, and the vestibular senses.

Read pages 197-200 and answer the following questions.

1. All somatosensory information is detected by the _____ of neurons rather than by separate _____ _____.

2. Some dendrites have specialized endings. List and describe the function of two of these endings. (See Figure 6.32 in your text.)

   1.

   2.

3. a. Warmth and coolness are probably detected by _____ kinds of detectors.

   b. Temperature detectors respond best to _____ in temperature, but they eventually _____ to changes in the temperature of the environment within limits.

4. a. Distinguish between touch and pressure.
   b. Describe the sensations you would feel on your arm from

      1. a small weight in the beginning and a few minutes later.

      2. an additional weight. (Nafe and Wagoner, 1941)

      3. a very heavy weight.

   c. Explain why you experienced these different responses.

5. Describe the method for determining the two-point discrimination threshold and explain how the results are interpreted. (See Figure 6.33 in your text.)

6. a. List the two components of pain.

   1.   2.

b. Outline evidence supporting this distinction by giving an example of

   1. drugs that affect the physical reaction to pain.

   2. surgical procedures that affect the emotional reaction to pain.

c. List the two types of pain sensation and give an example of stimuli that would cause each of them.

   1.   2.

d. What is the biological significance of the ability to experience pain? (Be sure to refer to the opening vignette.)

7. a. Summarize the experiences of people afflicted with sensations of a phantom limb as well as the accepted explanation. (Melzak, 1992.)

b. What treatment is, at least, temporarily successful?

c. According to Melzak, why may the phantom limb sensation be an inevitable reaction to amputation?

8. Before a competition, why have some weight lifters received injections of a local anesthetic near the tendons? What risk do they run?

9. Where are muscle spindles found and what is their function?

10. a. Study the vestibular apparatus of the inner ear shown in Figure 6.34 in your text and add labels to the leader lines in Figure 5.

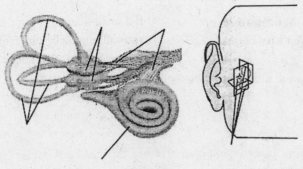

Figure 5

11. a. Describe how the semicircular canals detect head rotation.

b. Describe how the vestibular sacs detect head tilt.

c. Describe another useful function of the vestibular sacs.

LESSON II SELF TEST

1. The basilar membrane
   a. divides the cochlea into two parts.
   b. isolates the semi-circular canals from each other.
   c. surrounds the ossicles.
   d. lines the ear canal.

2. High- and medium-frequency sounds cause _____ of the basilar membrane to vibrate.
   a. the tip
   b. various regions
   c. the middle
   d. the upper half

3. We perceive the location of sounds by using
   a. rate and range.
   b. sound thresholds.
   c. orienting responses and arrival time.
   d. relative loudness and arrival time.

4. Members of the Deaf community
   a. have been deaf from birth.
   b. recognize their deafness is a deficit that needs correction.
   c. communicate visually using sign language.
   d. are relieved when their children have normal hearing.

5. American Sign Language is
   a. signed English.
   b. the universally accepted manual language.
   c. a full-fledged language.
   d. not as efficient a means of communication as a spoken language.

6. Foods do not taste as good when you have a head cold because
   a. fluid intake must be increased and the diminished taste of food has evolved as an important signal in regulating body fluids.
   b. congestion makes it difficult for food odours to reach receptors for your sense of smell.
   c. your saliva becomes thicker and blocks some receptor cells.
   d. fever impairs the functioning of receptor cells.

7. Research on olfaction
   a. has shown that we possess a very large number of receptors for specific odours.
   b. indicates the existence of four primary odours.
   c. has found that the olfactory bulbs send information directly to the limbic system.
   d. has shown that the human olfactory system is relatively insensitive when compared to animals.

8. Pacinian corpuscles detect
   a. warmth.
   b. coolness.
   c. pain.
   d. vibration.

9. If a small weight is placed on your motionless arm, you will eventually stop feeling its presence because sensory endings that respond to touch
   a. experience fatigue.
   b. only respond to movement.
   c. are self-inhibiting.
   d. require muscular contraction.

10. The _____ detect changes in the rotation of the head.
    a. semicircular canals
    b. vestibular sacs
    c. free nerve endings
    d. cilia

Answers for Self Tests

Lesson

1. d	Obj. 6-1	2. a	Obj. 6-2	3. b	Obj. 6-2	4. c	Obj. 6-3	5. b	Obj. 6-4
6. b	Obj. 6-5	7. c	Obj. 6-5	8. b	Obj. 6-6	9. a	Obj. 6-7	10. d	Obj. 6-7

Lesson II

1. a	Obj. 6-8	2. b	Obj. 6-8	3. d	Obj. 6-8	4. c	Obj. 6-9	5. c	Obj. 6-9
6. b	Obj. 6-10	7. c	Obj. 6-11	8. d	Obj. 6-12	9. b	Obj. 6-12	10. a	Obj. 6-12

CHAPTER 7

Perception

LESSON I

Read the interim summary on page 211 of your text to re-acquaint yourself with the material in this section.

7-1 Describe the primary visual cortex, the visual association cortex, and the effects of brain damage on visual perception.

Read pages 207-211 and answer the following questions.

1. a. Define *perception* in your own words.

   b. Where does perception take place?

2. Study Figure 7.1 in your text and review the visual pathway to the brain by arranging these steps in the correct sequence. Begin with visual information from the optic nerves.

   optic nerves / in the middle of the parietal lobe / the second level of visual association cortex / thalamus / the first level of visual association cortex / primary visual cortex in the occipital lobe / in the lower part of the temporal lobe / in the occipital lobe

3. Briefly explain how perception can be seen as a hierarchy of information processing.

4. a. Briefly describe the experimental procedure Hubel and Wiesel (1977, 1979) used to study the earliest stages of visual analysis. Be sure to explain the importance of microelectrodes and anesthesia in your answer.

   b. Why did they
      1. move the stimuli around on the screen?

      2. present stimuli with various shapes?

   c. According to Hubel and Wiesel, what is the relation between the geography of the visual field and primary visual cortex?

d. Explain why the map resembles a mosaic.

e. List some of the characteristics analyzed by these mosaic "tiles," which are usually called modules. Be sure to explain the relationship between this analysis and the receptive field.

5. Study Figure 7.2 in your text and explain how a line of a particular orientation is detected.

6. Explain why the primary visual cortex is not capable of analyzing an entire scene.

7. a. Study Figure 7.3 in your text and then add labels to the ovals and fill in the blanks in Figure 1.

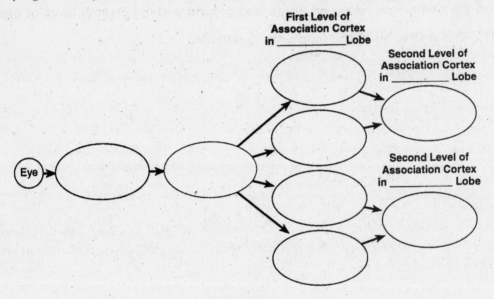

First Level of Association Cortex in _____ Lobe

Second Level of Association Cortex in _____ Lobe

Second Level of Association Cortex in _____ Lobe

Eye

Figure 1

b. Describe the PET-scan studies of the effects of different stimuli on localized brain activity. (See Figure 7.4 in your text.) Relate these results to the diagram in Figure 1, above.

8. a. If the primary visual cortex is damaged, what is the effect on a person's vision and perception?

b. What do the results suggest about the function of the visual association cortex?

c. Confirm your answer by trying the demonstration with the roll of paper described in your text.

9. If the visual association cortex is damaged, what is the effect on a person's vision and perception?

10. Describe the vision deficits shown by patients with

a. achromatopsia. (See Figure 7.5 in your text.)

b. bilateral damage to a particular subregion of visual association cortex. (Zihl et al., 1991)

c. Balint's syndrome.

d. visual agnosia. (Benson and Greenberg, 1969)

e. prosopagnosia. (Damasio et al., 1990)

Read the interim summary on page 222 of your text to re-acquaint yourself with the material in this section.

7-2 Describe the distinction between figure and ground and the Gestalt laws of grouping.

Read pages 212-214 and answer the following questions.

1. What is a boundary? What role does it play in distinguishing figure from ground? (See Figures 7.6 and 7.7 in your text.)

2. See Figures 7.8 and 7.9 in your text and explain the following statement: "The presence of a boundary is not necessary for the perception of form." Be sure to use the term *illusory contours* in your answer.

3. State and briefly explain the principle tenet of Gestalt psychology.

4. a. List the five Gestalt laws of grouping. (See Figures 7.10-7.13 in your text.)

   1.

   2.

   3.

   4.

   5.

   b. Now make sketches that illustrate each of the laws (or provide a brief verbal description).

7-3 Discuss current models of pattern perception.

Read pages 214-217 and answer the following questions.

1. Models of pattern perception have been developed by _____ psychologists.

2. Define *template* in your own words.

3. a. Briefly describe the template model of perception.

   b. Why is it difficult to accept this theory?

4. a. Define *prototype* in your own words.

   b. Briefly describe the prototype model of perception.

   c. Describe supporting evidence that demonstrated the capacity of the brain

      1. to retain images.

      2. to form and retain visual prototypes. Be sure to mention the term *habituation* in your answer. (Humphrey, 1974.)

5. a. Define *distinctive features* in your own words. (See Figure 7.14 in your text.)

   b. Briefly describe the distinctive features model of perception.

6. a. Look at Figure 7.15 in your text and find the letter Z in both columns—a task Neisser (1964) asked subjects to do.

   b. Use the distinctive features model of perception to explain your performance.

7. a. Look at Figure 7.16 in your text and discuss how contextual cues affect perception.

   b. What does your explanation suggest about a difficulty with the distinctive features model of perception?

8. a. According to Biederman (1987, 1990), what kind of features of objects are essential for object recognition?

   b. Study Figure 7.17 in your text and describe some of the geons proposed by Biederman.

   c. How may the visual system use geons to identify objects?

9. a. What perceptual finding may be a problem for Beiderman's model? (Humphrey & Khan, 1992, Tarr, et al., 1998)

   b. Even if our ability to perceive categories of objects involves _____, it seems unlikely they are involved in the perception of _____ objects.

10. The geon hypothesis may best explain the perception of what kind of objects? Why?

7-4 Describe and evaluate serial and parallel models of mental functions.

Read pages 218-219 and answer the following questions.

1. List the four major parts of a general-purpose computer and describe their functions. (See Figure 7.18 in your text.)

   1.

   2.

   3.

   4.

2. a. Define *artificial intelligence* in your own words.

   b. Describe an advantage and a disadvantage to this approach to understanding the way the brain works.

3. Explain why the modern general-purpose computer is referred to as a serial device.

4. Does the brain work fast enough to function efficiently as serial device? Explain.

5. Identify and describe a better model for understanding how the human brain works.

7-5 Describe neural network models and describe research on top-down and bottom-up perceptual processing.

Read pages 219-221 and answer the following questions.

1. Define *neural network* in your own words.

2. a. Describe the properties of the simple elements of a neural network. (See Figure 7.19 in your text.)

   b. Relate these properties to what you already know about neurons.

3. Discuss how neural networks can simulate brain plasticity.

4. Investigators have written computer programs to simulate neural networks. Compare the ability of these networks with the ability of the brain to recognize particular patterns.

5. Describe the kind of information analyzed by neural networks in the brain at each of the following locations in the visual system. (See Figure 7.20 in your text.)

   a. primary visual cortex

   b. subregions of visual association cortex of the occipital lobe

   c. visual association cortex of the temporal lobe

   d. visual association cortex of the parietal lobe

6. Is the serial computer a good model to explain brain function?

7. a. To understand the importance of context for accurate perception, look first at Figure 7.21 and then Figure 7.22 in your text.

   b. After showing subjects familiar scenes, what did Palmer show them next? (See Figure 7.23 in your text.)

   c. Name and explain the use of the device he used to present the stimuli.

   d. How accurately did subjects identify objects that fit the context of the original scene? did not fit the context? and in the no-context control condition?

e. What do these results suggest about the role of context in object identification?

8. Describe the following:

a. bottom-up processing.

b. top-down processing.

9. a. What task were monkey subjects trained to perform? (Haenny and Schiller, 1988)

b. How did neurons respond when the visual stimulus matched the pattern they had been trained to recognize?

c. If monkey felt a pattern of grooves at a particular orientation and then saw a matching visual pattern, how did neurons respond? (Haenny et al., 1988)

d. What do the results of this study suggest about contextual importance and top-down information processing?

10. Study Figure 7.24 in your text and explain why perception consists of both top-down and bottom-up information processing.

LESSON I SELF TEST

1. What is the name of the brain region where three dimensional form perception takes place?
   a. primary visual cortex
   b. first level of visual association cortex surrounding primary visual cortex
   c. second level of visual association cortex in the parietal lobe
   d. second level of visual association cortex in the lower temporal lobe

2. A person with visual agnosia can no longer
   a. see colours.
   b. recognize particular objects by sight.
   c. see where objects are located.
   d. read.

3. What we perceive can be classified into two broad categories:
   a. animate and inanimate.
   b. foreground and background.
   c. figure and ground.
   d. relevant and irrelevant.

4. Our perception of wind currents in a field of wheat illustrates the Gestalt law of
   a. proximity.
   b. similarity.
   c. closure.
   d. common fate.

5. Many psychologists prefer the prototype model of perception to the template model of perception because prototypes are
   a. not idealized representations of objects.
   b. more flexible than templates.
   c. representations of only one object.
   d. consistent with Gestalt laws of grouping.

6. An important difficulty with the distinctive features model of perception is
   a. the need for an almost limitless number of special circuits for feature detection.
   b. that the effects of context receive too much weight.
   c. the lack of an acceptable operational definition of "distinctive feature."
   d. that the perception of simple and complex features occurs at about the same speed.

7. Computers are an excellent basis for models of neural processes because they
   a. contain four major parts that correspond with particular regions of the brain.
   b. operate as quickly as the brain.
   c. are flexible and powerful.
   d. process information in parallel.

8. Parallel processors work
   a. simultaneously at several different tasks.
   b. one step at a time.
   c. slowly.
   d. the way neural synapses do.

9. Neural networks
   a. contain a central processor.
   b. lack input and output devices.
   c. employ memory banks that contain templates.
   d. can "learn" to recognize particular stimuli.

10. The use of context in perception is an example of
    a. trial and error.
    b. bottom-up processing.
    c. top-down processing.
    d. serial processing.

LESSON II

Read the interim summary on page 235 of your text to re-acquaint yourself with the material in this section.

7-6 Describe how we perceive space and motion and discuss the monocular and binocular cues for distance perception.

Read pages 223-227 and answer the following questions.

1. a. Animals with eyes in the front of the head can obtain both _____ and _____ cues, but animals with eyes on the side of the head can obtain only _____ cues. Why?

   b. Summarize Figure 7.25 in your text by listing the principal monocular and binocular cues for depth perception at the ends of the arrows in the figure below.

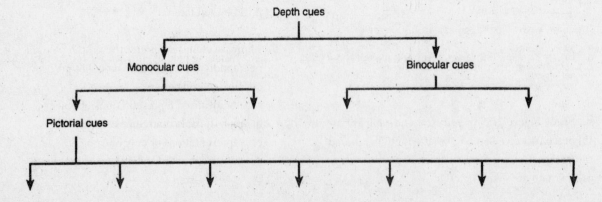

2. Under what circumstances do we make use of movement cues (motion parallax)?

3. Study Figure 7.26 in your text. When the eyes converge on a distant object the angle between them is
_____ than when they converge on a _____ object.

4. a. Try the demonstration in your text of holding your fingers in front of your eyes and explain the term *retinal disparity*.

   b. Define the term *stereopsis*.

   c. Study Figure 7.27 in your text and explain the role of retinal disparity in depth perception (Schiffman, 1996).

   d. Cite research recording the electrical activity of individual neurons that further supports your explanation.

5. Discuss monocular cues that can be illustrated in a painting or photograph.

   a. Almost everyone who sees Figure 7.28 in your text sees two groups of two objects, with the left-hand object being closer. Use the concepts of good form and interposition to explain why we do not usually see a complex figure and how we judge the location of each object.

   b. While you are hiking you see a church steeple in the distance. Explain how familiarity with sizes helps you determine how far away you are from the building.

   c. Study Figures 7.29 in your text and explain why we rely on linear perspective and ignore the size of retinal images to determine the size of an object.

   d. Study Figures 7.30 and 7.31 in your text and describe how cues provided by texture and haze influence distance perception.

   e. Study Figure 7.32 in your text and explain how cues provided by shading help us judge the distance of parts of an object.

   f. Study Figure 7.33 in your text and explain how elevation in relation to the horizon influences distance perception.

6. Discuss how monocular cues from head and body movements influence distance perception.

   a. If you gaze at a scene while moving your head from side to side, what is the location of objects that change the most in relation to head movements?

   b. Study Figure 7.34 in your text and using the phenomenon of motion parallax to explain how the relative location of features in the environment change as we move.

7-7 Discuss evidence that perceptual development may be influenced by cultural experience.

Read pages 227-230 and answer the following questions.

1. List the two broad classes of variables in which cultures can differ and give several examples of each.

   1.   2.

   Examples   Examples

Let's look more closely at ecological variables.

2. How may perceptual development be affected by

   a. geographical variables?

   b. cultural codes found in pictorial representations? (Reports cited by Berry et al., 1992.)

3. a. What did British Prime Minister William Gladstone observe in the writings of the ancient Greeks and what hypothesis did this observation suggest to him?

   b. Briefly describe how Magnus (1880) tested this hypothesis.

   c. What did his results suggest about the relationship between language and perceptual ability?

4. State the principle of linguistic relativity. Who is its best-known proponent?

5. According to this principle, colour names are _____ _____.

6. a. What did studies (Berlin and Kay, 1969; Kay, 1975) of a wide range of languages indicate about the number of primary colour terms?

b. What general name did they give to these colours?

7. What does agreement about the categories of colours that require names suggest is the basis for the selection of colour names by cultures?

8. Summarize research with the Dani people of New Guinea that supports this conclusion. (Heider, 1972; Rosch, 1973)

9. Refer to the study conducted by Roberson, et al. (2000).

   a. Describe how English speakers and Berinmo speakers categorized colours.

   b. What conclusions were drawn from this study?

10. a. Study Figure 7.35 in your text and describe the Müller-Lyer illusion.

   b. Which group of subjects in a study by Segal et al. (1966) was more susceptible to the Müller-Lyer illusion?

   c. What do these results suggest about the influence of culture experience on visual perception? (See Figure 7.36 in your text.)

11. What can we conclude about the effects of cultural experience on perceptual development?

7-8 Describe and discuss the phenomena of brightness and form constancy.

Read pages 230-231 and answer the following questions.

1. Explain the concept of brightness constancy in your own words.

2. a. Describe the equipment and procedure Katz (1935) used to demonstrate this phenomenon. (Study Figure 7.37 in your text.)

   b. How accurately did subjects match squares of different shades of gray on the right with the gray square in shadow?

   c. If subjects had compared colour shades based strictly on the amount of light reflected by the two squares, how would their accuracy rate have changed?

   d. What do the results suggest about the perception of brightness?

3. a. Explain the concept of form constancy.

   b. According to von Helmholtz, why does our perception of an object's size remain relatively constant? Be sure to use the term unconscious inference in your answer.

c. Study Figure 7.38 in your text and explain why we perceive the shape of the window as rectangular.

d. If an unfamiliar object produces a large retinal image how will we perceive its size if it is far away? nearby?

e. Study Figure 7.39 in your text and then turn it upside down. Now explain why this phenomenon occurs.

7-9 Discuss research on the perception of motion.

Read pages 231-235 and answer the following questions.

1. Briefly describe the waterfall phenomenon.

2. a. What did subjects in research by Tootell et al., (1995) report when the concentric rings they had been watching stopped?

   b. How did the metabolic activity of their brains, measured at the same time by brain scans, correspond to the length of the illusion?

3. a. How did Ball and Sekuler (1982) train subjects to detect the motion of a series of dots?

   b. What were the results of training? How long did the effects of training persist?

   c. What do the results suggest about the effects of practice on motion detection?

4. a. Try all three demonstrations about moving retinal images described in your text and then explain how the brain interprets the significance of perceived motion. (Study Figure 7.40 in your text.)

   b. State the general rule for determining how objects of different sizes appear to move in relationship to each other.

   c. Describe how Johansson (1973) demonstrated the kinds of information that can be obtained from movement and list some of the features that the subjects could detect.

   d. What additional information can people determine with reasonable accuracy? (Kozlowski and Cutting, 1977; Barclay et al., 1978)

5. a. After each rapid steplike eye movement, or _____, the eye stops briefly to rest and gather information. These stops are called _____.

   b. Study Figures 7.41 and 7.42 in your text and, using the concept of fixation, explain why one of the figures is more difficult to evaluate.

6. a. Explain the phenomenon of backward masking in your own words. (Werner, 1935)

   b. Summarize Breitmeyer's (1980) explanation for this phenomenon.

   c. Study Figure 7.43 in your text and explain what would happen if backward masking did not take place.

7. Describe the phi phenomenon and give an example of an important application of this phenomenon.

LESSON II SELF TEST

1. Convergence as a cue for distance perception depends on information
   a. about the angle between the eyes.
   b. about the amount of disparity, produced by images of the objects on both retinas.
   c. obtained from monocular vision.
   d. about the size of objects midway between the target object and the eyes.

2. A stereoscope can be used to demonstrate the role of _____ in depth perception.
   a. backward masking
   b. retinal disparity
   c. negative afterimages
   d. motion parallax

3. Which monocular cue cannot be represented realistically in a drawing?
   a. texture
   b. interposition
   c. elevation
   d. motion parallax

4. The principle of linguistic relativity states that language
   a. is the most important component of cultural identity.
   b. imperfectly reflects abstract ideas and concepts.
   c. not only voices ideas and perceptions but shapes them as well.
   d. is the best indicator of potential for cultural development.

5. Various studies to identify colour terms in a wide range of languages concluded that
   a. colour names are purely cultural conventions.
   b. the physiology of the visual system and cultural conventions determine the selection of colour names.
   c. with the exception of black and white, the selection of focal colours varied among cultures.
   d. nonfocal colours reflect nature and focal colours reflect cultural conventions.

6. A gray card in sunlight looks darker than a white card in the shade. This is an example of
   a. brightness constancy.
   b. form constancy.
   c. habituation.
   d. counterbalancing.

7. When we approach an object or when it approaches us, we perceive its size
   a. as getting bigger.
   b. as constant.

c. in proportion to the size of the retinal image it produces.

d. from the size of the afterimage.

8. Our ability to distinguish between movements of a retinal image caused by eye movements and those caused by the movements of objects depends on
   a. feedback from the eye muscles.
   b. perception of relative motion.
   c. top-down processing.
   d. the brain's "knowledge" that it has moved the eyes.

9. We would have difficulty reading if it were not for
   a. backward masking.
   b. phi phenomenon.
   c. motion parallax.
   d. binocular vision.

10. If it were not for the existence of the phi phenomenon, we would not have
    a. serial computers.
    b. lasers.
    c. television.
    d. CT scanners.

Answers for Self Tests

Lesson I

1. d	Obj. 7-1	2. b	Obj. 7-1	3. c	Obj. 7-2	4. d	Obj. 7-2	5. b	Obj. 7-3
6. d	Obj. 7-3	7. c	Obj. 7-4	8. a	Obj. 7-4	9. d	Obj. 7-5	10. c	Obj. 7-5

Lesson II

1. a	Obj. 7-6	2. b	Obj. 7-6	3. d	Obj. 7-6	4. c	Obj. 7-7	5. b	Obj. 7-7
6. a	Obj. 7-8	7. b	Obj. 7-8	8. d	Obj. 7-9	9. a	Obj. 7-9	10. c	Obj. 7-9

CHAPTER 8

Memory

LESSON I

Read the interim summary on page 243 of your text to re-acquaint yourself with the material in this section.

8-1 Explain the difference between sensory memory, short-term memory, and long-term memory, and describe research on sensory memory.

Read pages 240-243 and answer the following questions.

1. a. Define *memory* in your own words.

   b. List and define the three components of the structure of memory.

      1.

      2.

      3.

2. Briefly explain two different approaches to the study of the structure of memory. (Howard, 1995)

3. Compare the characteristics of the following three kinds of memory. (Atkinson and Shiffrin, 1968)

   a. Sensory memory

      1. duration

      2. capacity

   b. Short-term memory

      1. duration

      2. capacity

   (Be sure to try the demonstration on page 241 in your text that illustrates the capacity of short-term memory.)

   c. Long-term memory

      1. duration

      2. capacity

4. Why do some psychologists object to the model of memory presented in Figure 8.1 in your text?

5. What kind of memory do each of the following situations illustrate?

    a. You recall nursery rhymes you learned as a child.

    b. You look up an address and remember it long enough to write it on the envelope.

    c. You think you just saw a shooting star, but you are not really sure.

    d. Although you have not played Gin Rummy in years, you agree to play with your younger cousin. You are surprised at how easily you can remember the rules.

6. Visual sensory memory is referred to as _____ memory and auditory sensory memory is referred to as _____ memory.

7. Summarize results of research by Sperling (1960) on iconic memory.

    a. Describe the stimulus and explain how Sperling presented it to subjects. (See Figure 8.2 in your text.)

    b. Describe the whole-report procedure.

    c. How many letters did subjects usually recall?

    d. What did Sperling think might account for their responses?

    e. Describe the partial-report procedure.

    f. Why did he present the tone *after* the letters were flashed?

    g. How accurately were subjects able to recall a specific line now?

    h. How accurately were subjects able to recall a specific line when the time between the flashing the letters and hearing the tone was extended?

    i. What do these results suggest

        1. about the duration of iconic memory?

        2. is the reason that subjects could not recall more than four or five letters?

8. Briefly explain the role of echoic memory in speech comprehension.

9. Summarize research by Darwin et al. (1972) on the duration of echoic memory.

   a. Describe the stimuli and explain how they were presented to the subjects.

   b. In general, how did the length of the delay between the stimulus and the visual cue affect the accuracy of responses?

   c. What do these results suggest about the duration of echoic memory?

Read the interim summary on pages 250-251 of your text to re-acquaint yourself with the material in this section.

8-2 Describe research on the encoding of information in short-term or working memory and the limits of working memory.

Read pages 243-246 and answer the following questions.

1. Try the letter and number demonstrations in your text and then explain why Figure 8.3 may more accurately portray short-term memory for verbal information than Figure 8.1 does.

2. Some psychologists prefer to refer to short-term memory as _____ _____ because it contains both _____ information and information retrieved from _____-_____ memory. (Baddeley, 1986, 1993) Working memory represents our ability to remember what we _____ _____ and think about it in terms of what we _____ _____. (Haberlandt, 1994)

3. a. When subjects are asked to freely recall words that have been read to them from a long list, what words do they recall best and what do we call these tendencies?

   b. According to Atkinson and Shiffrin (1968), what may account for the primacy effect? the recency effect?

   c. What do these effects suggest about memory?

4. a. How did Peterson and Peterson (1959) prevent subjects from rehearsing a three consonant stimulus?

   b. How did this additional task affect the accuracy of recall? (See Figure 8.4 in your text.)

   c. What do the results suggest about the length of time stimuli remain in short-term memory?

5. a. How many items of information can be retained in short-term memory? (Miller, 1956)

   b. Explain the concept of chunking in your own words.

c. Why is it advantageous to be able to combine information into "chunks?"

d. Now use this information to explain why few people can accurately repeat the fifteen seemingly random words and why these words can easily be remembered when arranged differently.

e. What characteristic of the stimulus appears to determine the capacity of short-term memory?

8-3 Describe the behavioural and neurological evidence for the existence of phonological short-term memory.

Read pages 246-247 and answer the following questions.

1. List the two types of information stored in working memory for which there is good evidence.

   1.   2.

2. Define *phonological short-term memory* in your own words.

3. a. What results did Conrad (1964) obtain when he asked subjects to write down letters from lists they had been shown?

   b. What did the nature of their errors suggest about the way visual information is encoded?

4. a. However, Hintzman (1967) suggested that the errors could also reflect a form of _____ coding.

   b. Explain the process of subvocal articulation in your own words.

5. Explain why

   a. Conrad (1970) chose deaf children as subjects when he replicated his experiment.

   b. some children still made "acoustical" errors.

   c. these results confirm the presence of articulatory coding in short-term memory.

6. a. Study Figure 8.5 in your text and then add labels to the leader lines of Figure 1 on the next page.

7. a. Conduction aphasia is a profound deficit in _____ _____ _____ caused by damage to a region of the _____ _____ _____.

b. How does conduction aphasia affect speech

    1. comprehension?

    2. production?

    3. repetition?

c. Study Figure 8.6 in your text and carefully explain the presumed reason why the lesion that causes conduction aphasia disrupts the ability to repeat words.

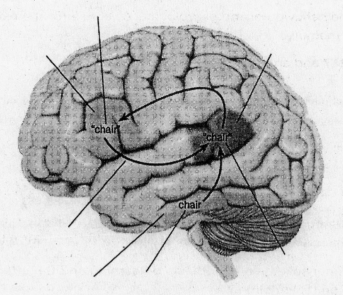

Figure 1

8-4 Describe visual short-term memory and explain how information is lost from short-term memory.

Read pages 247-250 and answer the following questions.

1. a. Explain why it was easier for chess experts than novices to recall the position of pieces in a real game. (DeGroot, 1965)

    b. What happened when the pieces were placed haphazardly on the board? What is the explanation for this finding?

    c. Explain how this research applies to an expert hockey player like Wayne Gretzky (Gzowski, 1981).

2. a. Study Figure 8.7 in your text and describe the pairs of shapes that subjects were asked to compare in a study by Shepard and Metzler (1971).

    b. When asked to describe how they made a particular comparison, what did subjects report?

    c. Study Figure 8.8 in your text and describe the variable that affects a person's decision time.

d. What is the possible utility of this ability?

3. The most important cause for the loss of information from short-term memory may be _____.

4. a. Waugh and Norman (1965) conducted research on the disappearance of information in short-term memory. Explain the task they taught to subjects. (Be sure to use the term the *probe digit* in your answer.)

   b. Describe the two experimental conditions in which the lists were presented and explain why the researchers followed this procedure.

   c. Which factor influenced performance the most—rate or number of items? (Study Figure 8.9 in your text.)

   d. What do the results suggest about the principal reason why information in short-term memory disappears?

Read the interim summary on pages 257-258 of your text to re-acquaint yourself with the material in this section.

8-5 Discuss the consolidation hypothesis of learning and the effects of deep and shallow processing on remembering.

Read pages 251-255 and answer the following questions.

1. Identify two types of learning.

   1.   2.

2. Give your own examples of memory formation as

   a. an active process.

   b. a passive process.

3. a. Define *consolidation* in your own words.

   b. Explain the consolidation hypothesis of memory formation.

4. a. Now define *retrograde amnesia* in your own words.

   b. Describe how head injury can cause retrograde amnesia. Refer to the disruption of short-term memory.

5. State two assumptions about the consolidation process drawn from the effects of head injury.

   1.

   2.

6. Now state two assumptions of the consolidation theory that have been challenged by recent research.

   1.

   2.

7. Describe the two kinds of rehearsal suggested by Craik and Lockhart (1972).

   a. maintenance rehearsal

   b. elaborative rehearsal

8. Summarize research on the effectiveness of elaboration by Craik and Tulving (1975).

   a. Describe the task subjects were asked to perform. Be sure to mention the complexity of the sentences.

   b. What were the subjects asked to do next?

   c. Describe the circumstances in which subjects had the best recall of words they had used.

   d. What do these results suggest about the way to organize material to facilitate remembering it?

9. Craik and Lockhart (1972) suggested a useful framework for understanding how information enters long-term memory. Explain what they meant by:

   a. shallow processing and surface features.

   b. deep processing and semantic features.

10. a. Define *effortful processing* and *automatic processing* in your own words.

b. List several kinds of information that are encoded by these means.

c. What is a benefit of being able to process information automatically?

11. State two conclusions about these aspects of the elaborative encoding of information

   a. benefits of rehearsal

   b. encoding specificity

12. Summarize research on the importance of encoding specificity. Explain why subjects

   a. reported that a list of words that had been read aloud to them contained only musical terms. (Flexser and Tulving, 1978)

   b. had more difficulty recalling a passage without a title than with a title. (Dooling and Lachman, 1971).

   c. had no improvement in recall if they were given the title of the passage after reading and processing it. (Bransford and Johnson, 1972)

13. What do the results of these studies suggest about the best time to attempt to make information meaningful?

14. Briefly summarize criticisms of these aspects of the depth of processing model of memory.

   a. definitions of terms

   b. unobservable behaviour

   c. superficial and deep features of stimuli

LESSON I SELF TEST

1. Sperling used a tachistoscope to show subjects a set of nine letters. They could not recall more than four or five of them correctly because
   a. the set of letters was greater than the capacity of iconic memory.
   b. the visual stimulus fades quickly from iconic memory.

   c. items in iconic memory cannot be chunked efficiently.
   d. stimuli are not accurately represented in sensory memory.

2. Echoic memory is important for
   a. spelling.

b. comprehension of sounds.

c. sound location.

d. reading.

3. Short-term memory

a. stores unrehearsed information.

b. has a limited capacity that can be increased through rehearsal.

c. is difficult to distinguish from the later stages of perception.

d. receives both new information and information from long-term memory.

4. Stimuli remain in short-term or working memory about _____ seconds unless they are _____.

a. 10; rehearsed

b. 20; rehearsed

c. 10; emotionally charged

d. 20; already familiar

5. The fact that deaf people sometimes make acoustical errors when they repeat letters presented to them on a screen implies that

a. proactive inhibition is responsible for errors in short-term memory.

b. auditory information fades faster than visual information.

c. phonological short-term memory uses an articulatory code.

d. the short-term memory of deaf people is less accurate than that of people who can hear.

6. People with conduction aphasia have difficulty

a. repeating precisely what they hear.

b. reading aloud.

c. writing.

d. following verbal instructions.

7. The superior ability of expert chess players to remember positions of pieces from an actual game underscores the

a. advantages of chunking information.

b. robustness of the primary and recency effects.

c. fact that information coding is negatively affected by complexity.

d. ability to manipulate information in long-term memory.

8. The most important reason that information in short-term memory is lost is

a. decay.

b. displacement.

c. insufficient rehearsal.

d. our inability to retrieve it.

9. The consolidation hypothesis of memory asserts that

a. short-term and long-term memory are physiologically different.

b. the transfer of information from short-term to long-term memory occurs only for nonverbal material.

c. the transfer of information from short-term to long-term memory requires rehearsal.

d. the distinction between short-term and long-term memory is only apparent, not real.

10. The levels of processing hypothesis of memory asserts that

a. memories are more effectively established through elaborative rehearsal.

b. people engage in two kinds of rehearsal: verbal and nonverbal.

c. greater knowledge facilitates recall of knowledge.

d. how we encode information has no effect on our ability to recall it later.

LESSON II

8-6 Describe techniques for improving long-term memory.

Read pages 255-257 and answer the following questions.

1. a. Define *mnemonic system* in your own words.

   b. Explain these storage features of mnemonic systems.

      1. complexity

      2. organization

2. Briefly explain how information is organized using the

   a. method of loci. (See Figure 8.10 in your text.)
   b. peg-word method. (See Figure 8.11 in your text. Miller et al., 1960)

3. a. To demonstrate the usefulness of narrative stores in memorizing information Bowers and Clark (1969) asked subjects to memorize lists of nouns. Summarize the instructions they gave to the narrative group and the control group.
   b. Which group had superior recall for all of the lists?

4. a. How can songs improve memory? Discuss the evidence that supports this notion. (Wallace 1994)
   b. What is an alternative explanation for why songs aid remembering? Be sure to discuss the study conducted by Kilgour et al. (2000).

5. Finally, what is a limitation of the use of mnemonic systems?

Read the interim summary on page 263 of your text to re-acquaint yourself with the material in this section.

8-7 Discuss research on the distinction between episodic and semantic memory and the distinction between explicit and implicit memory.

Read pages 258-260 and answer the following questions.

1. Summarize research by Sachs (1967) on the relative importance of specific words and meaning in long-term memory.

   a. Describe the task that the subjects were asked to perform. Explain the ways that the test and comparison sentences could differ from each other.

b. Study Figure 8.12 in your text and describe the results.

c. What conclusions can be made concerning long-term memory?

2. a. Define the terms *episodic memory* and *semantic memory* proposed by Tulving in your own words and give your own example of each.

b. Explain why it is inaccurate to conclude that these types of memories represent different memory systems.

c. How has Tulving (1983, 1984) revised his model?

3. Define *explicit memory* and *implicit memory* in your own words and give several examples of each from your own experience.

8-8 Describe anterograde amnesia in humans and laboratory animals, and discuss the implications for the organization of long-term memory.

Read pages 260-263 and answer the following questions.

1. Identify the two groups of subjects that researchers have studied to understand the biology of human memory. (Spear and Riccio, 1994)

2 a. What kinds of brain damage lead to anterograde amnesia? (Parkin, 1991)

b. In general, what information can people with anterograde amnesia remember and talk about? cannot remember and talk about?

3. a. Why did patient H.M. undergo bilateral removal of part of the temporal lobes?

b. Although the operation was successful in treating his condition, what was a side effect of surgery?

4. Briefly describe the case of patient H.M. following surgery.

a. Why has H.M. been studied so thoroughly?

b. Place an *N* or an *I* in each blank to indicate whether H.M.'s ability in the following areas remains *normal* or has been *impaired* by his surgery.

_____ recall of explicit memories learned prior to surgery

_____ ability to store new episodic information after surgery in long-term memory

_____ verbal short-term/working memory

_____ formation of new explicit memories

_____ formation of new implicit memories

  c. How does H.M. spend most of his time?

  d. What has H.M. said that indicates that he is aware of his condition?

5. H.M. and other people with anterograde amnesia are able to learn some new tasks.

  a. Explain why, once H.M. had seen the complete drawings of the elephant and the umbrella, he later recognized the incomplete drawings. (See Figure 8.13 in your text. Milner, 1970)

  b. What are some other specific tasks that people with anterograde amnesia are able to learn? (Squire, 1987)

6. Chun and Phelps (1999), however, found that not all implicit memories are spared in anterograde amnesia. Discuss their experiment and the results. Be sure to include procedural memory and predictive relations in your answer.

7. Subject with anterograde amnesia are not able to form any new _____ memories; nevertheless, they are able to form many, but not all, new _____ memories.

8. What is the name of the part of the brain that seems to be involved in the formation of new explicit memories and where is it located? (Refer back to Figure 4.32 in your text.)

9. Review the important connections between the hippocampus and other regions of the brain to explain why it may play an influential role in long-term memory formation. (Gluck and Myers, 1995)

10. What may account for the fact that few of us remember events that occurred when we were infants?

11. The hippocampus may also be important for _____ and _____ explicit memories of episodic experiences.

12. Rosenbaum et al. (2000) studied the memory ability of a man with extensive damage to his hippocampus.

  a. List the tasks that this individual could and could not perform.

  b. This demonstrates that he was unable to use what kind of information?

13. a. Which area of the brain, when damaged, leads to impaired implicit memory? What disease destroys this area?

 b. Discuss the evidence obtained by Doyon et al. (1998) which demonstrated that damage to this area interferes with implicit memory.

14. a. How did Duva et al. (1997) study the effect on spatial memory of lesions on the dorsal area of the hippocampus?

 b. How did they explore the effect of these lesions on "object recognition?"

15. a. When mice have been bred without NMDA receptors in the hippocampus, what deficits do they demonstrate? (Rampon et al., 1998)

 b. What is the hippocampus a distinctive brain structure?

 c. Discuss the evidence provided by Gould et al. (1999) which demonstrated that new cell growth in the hippocampus plays a role in memory.

 d. Explain how Greenough et al. (1999) explain the findings of Gould et al. (1999).

Read the interim summary on page 271-272 of your text to re-acquaint yourself with the material in this section.

8-9 Explain how long-term memories may alter the structures of the brain, how information is remembered, and how information can be remembered more efficiently.

Read pages 264-266 and answer the following questions.

1. If remembering is automatic, how can you explain the fact that we often make a deliberate effort to remember something? What is it that we are doing?

2. a. Study Figure 8.15 in your text and, if you have not already done so, try the exercise. (Stroop, 1935; Macleod, 1991)

 b. How does the Stroop effect support the statement "Remembering is automatic."?

3. a. Review what researchers have learned about the tip-of-the-tongue experience. (James, 1893; Brown and McNeill, 1966; Brown, 1991)

 b. Refer to the tip-of-the-tongue experience to explain why even information that is difficult to recall is still retrieved automatically.

4. a. Define *recollection* and *retrieval cues* in your own words. (Baddeley, 1982)

   b. Explain how retrieval cues, such as contextual variables, affect recollection.

5. a. In what two environments did scuba divers, serving as experimental subjects, learn lists of words and then later recall them? (Godden and Baddeley, 1975)

   b. How did where the divers learned the words lists affect their recall?

   c. What do the results suggest about the affect of learning context on recollection?

6. Summarize research on the duration of memories of experimental tasks and real life experiences.

   a. What task did Ebbinghaus set for himself?

   b. How did the passage of time affect his recall? (See Figure 8.16 in your text.)

   c. What did the subjects in research by Bahrick (1983, 1984a, 1984b) have in common?

   d. What kinds of information were they asked to remember in the recall tests?

   e. How was their recall affected by the passage of time? (See Figure 8.17 in your text) the degree to which the information was learned?

   f. When is information such as peoples' names most likely to be forgotten? (Kausler, 1994)

8-10 Explain how the accuracy of remembered information is affected by cultural context and discuss attempts to reconstruct events.

Read pages 266-268 and answer the following questions.

1. What do some researchers suggest is the relationship between remembering and culture? (Mistry and Rogoff, 1994)

2. a. In tests of free recall of previously learned lists of material, how well did American children do? Guatemalan Mayan children? (Rogoff and Waddell, 1982)

   b. Why were the scores of American children anticipated?

3. a. Later these researchers had both groups of children participate in a different learning task. Why?

b. Describe both the task and the children's performance.

c. What do the results suggest about the effects of cultural experience on remembering?

4. a. Now compare the abilities of a child from each group to retell a story to an adult. (Mistry and Rogoff, 1994)

b. Why is it inaccurate to conclude that the Mayan child did not remember the story very well?

5. To what extent does culture appear to influence learning and remembering?

6. After listening to subjects retell a story or draw a picture they had previously seen, what did Bartlett (1932) conclude about memory formation?

7. Explain how the form of a question can affect the way details of an event are recalled.

a. How did leading questions asked by the Loftus and Palmer (1974) influence subjects'

1. estimates of vehicle speed on impact? (Study Figure 8.18 in your text.)

2. later recall of other accident details?

b. How did even very subtle leading questions influence subjects' reports of what they saw in a film about an automobile accident? (Loftus and Zanni, 1975)

c. How can the use of leading questions affect judicial proceedings?

8. Carefully explain what the effect of leading questions on remembering suggests about the way and the efficiency with which information is organized and stored in memory.

8-11 Explain how remembering is affected by interference from other information.

Read pages 268-269 and answer the following questions.

1. Explain how remembering may be affected by interference and cite research to support your answer. (See Figure 8.19 in your text. Jenkins and Dallenbach, 1924)

2. Sometimes our ability, to retrieve new information is reduced by information we learned previously—a phenomenon we call _____ _____. At other times our retrieval ability is affected by information we learned more recently—a phenomenon called _____ _____.

3. Study Figure 8.20 in your text and explain how researchers test for the effect of retroactive inhibition and proactive inhibition.

4. Explain why some researchers believe that the results of laboratory tests on retrieval may not reflect the effect of interference on the retrieval of information in real life.

5. Identify the concepts (listed below) illustrated in the following situations.

_____ "I was surprised that he could not remember more of what happened," Lucia said to her mother after visiting her friend in the hospital. "He doesn't even remember the bus hitting the tree."

_____ "I can't remember the name of the travel agency, but I remember noticing that the ad in the directory is near the bottom left part of the page."

_____ "It was so easy to learn our new telephone number," Gerard said to his grandmother. "It's almost the same as our old postal code."

_____ "Dad is recovering physically from his stroke, Tri told his cousin. "He talks so easily, you might not think anything is wrong until you realize he hasn't remembered anything from your last visit—or even that you visited!"

_____ "That's your fourth strike in six frames," Andy said. "How do you get just the right curve to the ball?" "I really don't know," Alison replied, a little self-consciously.

_____ "I don't think I can give you any more help," Grandpa told Alex, who was trying to draw a family tree for his social studies class. "Oh please, Grandpa," Alex said. "You can remember this name. Do you think he was named after a relative? Would it seem like an unusual name today?"

Choices: implicit memory, retrograde amnesia, elaborative rehearsal, anterograde amnesia, episodic memory, shallow processing

8-12 Describe the technique of hypnotic memory enhancement, and discuss the accuracy of induced memories.

Read pages 270-271 and answer the following questions.

1. When police use hypnosis to help witnesses remember details that might aid a criminal investigation, what kind of instructions do they give them when using the

a. most common method?

b. television technique? (Reiser and Nielsen, 1980)

2. What information did the Chowchilla bus driver recall under hypnosis? Why? (Kroger and Doucé, 1979)

3. What kind of instructions are given to witnesses during a nonhypnotic

    a. guided memory session? (Malpass and Devine, 1981)

    b. cognitive interview? (Geiselman et al., 1984)

4. List three dangers of hypnotic memory enhancement. (Orne et al., 1988)

    1.

    2.

    3.

5. Summarize evidence that hypnosis can modify existing memories of witnesses.

    a. How do we know that the hypnotic visualization given by a rape victim was completely imaginary? (Orne et al., 1988)

    b. Explain why witnesses sometimes give inaccurate information under hypnosis.

6. When subjects who had slept soundly were questioned about their night's sleep, what did they reply

    a. under hypnosis?

    b. after they were hypnotized?

    c. even after they were told about the hypnotist's suggestion? (Laurence and Perry, 1983)

7. a. Carefully describe how hypnosis may alter the details and undermine the accuracy of eyewitness testimony.

    b. Explain why eyewitness testimony is such compelling evidence when presented in court.

8. a. Explain the dangers of using testimony from hypnotized witnesses that make it inadmissible in most North American courts.

    b. Explain why a hypnotized witness may hinder rather than help a police investigation.

    c. What is probably a better way of learning the truth during an investigation and trial?

LESSON II SELF TEST

1. Mnemonic systems
   a. simplify information.
   b. make information more elaborate.
   c. are useful for all kinds of information.
   d. are often more time–consuming to learn than the information itself.

2. Episodic memory and semantic memory
   a. involve different kinds of information.
   b. are separate, independent memory systems.
   c. exist for each sensory modality.
   d. store the same information in different ways.

3. The best way to reveal implicit memory is to ask the subject
   a. a series of oral questions.
   b. a series of implicit questions.
   c. to demonstrate a skill.
   d. to demonstrate a skill and describe each action.

4. Patients like H.M.
   a. can never learn any new information.
   b. have an implicit memory deficit.
   c. cannot recall explicit memories formed before brain damage.
   d. have relatively normal short-term memory.

5. Anterograde amnesia results from damage to the
   a. pons.
   b. hippocampus.
   c. amygdala.
   d. occipital lobes.

6. The Stroop effect demonstrates that remembering is
   a. creative.
   b. compulsive.
   c. automatic.
   d. transient.

7. What we remember about an experience and store in long-term memory is generally
   a. a few striking details.
   b. a faithful representation of the events.
   c. only that information that is inconsistent with what we already know.
   d. only that information that we rehearse.

8. Retroactive interference
   a. occurs when recent learning interferes with previous learning.
   b. occurs when previous learning interferes with recent learning.
   c. only occurs when previous learning is particularly meaningful.
   d. only occurs when people are trying to recall exciting past events.

9. Hypnosis can only enhance people's _____, not their _____.
   a. memory; co-operation
   b. memory; motivation to help
   c. recollection; confidence
   d. recollection; memory

10. Hypnotized eyewitnesses
    a. are unable to lie.
    b. have insight and abilities they do not possess when not hypnotized.
    c. can sometimes be induced to remember false information.
    d. remember events accurately.

Answers for Self Tests

Lesson I

1. b	Obj. 8-1	2. b	Obj. 8-1	3. d	Obj. 8-2	4. b	Obj. 8-2	5. c	Obj. 8-3
6. a	Obj. 8-3	7. a	Obj. 8-4	8. b	Obj. 8-4	9. a	Obj. 8-5	10. a	Obj. 8-5

Lesson II

1. b	Obj. 8-6	2. a	Obj. 8-7	3. c	Obj. 8-7	4. d	Obj. 8-8	5. b	Obj. 8-8
6. c	Obj. 8-9	7. a	Obj. 8-10	8. a	Obj. 8-11	9. d	Obj. 8-12	10. c	Obj. 8-12

CHAPTER 9

Consciousness

LESSON I

Read the interim summary on page 280 of your text to re-acquaint yourself with the material in this section.

9-1 Outline three historical philosophical positions on the nature of consciousness and discuss the possible relationship between consciousness and the ability to communicate.

Read pages 276-279 and answer the following questions.

1. What do we mean by *consciousness?*

2. Compare the three philosophical positions on the nature of consciousness with regard to beliefs about the source of consciousness and the possibility of understanding it. (Flanagan, 1992)

3. What approach to the study of consciousness is likely to be unproductive? productive?

4. What behavioural capacity with clear adaptive significance may have given rise to consciousness?

5. We directly experience our own consciousness, but what is the only evidence we have of someone else's consciousness?

6. What two general capacities are necessary in order to communicate with others and ourselves?

7. What observations suggest we use brain mechanisms involved in speech when we think?

8. Discuss the following observations which suggest that other animals possess varying degrees of consciousness?
   a. communication

   b. brain mechanisms involved in explicit memory

   c. mirror images

9. Discuss the behaviour of two individuals whose frontal lobes were damaged prior to the age of two (See Figure 9.1 in your text. Anderson et al. (1999).

    a. On what kinds of tests did these individuals show normal scores? On what kinds of questions did they perform poorly?

    b. What other behaviours demonstrated that these individuals could not tell the difference between right and wrong?

    c. What questions do these individuals raise concerning the frontal lobes?

Read the interim summary on page 287-288 of your text to re-acquaint yourself with the material in this section.

9-2 Describe selective attention, discuss its importance, and describe research on how we attend to auditory information.

Read pages 280-282 and answer the following questions.

1. Define *selective attention* in your own words.

2. What did Sperling's (1960) study demonstrate about the role of selective attention in transferring information from sensory memory into short-term memory?

3. a. Describe three ways that attention may be controlled and give an example of each. What is the purpose of attentional mechanisms?

    b. Explain how attention affects
      1. short-term memory.

      2. explicit and implicit long-term memory. (You may wish to review the concepts of explicit and implicit memory in Chapter 8.)

4. According to Broadbent (1958), what may be the function of a system of selective attention?

5. a. Describe a dichotic listening task.

    b. Using this procedure how were subjects in research by Cherry (1953) asked to respond to one of the messages? Why?

    c. What effect did shadowing have on their ability to recall information from the unattended ear?

d. What is one possible explanation for this lack of recall? (See Figure 9.2(a) in your text.)

e. Cite two experiments that refute this explanation. (Moray, 1959; Nielsen and Sarason, 1981.)

f. Because subjects do respond to particular kinds of information presented to the unattended ear, what is happening to the information? (See Figure 9.2(b) in your text.)

6. a. Describe the task McKay (1973) used to demonstrate the effects of information presented to the unattended ear.

b. Describe and explain the results.

7. a. Study Figure 9.3 in your text and describe how Treisman (1960) tested people's skill at shadowing a message.

b. Describe and explain the results.

c. Explain the practical value of selective attention by referring to the cocktail-party phenomenon illustrated in See Figure 9.4 in your text.

9-3 Describe research on how we attend to visual information and the brain mechanisms of selective attention.

Read pages 283-285 and answer the following questions.

1. a. Describe what subjects saw on the video-display screen during the experiment by Posner and his colleagues. (Posner et al., 1980)

b. How were their response times affected by the kind of warning stimulus they saw? (Study Figure 9.5 in your text.)

c. Explain what different response times indicated about selective attention. Be sure to explain why subjects were asked to gaze at the fixation point.

2. a. Define "inhibition of return" in your own words.

b. Describe research by O'Donnell and Pratt (1996) that indicates how attention may be directed.

3. a. How successfully did subjects follow videotapes of scenes such as the one illustrated in Figure 9.7 in your text? (Neisser & Beckler, 1975)

b. What may have influenced the event that the subjects followed and remembered?

4. When subjects were asked if they recognized a series of shapes that had originally been presented as overlapping coloured pairs, how did they respond? (See Figure 9.8 in your text. Rock and Gutman, 1981)

5. Describe research that demonstrated what happens to unattended visual information. (Neisser, 1969)

6. a. List the three ways that coloured rectangles subjects watched on a computerized display changed? (Corbetta et al., 1991)

   1.   2.   3.

   b. While subjects watched the display of changing rectangles, paying attention to a particular attribute, what activity did the experimenters monitor?

   c. What did PET scans confirm about brain activity and selective attention? (See Figure 9.9 in your text.)

7. Briefly summarize research with monkeys by Luck et al. (1993) that showed similar results.

9-4 Explain how meditation may produce changes in consciousness.

Read pages 286-287 and answer the following questions.

1. _____ techniques to alter consciousness through _____-_____ can be found in almost every _____. They can be divided into techniques to _____ attention to commonplace events and techniques to _____ attention from stimuli around us.

2. a. What is the desired effect of most meditation techniques?

   b. How does concentrating on a single source during meditation differ from concentrating on a compelling book?

3. List the primary goals of withdrawal of attention.

   1.

   2.

4. Discuss an advantage and disadvantage of habituation.

5. Review some of the ways to reduce habituation to our surroundings.

   a. What is the easiest way to reduce habituation? What is an accompanying worthwhile side effect?

   b. Why do many ancient traditions suggest doing routine tasks differently?

   c. Why do people find dangerous activities such as mountain climbing appealing?

   d. How does a period of meditation alter our impression of our surroundings? Why?

Read the interim summary on page 291 of your text to re-acquaint yourself with the material in this section.

9-5 Explain the significance of the symptoms of isolation aphasia, visual agnosia, and the split-brain syndrome to our understanding of consciousness.

Read pages 288-290 and answer the following questions.

1. If human consciousness is related to human speech, what kind of brain mechanisms may then be involved in consciousness?

2. a. As a result of carbon monoxide poisoning, a woman suffered severe brain damage. Carefully describe the areas of the brain that were and were not damaged. (Geschwind et al., 1968)

   b. Describe how brain damage affected her

     1. speech production.

     2. speech comprehension.

     3. ability to repeat speech.

     4. ability to learn new sequences of words.

   c. In addition, how did the brain damage affect her awareness of herself and her surroundings?

   d. What is this syndrome called?

   e. What does this case contribute to our understanding of consciousness?

3. a. How did brain damage from blood vessel inflammation affect the man's ability, to recognize objects or pictures of objects by sight?

b. What did the man often do when he was shown a picture of a particular object? (Margolin et al., 1985)

c. Study Figure 9.10 in your text and carefully explain how visual information may have been processed by the man's brain following brain damage.

d. What does this case contribute to our understanding of consciousness?

4. a. Why is a split-brain operation performed and what brain connection is severed?

b. How does surgery affect the functioning of the two hemispheres of the brain and the behaviour of the patient?

c. Although surgery profoundly alters the brain, why are behavioural changes often difficult to detect?

d. Study Figure 9.11 in your text and explain why olfaction is an exception to the crossed representation of sensory information in the brain. Describe research on the behaviour of split-brain patients when odours are presented to the left and right nostril.

e. What does this case contribute to our understanding of consciousness?

LESSON I SELF TEST

1. The earliest philosophical position on the nature of consciousness considered consciousness to be a
   a. natural phenomenon limited to human beings.
   b. mysterious phenomenon and beyond human understanding.
   c. natural phenomenon, which we cannot understand for a variety of reasons.
   d. poorly defined phenomenon too individualistic to understand.

2. Which is the most accurate statement about consciousness?
   a. The ability to communicate symbolically with ourselves may give rise to consciousness.
   b. Consciousness is not an essential human trait because the evolutionary function of consciousness has never been discovered.
   c. The language area of the brain is the most likely location of the center of consciousness.
   d. It is unlikely we will understand human consciousness because the necessary research would be unethical.

3. Auditory or visual information that people do not pay attention to
   a. cannot affect behaviour.
   b. usually does not enter consciousness.
   c. does not affect verbal processing.
   d. normally produces only episodic memories.

4. Subjects who were asked to pay attention to one or two overlapping coloured shapes later recognized
   a. only those coloured shapes they had been instructed to follow.
   b. only those shapes that were familiar objects regardless of their colour.
   c. only the first few and last few shapes they saw, regardless of their colour.
   d. all the shapes they had seen, regardless of their colour.

5. PET scans of human subjects who watched coloured rectangles for changes in either shape, colour, or speed of movement showed increased levels of brain activity
   a. that varied directly with the speed at which the rectangles were displayed.
   b. only until subjects accurately learned to anticipate changes in the attributes of the rectangles.
   c. in regions that analyze shape, colour, or speed of movement.
   d. each time the subjects were instructed to follow a different attribute of the rectangles.

6. Withdrawal of attention
   a. is the goal of most meditation exercises.
   b. is most easily achieved through self-control.
   c. heightens self-awareness.
   d. reduces or may even eliminate the "rebound phenomenon."

7. Techniques for _____ awareness help reduce _____.
   a. increasing; the need for symbolic communication
   b. decreasing; the tendency to regard the surrounding environment as commonplace
   c. increasing; habituation
   d. decreasing; age related apathy

8. The case of the man who could not recognize objects by sight suggests that consciousness
   a. is simply an activity of the brain's speech mechanism.
   b. is synonymous with the ability to talk about perceptions and memories.
   c. and self-awareness are different phenomena.
   d. is necessary for learning.

9. The right hemisphere of a person who has had a split-brain operation cannot
   a. perceive sensory information.
   b. understand verbal instructions.
   c. produce speech.
   d. control movements of the right hand.

10. The effects of the split-brain operation confirm that
    a. consciousness developed in the right hemisphere.
    b. the left hemisphere is more adept at analyzing sensory information that the right hemisphere.
    c. all cognitive processes are located in the left hemisphere.
    d. information does not reach consciousness unless it reaches those parts of the brain responsible for verbal communication.

LESSON II

Read the interim summary on page 295 of your text to re-acquaint yourself with the material in this section.

9-6 Describe the characteristics of hypnosis and discuss two explanations of this phenomenon.

Read pages 291-293 and answer the following questions.

1. a. Hypnosis, or _____, is an unusual form of _____ _____.

   b. Hypnosis is a fascinating phenomenon, but why is it important to the study of psychology?

c. Briefly explain the discovery and first uses of hypnosis.

2. The only necessary condition for successful hypnosis is the subject's _____ that he or she will be hypnotized.

3. List and describe the three types of hypnotic suggestions.

4. Briefly explain the following characteristics of hypnosis.

   a. misperceptions about reality

   b. posthypnotic suggestibility

   c. posthypnotic amnesia

5. a. What does research indicate has really occurred when people who have been hypnotized experience changes in perception?

   b. Study the Ponzo illusion in Figure 9.12 in your text and describe how Miller et al. (1973) demonstrated differences in hypnosis-induced blindness and physical blindness.

   c. What do the perceptions of subjects following hypnosis suggest about its effects on the visual and verbal systems?

6. List the two general views of hypnosis.

   1.   2.

7. Discuss the sociocognitive approach to hypnosis.

   a. Explain Spanos' (1991) argument that hypnotic behaviours are social behaviours.

   b. What false information did Orne present in lecture and how did it later hypnotized subjects who had heard that lecture?

   c. To what experience does Barber (1975) compare the suspension of self-control that occurs during hypnosis?

8. Discuss the dissociation approach to hypnosis.

   a. Describe how dissociation theories use the distinction between psychological processes and our awareness of those processes to explain hypnosis.

b. Explain Hilgard's (1991) dissociation theory of hypnosis.

c. Describe dissociated control theories of hypnosis. (Bowers and Davidson, 1991; Kilstrom, 1998)

9. Neither the sociocognitive approach nor the dissociation approach seems complete. A better account of hypnosis may involve a _____ of the two theories.

9-7 Describe and evaluate evidence that hypnosis can induce people to perform antisocial acts, and describe beneficial uses of hypnosis.

Read pages 293-295 and answer the following questions.

1. Summarize research suggesting that hypnotized people can be induced to perform antisocial or even dangerous acts.

   a. Briefly describe how hypnotized subjects responded when they thought they been given a

      1. "pistol." (Ladame, 1887)

      2. "knife." (Liégois, 1889)

   b. Discuss the arguments which suggested that these early experiments are unconvincing?

   c. In more dangerous experiments (Rowland, 1939), how did hypnotized subjects respond when they were asked to

      1. pick up a rattlesnake?

      2. throw sulphuric acid at the experimenter?

   d. What did Rowland conclude about hypnotic coercion?

2. Why do Orne and Evans (1965) believe these studies are not as convincing as they first appear?

3. a. All five of the subjects in an experiment by Orne and Evans (1965) that was similar to the one performed by Rowland did perform ostensibly dangerous acts. How did the subjects perceive their risk?

   b. How did control subjects, all of whom performed the experimental tasks, perceive their risk?

4. Explain why research on hypnosis and antisocial behaviour must include appropriate control groups. Cite further research by Coe et al., (1973) on a scheme to sell heroin to support your answer.

5. Discuss two reasons why ethical research cannot determine whether hypnosis can induce subjects to perform antisocial acts.

   1.

   2.

6. a. Describe some beneficial uses of hypnosis.

   b. State two reasons why the use of hypnosis to induce analgesia is not more widespread.

   1.

   2.

   c. Briefly describe how phobias may be treated using hypnosis.

Read the interim summary on pages 301-302 of your text to re-acquaint yourself with the material in this section.

9-8 Name and describe the stages of sleep, and indicate how they are measured.

Read pages 295-297 and answer the following questions.

1. Sleep is a state of _____ _____.

2. Describe the purpose of the following equipment and records.

   a. polygraph

   b. electroencephalogram (EEG)

   c. electromyogram (EMG)

   d. electrocardiogram (EKG)

   e. electro-oculogram (EOG)

3. Describe the sleep laboratory, explain how a subject is prepared to spend the night there, and explain how data are recorded. (See Figure 9.13 in your text.)

4. Describe beta activity and alpha activity and identify the stages of consciousness that accompany them.

5. Study Figure 9.14 in your text and then add the following labels to Figure 1 below: Alpha activity, Awake, Beta activity (2), Delta activity (2), REM sleep, Stage 1 sleep, Stage 2 sleep, Stage 3 sleep, Stage 4 sleep, Theta activity (2). (Numbers in parentheses indicate that a label should appear more than once.)

6. Note the number of episodes of REM sleep that occur during a night's sleep and describe their length and the interval between them. (See Figure 9.15 in your text.)

7. During REM sleep what happens to the ability to move? What happens to the genitals?

8. To review some of the stages that occur during a night's sleep study Table 9.1 in your text.

9-9 Discuss research on sleep deprivation to determine the functions of sleep and discuss the function of dreams.

Read pages 297-299 and answer the following questions.

1. a. Describe the sleep pattern of the Indus dolphin. (Pilleri, 1979)

   b. What does this unusual sleep pattern suggest about the universal necessity of sleep?

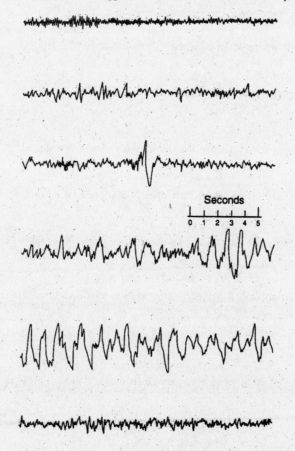

Figure 1

2. Explain the rationale of studying the effects of sleep deprivation to determine the functions of sleep.

3. Summarize the effects of sleep deprivation on the body and brain.

   a. State two conclusions about the effects of sleep deprivation on physical exercise and physiological stress drawn from a review of more than fifty experiments. (Horne, 1978)

      1.

      2.

   b. How well did sleep-deprived subjects perform on short intellectual tasks? more complex intellectual tasks? tasks that required vigilance? (Horne and Pettitt, 1985)

   c. Cite research (Sakai et al., 1979) and behavioural evidence that the brain may be resting during Stage 4 sleep.

4. Explain the rationale for studying the effects of exercise on sleep to determine the functions of sleep.

5. Summarize changes in slow-wave sleep of

   a. healthy subjects who spent six weeks resting in bed. (Ryback and Lewis, 1971)

   b. completely immobile quadriplegics and paraplegics. (Adey et al., 1968)

6. a. What kind of exercise does appear to increase the demand for slow-wave sleep?

   b. Describe how Horne and Minard (1985) tested the effects of increased mental activity on subsequent slow-wave sleep.

      1. What were the subjects first told they would be doing during the experiment, and how were the plans changed?

      2. What changes were observed in their slow-wave sleep that night, and what do the results suggest about the function of sleep?

7. Compare the kinds of dreams reported by people awakened from REM sleep and slow-wave sleep.

8. Explain why someone might claim, "I haven't had a dream in years."

9. What do the reports of people awakened from REM or slow-wave sleep indicate about sleep and consciousness?

10. List the two major approaches to the study of dreaming.

    1.   2.

11. a. Freud believed that all dreams represent _____ _____.

    b. Describe Freud's concepts of latent content and manifest content.

    c. What is a drawback to Freud's approach to understanding the symbolism of dreams?

12. Outline the physiological explanation of dreaming proposed by Hobson (1988).

    a. What change in the brain triggers REM sleep?

    b. What changes result from the activation of the visual system?

    c. Compare the content of a dream with the accompanying eye movements. (Dement, 1974)

    d. What topics tend to occur in a person's dreams?

    e. According to Hobson, how does the brain try to unify the fragmentary images of a dream?

9-10 Discuss the effects of REM sleep deprivation, possible functions of REM sleep, and the brain mechanisms of sleep.

Read pages 299-301 and answer the following questions.

1. a. Describe how researchers selectively deprive subjects in the sleep laboratory of REM sleep.

   b. How do researchers treat control subjects in the same experiment? Why?

2. When a person who has been deprived of REM sleep is allowed to sleep normally, what changes in REM sleep patterns occur? Be sure to mention the rebound phenomenon.

3. In general, what are the effects of REM sleep deprivation? (Lavie et al., 1984; Gironell et al., 1995)

4. a. What limited effect does REM sleep deprivation have on the ability of laboratory animals to learn a complex task?

   b. What does this kind of research suggest is the role of REM sleep in learning?

5. a. Summarize changes in REM sleep patterns from about thirty weeks after conception through adulthood. (Roffwarg et al., 1966; Petre-Quadens and De Lee, 1974; Inoue et al., 1986)

   b. When during an individual's life does the highest proportion of REM sleep occur and what does this suggest about a function of REM sleep?

   c. How did Mirmiran and his colleagues deprive infant rats of REM sleep? (Mirmiran, 1995)

   d. What later changes did they observe in the animals?

   e. What alternative explanation for these changes may also be correct?

   f. What did Marks et al. (1995) observe in animals who had been deprived of REM sleep without the use of drugs?

   g. What limited conclusion about the functions of REM sleep can be made?

6. Mammals possess _____ biological clocks that influence sleep patterns. The first, which is located in the _____ _____ _____, controls _____ _____ and oscillates _____ a day. The second controls the _____ _____-_____ cycle as well as cycles of _____-_____ and _____ sleep and oscillates _____ times a day. It is located somewhere in the _____. (See Figure 9.16 in your text.)

7. Define *circadian rhythms* and *basic rest-activity cycle* in your own words.

8. Describe the changes in the biological clock controlling human circadian rhythms under constant illumination and normal illumination.

9. a. What observation suggested the basic rest-activity cycle to Kleitman (1961)?

   b. What is the duration of this cycle?

10. Study Figure 9.17 in your text and add labels to Figure 2 below to explain the control of REM sleep.

11. a. What is the first step in the control of REM sleep and what observation suggested it?

    b. List three circuits of neurons that then become active. What activities do they control?

    c. How do serotonin-secreting neurons affect the activity of REM-ON neurons?

    d. And how are the serotonin-secreting neurons and then REM-ON neurons affected by drugs such as LSD? antidepressant drugs?

    e. What does the effect of antidepressant drugs suggest about a cause for mood disorders?

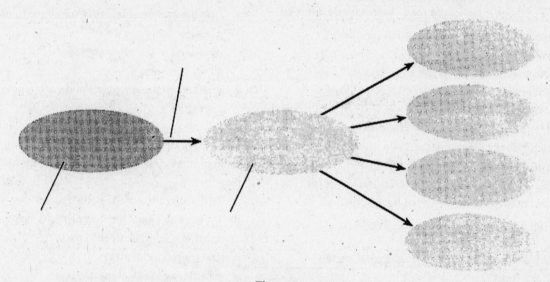

Figure 2

12. What brain region may be involved in the control of slow-wave sleep? Cite research to support your answer. (McGinty and Sterman, 1968; Szymusiak and McGinty, 1986; Sterman and Clemente, 1962a, 1962b)

LESSON II SELF TEST

1. In order for a person to be hypnotized he or she must
   a. be completely relaxed.
   b. become drowsy as the hypnotist speaks.
   c. fixate the eyes on a slowly moving object.
   d. understand that he or she is to be hypnotized.

2. Which of the following is true of the dissociation theory of hypnosis?
   a. It was developed by Spanos.
   b. It argues that hypnosis should not be viewed as a special state of consciousness.
   c. It uses the distinction between process and awareness.
   d. Psychologists agree that it is the best approach to hypnosis.

3. It is unlikely that research will settle questions about hypnotic coercion because
   a. most studies have not measured how deeply subjects were hypnotized.
   b. most studies failed to use appropriately dangerous acts because of ethical and legal concerns.
   c. few studies have accounted for differing cultural definitions of what constitutes a moral code violation.
   d. the experimental setting assures that subjects and others will be protected from harm and blame.

4. Which of the following records electrical signals from the heart?
   a. EEG
   b. EMG
   c. EKG
   d. EOG

5. _____ is to alertness as _____ is to Stage 4 sleep.
   a. delta activity; beta activity
   b. delta activity; alpha activity
   c. beta activity; delta activity
   d. alpha activity; delta activity

6. Bouts of REM sleep
   a. occur during all stages of sleep.
   b. are accompanied by muscular paralysis.
   c. occur at irregular intervals throughout the night.
   d. are accompanied by delta activity in the EEG.

7. Sleep deprivation studies suggest that sleep is required
   a. to rest the body.
   b. to keep the body in good physiological shape.
   c. to rest the brain.
   d. all of the above.

8. Hobson suggests that the plots and images of a dream are
   a. an attempt to resolve unconscious conflicts and desires.
   b. the products of activation of recent memories that the brain ties together somehow to make a plausible story.
   c. unrelated to the physiological functions of REM sleep.
   d. affected by the memories and experiences of our ancestors.

9. REM sleep deprived subjects who are permitted to sleep normally again _____ during the next night or two.
   a. have difficulty entering REM sleep
   b. experience characteristics of REM sleep intruding in other sleep stages
   c. show a rebound effect
   d. experience bouts of insomnia

10. The basic rest-activity cycle (BRAC) for humans
    a. is controlled by neurons in the hippocampus.
    b. is a ninety-minute period.
    c. determines our circadian rhythms.
    d. is affected by periods of light and dark.

Answers to Self Tests

Lesson I

1. b	Obj. 9-1	2. a	Obj. 9-1	3. b	Obj. 9-2	4. a	Obj. 9-3	5. c	Obj. 9-3
6. a	Obj. 9-4	7. c	Obj. 9-4	8. b	Obj. 9-5	9. c	Obj. 9-5	10. d	Obj. 9-5

Lesson II

1. d	Obj. 9-6	2. c	Obj. 9-6	3. d	Obj. 9-7	4. c	Obj. 9-8	5. c	Obj. 9-8
6. b	Obj. 9-8	7. c	Obj. 9-9	8. b	Obj. 9-10	9. c	Obj. 9-11	10. b	Obj. 9-11

CHAPTER 10

Language

LESSON I

Read the interim summary on page 317 of your text to re-acquaint yourself with the material in this section.

10-1 Explain the functions of language and describe the recognition of individual speech sounds and continuous speech.

Read pages 306-308 and answer the following questions.

1. Describe the field of psycholinguistics and explain how it differs from the field of linguistics.

2. What are some of the significant advantages we humans enjoy because we can engage in verbal behaviour?

3. a. List three factors that influence our perception of speech sounds.

   b. Define the term *phoneme* in your own words.

   c. Carefully explain why we can distinguish between *pa* and *ba*. Be sure to use the terms *voice-onset time* and *voicing* in your answer.

4. Lisker and Abramson (1970) asked subjects to listen to computer-generated sounds of a puff followed by *ah*.

   a. What two phonemes did subjects report hearing?

   b. Study Figure 10.1 in your text and explain how subjects used voice-onset time to distinguish between them.

5. Summarize research that suggests that psychologically the fundamental unit of speech is not an individual phoneme, but groups of phonemes.

   a. How easily did Liberman et al. (1967) isolate the phoneme /d/ from the syllables *doo* and *dee*?

b. How did Ganong (1980) demonstrate that the sounds that follow a phoneme are important for speech perception?

6. a. How accurately did subjects understand individual words isolated from normal conversation? presented in the original context? (Pollack and Pickett, 1964)

b. The effect of context on the perception of words is an example of _____-_____ processing.

10-2 Explain how we derive our comprehension of speech through the syntax of a language, as well as the relationship between semantics and syntax, and knowledge of the world.

Read pages 309-311 and answer the following questions.

1. a. What is a synonym for syntax?

b. Explain syntactical rules in your own words.

c. Our understanding and use of syntax is _____.

2. a. Briefly describe how subjects in research by Reber and Allen (1978) acquired the grammar rules for the letters M, V, R, T, and X.

b. How accurately did subjects later identify "grammatical" strings of these letters and how clearly did they explain the reasons for their choices?

c. What do these results suggest about the automatic acquisition and use of syntactical rules? (Be sure to refer to *implicit* and *explicit memories* in your answer.)

d. State the results of two studies of patients with anterograde amnesia to support your answer. (Knowlton et al., 1991; Gabrieli et al., 1988)

3. List the six syntactical cues that speakers and listeners rely on for accurate communication.

   1.   4.

   2.   5.

   3.   6.

4. What kinds of information do word order and word class provide?

5. a. Define these terms in your own words and give several examples of each type.

   1. function words

   2. content words

   3. affixes

   b. Explain why subjects more easily remembered a longer word string with affixes than a shorter string without them. (Epstein, 1961)

6. a. What is a synonym for semantics?

   b. Describe how word meaning and function words help make the syntax of a sentence clear.

   c. Explain how content words—even without accompanying function words—help make the meaning of a sentence clear.

7. Define *prosody* in your own words and give two examples of the use of prosody in speech.

8. a. Explain what Chomsky (1957, 1965) means by the deep structure and the surface structure of a sentence.

   b. Study Figure 10.2 in your text and explain what the sentence "Rosa always date shranks" reveals about some of the steps in the transformation of deep structure to surface structure. (Fromkin, 1973)

   c. Which of Chomsky's views do most psychologists agree with? disagree with? (Tannhaus, 1988; Bohannon, 1993; Hulit and Howard, 1993)

9. a. Define *scripts* in your own words. (Schank and Abelson, 1977)

b. Explain why scripts are an important aid to speech comprehension. (Hunt, 1985)

10-3 Describe evidence about the nature of speech production and comprehension from the study of aphasia.

Read pages 311-315 and answer the following questions.

1. Describe how Broca's aphasia affects speech production.

2. Study Figure 10.3 in your text and describe the location of Broca's area and the extent of brain damage that impairs normal speech.

3. a. What did Wernicke (1874) suggest is the function of Broca's area?

b. What anatomical data reinforces this conclusion?

4. a. Describe agrammatism that sometimes results from damage to Broca's area. (Saffran et al., 1980)

b. Contrast the accuracy of the responses of people with Broca's aphasia and normal people to a series of pictures Schwartz and her colleagues showed them? (Schwartz et al., 1980)

c. What aspect of grammar is apparently disrupted by damage to Broca's area?

5. a. How accurately do Broca's aphasics follow a series of commands? (Boller and Dennis, 1979)

b. What do results such as these suggest is an important function of the left frontal lobe?

6. a. Discuss the evidence of Dronkers (1996) demonstrating the brain regions involved in articulation problems. Be sure to include the terms insula in your answer. (See Figure 10.4 of your text)

b. Stromswold et al. (1996) used which technique to investigate the brain region involved in agrammatism? Which area was involved in interpreting difficult syntactic sentences?

7. a. Refer to Figure 10.3 and describe the location and function of Wernicke's area in understanding normal speech.

   b. Again study Figure 10.3 in your text and describe the extent of brain damage that causes Wernicke's aphasia.

8. Compare the fluency, articulation, prosody, and grammar of the speech of patients with Broca's aphasia and Wernicke's aphasia.

9. a. How is the speech comprehension of people with Wernicke's aphasia usually tested and how accurately do subjects respond?

   b. Explain why these deficits suggest Wernicke's aphasia is a receptive aphasia.

10. List three characteristic deficits resulting from damage to Wernicke's area and surrounding cortex.

   1.   3.

   2.

11. Explain the distinction between recognizing and comprehending a word.

12. a. What type of brain damage results in pure word deafness?

   b. Describe how the following abilities are affected in cases of pure word deafness.

      1. speech comprehension and recognition of emotion

      2. nonspeech comprehension

      3. speech production

      4. nonverbal communication

   c. How do people with Wernicke's aphasia react to their own speech difficulties?

13. a. What type of bran damage results in isolation aphasia?

   b. Describe the two characteristic symptoms of this disorder. (Refer to Figure 10.3.)

   c. Now describe how isolation aphasia differs from Wernicke's aphasia.

   d. Study Figure 10.5 in your text and explain the functions of the connections shown there.

10–4 Discuss the brain mechanisms that underlie our ability to understand the meaning of words.

Read pages 315-317 and answer the following questions.

1. a. When PET scanners have been used to study the brains of language-impaired people, which regions show low activity in people with

    1. Broca's aphasia?

    2. Wernicke's aphasia? (Karbe et al., 1989, 1990; Metter, 1991, Metter et al., 1990)

  b. How do these findings contribute to an understanding of aphasia?

2. When PET scanners have been used to study the brain of normal people, which region showed activity when normal people listened passively to a list of nouns? repeated the nouns? thought about verbs associated with those nouns? (See Figure 10.6 in your text. Petersen et al., 1988)

3. Using a fMRI, which regions of the brain did Binder et al. (1997) show were involved in understanding word meaning?

4. Words have meaning for us because they evoke particular _____, which are not stored in primary _____ _____, but in other parts of the brain.

5. Study Figure 10.7 in your text and follow the pathway responsible for recognizing and comprehending a spoken word.

6. a. Following a stroke that damaged part of the right parietal lobe, which plays a role in spatial perception, what kind of difficulty did a patient have in describing spatial relationships?

  b. She could understand some meanings of particular words, but not other meanings. Use examples to explain her difficulty.

7. Name and describe the specific comprehension difficulty associated with damage to the association cortex of the left parietal lobe.

Read the interim summary on page 324 of your text to re-acquaint yourself with the material in this section.

10–5 Describe the role eye-tracking experiments in the study of reading and discuss research on the distinction between phonetic and whole-word recognition.

Read pages 317-321 and answer the following questions.

1. a. The rapid jumps or _____ that your eyes are making as you read this sentence can be followed using a device called an _____ _____. You do not perceive the letters and words while your eyes are moving, but only during the brief pauses or _____ between jumps.

   b. Study Figure 10.8 and describe two ways that the fixations of good readers differ from those of poor readers.

   c. University students reading for meaning fixate on a higher percentage of content words than function words. Can we attribute this pattern to the fact that function words are usually shorter than content words? Explain. (Reichle et al., 1998; Carpenter and Just, 1983)

2. a. How do we analyze a sentence we are reading? (Rayner and Pollatsek, 1983)

   b. Explain how these variables affect our analysis.

      1. familiarity (Rayner et al., 1996)

      2. preceding unusual words (Thibadeau et al., 1982)

      3. word length or character complexity when familiarity is constant (See Figure 10.9 in your text. Carpenter and Just, 1983; Just et al., 1983)

3. a. What is the difference between word recognition through whole–word reading and phonetic reading?

   b. What factor determines which reading method will prevail? (Study Figure 10.10 in your text which illustrates some aspects of the reading process.)

   c. Why is whole-word recognition an essential skill for English speakers?

4. Define *dyslexia* and distinguish between acquired dyslexia and developmental dyslexias.

5. Complete this table summarizing some of the characteristics of acquired dyslexias after studying Figures 10. 11 and 10.12 in your text.

	Surface Dyslexia	Phonological Dyslexia	Direct Dyslexia
Reading method disrupted			
Words read easily			
Words read with difficulty			
Comprehension of words			

6. a. All of the dyslexias in the previous table result from damage to one of two regions on the left side of the brain. Name them.

   b. Explain why some people with phonological dyslexia may still be excellent readers.

   c. What does phonological dyslexia indicate about the brain mechanisms involved in reading?

   d. What other syndrome that you have already studied resembles direct dyslexia? (Schwartz et al., 1979; Lytton and Brust, 1989)

7. a. When do developmental dyslexias first appear?

   b. What does a familial tendency toward dyslexia suggest about its cause?

   c. What anatomical abnormalities also suggest that developmental dyslexia is an hereditary disorder. (Galaburda and Kemper, 1979; Galaburda et al., 1985; Galaburda, 1993; Galaburda et al., 1994)

   d. When contrasted with people without dyslexia, people with dyslexia do not use _____ and _____ areas in _____.

8. a. What kind of visual stimuli did Petersen et al. (1990) show subjects?

   b. Study the PET scans of the subjects shown in Figure 10.13 in your text and identify the stimuli that activated primary visual cortex? a region of visual association cortex?

   c. What do these results suggest about the cause of some forms of dyslexia?

10–6 Describe research on the way that readers comprehend the meaning of words and sentences.

Read pages 322-324 and answer the following questions.

1. We learn the meanings of words though _____.

2. Briefly explain how we may learn to understand the meaning of

   a. concrete content words.

   b. abstract content words.

   c. function words.

3. a. Define the phenomenon of semantic priming in your own words.

   b. Now use this concept to explain how memories may be evoked by the perception of words and cite research to support your answer. (Johnston and Dark, 1986; Morton, 1979; McClelland and Rumelhart, 1981)

4. Draw possible neural representations, based on the one in Figure 10.14 in your text, for the concepts linked to these sentences.

   The bed was moved.   The bed was made.

5. Explain why subjects made a shorter fixation on the word *popcorn* when it followed *buttered* than when it followed the word *adequate*. (Zola, 1984)

6. Now explain why subjects who read *put on his sweatshirt* rather than *took off his sweatshirt* later recognized the word *sweatshirt* more quickly. (Glenberg et al., 1987)

7. Describe the two types of memory involved in reading.
   1.
   2.

LESSON I SELF TEST

1. The fundamental unit of speech is the
   _____, but psychologically the
   fundamental unit is a _____.
   a. phoneme; phrase
   b. syllable; word
   c. phoneme; syllable
   d. spoken sound; written letter

2. Subjects who learned the rules combining *M, V, R,
   T* and *X,*
   a. forgot almost all of them when retested later.
   b. demonstrated the automatic nature of the use of
      syntax.
   c. had clear insight into their own behaviour.
   d. explained how they had solved the task.

3. Content words help us to determine the
   _____ of a sentence and function words
   help us determine its _____.
   a. meaning; syntax.
   b. structure; semantics
   c. clarity; intent
   d. meaning; implications

4. Most investigators believe the primary deficit of
   Wernicke's aphasia is
   a. loss of speech comprehension.
   b. an inability to speak fluently.
   c. disrupted neural representations of concepts.
   d. loss of whole-word reading skills.

5. The speech of people with Broca's aphasia is
   a. fluent but meaningless.
   b. labored but meaningful.
   c. superficially grammatical.
   d. full of function words but contains few content
      words.

6. The woman who could no longer recognize spatial
   relations as a result of a stroke demonstrated that
   the meanings of words
   a. are encoded as visual representations.
   b. are independent of their context.

   c. are linked to motor skills.
   d. are represented in neural circuits in various
      regions of association cortex.

7. By using eye movements to study the reading
   process, researchers have learned that
   a. Fixations in a forward and backward direction
      are characteristics of good readers.
   b. poor readers spend less time examining each
      word.
   c. punctuation does not usually affect reading
      speed.
   d. the amount of time we fixate on a word is
      proportional to its length.

8. Phonetic word recognition is
   a. preferred by experienced readers.
   b. faster than whole-word recognition.
   c. essential for reading irregularly spelled words.
   d. used to read unfamiliar words.

9. People with surface dyslexia cannot
   a. sound out words.
   b. read using the whole-word method.
   c. understand the words they read.
   d. increase their vocabularies.

10. The phenomenon of semantic priming suggests that
    memories
    a. about different aspects of word meanings are
       linked together in the brain.
    b. established through direct experience rather
       than vicarious experience are more complex.
    c. of the meanings of words are triggered only
       when explicit memory is active.
    d. for concrete and abstract content words are
       acquired in similar ways.

LESSON II

Read the interim summary on pages 334-335 of your text to re-acquaint yourself with the material in this section.

10-7 Describe the perception of speech sounds by infants and the acquisition of speech from the prespeech period through the two-word stage.

Read pages 324-327 and answer the following questions.

1. Explain why newborn preferences for a particular voice and passage suggest that some learning takes place prenatally. (DeCasper and Fifer, 1980; DeCasper and Spence, 1986)

2. What is the response of

    a. newborns in the delivery room to a sound in the room? (Wertheimer, 1961)

    b. two- or three-week-old infants to the sound of a voice or other sound?

    c. two-month-old infants to the sound of an angry or pleasant voice?

    d. What is your response to the question, "How well developed is the infant auditory system?"

3. Describe the technique Eimas et al. (1971) used to demonstrate that even very young infants can make fine discriminations. Table 10.1 in your text lists some of the infant responses to speech sounds.

4. a. What sounds do infants make at birth? one month? six months? (Kaplan and Kaplan, 1970)

    b. How do we know that adult speech influences infant preferences? (Mehler et al., 1988) infant babbling? (Boysson-Bardies et al., 1984)

5. a. Describe the procedure Kuhl and her colleagues used to study the ability of infants to distinguish between different vowel sounds. (See Figure 10.15 in your text.)

    b. Compare the reactions of American and Swedish infants to changing vowel sounds.

    c. What do the results suggest about the

       1. period during which the linguistic environment begins to affect an infant's perceptual mechanisms?

       2. need to understand speech sounds in order to perceive differences between them?

3. the difficulty native speakers of Japanese learning English have distinguishing between /l/ and /r/?

6. Explain how language acquisition may be a matter of becoming less discriminating of speech sound (Polka and Werker, 1994)

7. What are some of the characteristics of infant babble. (Menn and Stoel-Gamon, 1993)

8. a. Describe the first sounds, their origin, and the speech features of one-year-olds across all languages and cultures.

   b. Describe *protowords* and how infants use them. (Menn and Stoel-Gammon, 1993; Halliday, 1975)

   c. Which skill develops first—the ability to produce a sound or the ability to recognize it? Give an example. (Dale, 1976)

9. a. Early language acquisition takes place within a context of changing _____, _____, and _____ skills.

   b. Which three abilities work together to establish the foundation of more sophisticated speech? (Werker & Tees, 1999)

10. a. Make a general statement about the grammar of two-word speech of children everywhere. (Owens, 1992)

    b. State three reasons why young children cannot form complex sentences. (Locke, 1993)

10-8 Describe the way that adults talk to children, the acquisition of rules of grammar, and the acquisition of the meanings of words.

Read pages 327-329 and answer the following questions.

1. a. When adults speak to children, they use _____-_____ _____ which is marked by short, simple, repetitive sentences.

   b. What are some of the characteristics of child-directed speech that were identified by the de Villiers (1978)? Can you think of some examples from your own experience with young children?

c. What are some of the frequent topics of child-directed speech? (Snow et al., 1976) How do caregivers teach children the meaning of words? (Newport, 1975; Snow, 1977)

d. Describe a way that adults teach children more complex forms of speech. (Brown and Bellugi, 1964)

2. a. What is the most important factor controlling adults' speech to children?

b. How do adults adjust their speech to maintain a child's attention? (Stine and Bohannon, 1983)

c. How do infants and children direct the topic of conversation and how is learning affected? (Bohannon, 1993; Tomasello and Farrar, 1986)

d. What is the best strategy to follow in order to improve language and other skills?

3. a. What kind of words do children tend to use first? Why? (Brown and Fraser, 1964)

b. Continue to describe how children increase the length and complexity of their sentences. (Bloom, 1970)

c. Define *inflections* in your own words and explain why they, along with function words, are difficult to learn to use properly. Table 10.2 in your text shows the order in which children learn to use some English inflections and function words.

d. Explain why children learn to use the correct forms of irregular verbs first.

e. Now explain how learning about inflections temporarily hinders the continued use of these correct forms.

4. How do children learn to use and understand words and which words do they learn first? (Ross et al., 1986; Pease et al., 1993)

5. Define *overextension* and *underextension* in your own words. Explain why children make these errors when they are learning the meaning of words.

10-9 Discuss the controversy about the existence of an innate language acquisition device and discuss the role of reinforcement in language acquisition.

Read pages 329-332 and answer the following questions.

1. Summarize the arguments surrounding the assertion that language acquisition is an innate ability.

   a. How does Chomsky (1965) describe adult speech?

   b. What has the fact that most children learn to speak correctly in spite of imperfect models suggested about the ability to learn a language to some researchers? (Chomsky, 1965; Lennenberg, 1967; McNeill, 1970)

2. Summarize four points of a general theory about the function of cognitive structures involved in language acquisition concerning

   a. formation of grammar hypotheses and their testing

   b. existence and role of language acquisition device

   c. role of reinforcement

   d. best time for language acquisition (Pinker, 1990)

Now examine the evidence for each of these four points.

3. a. What widely accepted belief about the way children make and use hypotheses about grammar rules deters research?

   b. What may be a better use of these hypotheses in the study of language acquisition?

4. a. Describe the concept of language universals in your own words and give some examples.

   b. Discuss observations that suggest that not all language universals are the product of innate brain mechanisms and how these observations challenge the assertion that a language acquisition device exists. (Hebb et al., 1973;

   c. Outline Pinker's (1990) assertion and write the sentences that he gave in support of it.

   d. If Pinker's conclusion is correct, what assumption about the grammatical rules that children and linguists use must also be correct?

   e. Briefly discuss evidence that supports and questions the use of these rules.

5. a. Brown and Hanlon (1970) recorded and analyzed dialogue between parents and children. How did parents respond to their children's ungrammatical speech? grammatical speech? truthful speech?

b. What do these findings suggest about the role of reinforcement in learning to speak grammatically?

c. However, Bohannon and Stanowicz (1988) observed that adults do respond differently to grammatical and ungrammatical speech. Describe their observations and what they suggest about the role of reinforcement.

d. What did Newport et al. (1977) conclude about the quality of speech young children in industrialized English-speaking societies hear, and what does this conclusion suggest about the accuracy of Chomsky's description of adult speech?

6. a. How, according to some researchers, do some societies regard the importance of what children try to say to adults? How do these children eventually learn to speak correctly? (Pinker, 1990)

b. What kinds of social interaction does this reasoning overlook and what kind of research is required to confirm or dispel it?

c. What do the experiences of the hearing children of deaf parents confirm about

1. language acquisition through overhearing?

2. the importance of child-directed speech? (Bonvillian et al., 1976; Furrow et al., 1979; Furrow and Nelson, 1986)

d. How does the need for social interaction provide the motivation for learning to speak correctly?

7. a. Summarize research that the language acquisition device works best in childhood.

1. learning sign language by the deaf (Newport and Supalla, 1987)

2. learning English by Asian children (Johnson and Newport, 1989)

b. List some other variables correlated with age that might influence language acquisition.

8. Explain how the ease with which children learn a language has been interpreted by people on both sides of the debate.

10-10 Describe research on the abilities of other primates to communicate verbally.

Read pages 332-334 and answer the following questions.

1. a. Why did early attempts to teach chimpanzees to communicate with humans fail? How did the Gardners overcome this limitation?

   b. Briefly summarize some of Washoe's language skills.

   c. Compare her rate of progress with that of young children learning to speak.

   d. Why do Terrace et al. (1979) challenge the assertion that the skills these animals have learned is verbal behaviour? How have these criticisms been answered? (Fouts, 1983; Miles, 1983; Stokoe, 1983)

   e. Explain why research such as Project Washoe is useful.

2. a. Briefly describe some of the skills that Premack (1976) taught Sarah.

   b. What two important abilities did Sarah demonstrate by learning to work with plastic disks?

3. a. How did Savage-Rumbaugh (1990) teach Kanzi to communicate with humans?

   b. How else did Kanzi try to communicate with his human companions?

   c. Describe how the researchers later tested his language recognition and describe his responses. (See Table 10.3 in your text for examples of the behaviour.)

4. What do primate studies suggest about the nature of verbal ability and the conditions that facilitate verbal behaviour?

5. a. Explain how researchers made certain that Washoe, and not humans, taught Loulis to sign. (Fouts et al., 1983)

   b. Describe Washoe's attempt to teach signs to him.

LESSON II SELF TEST

1. Research using a pacifier with a pressure-sensitive switch demonstrated that infants
   a. stop sucking when they hear a novel sound.
   b. suck more slowly as habituation occurs.
   c. can distinguish between angry and pleasant voices.
   d. cannot yet distinguish speech sounds.

2. Infant babbling
   a. appears to be an attempt to communicate verbally.
   b. reflects the sounds and rhythm of the speech the infant hears.
   c. suggests that very young infants cannot discriminate between vowel sounds.
   d. is the same everywhere.

3. Protowords
   a. result when a child's caregivers use and encourage "baby talk."
   b. are preverbal attempts of young children to communicate with each other.
   c. are unique strings of phonemes invented by the child.
   d. support the hypothesis that children's speech follows different grammar rules than adult speech does.

4. When adults speak to children, they
   a. rarely make allowances for the age of the child.
   b. place the name of the object they are describing at the beginning of the sentence.
   c. use modifiers to convey subtle distinctions.
   d. pronounce words clearly and exaggerate *intonation*.

5. The most important factor controlling adults' speech to children is the child's
   a. sex.
   b. attractiveness.
   c. attentiveness.
   d. vocabulary.

6. Inflections are
   a. special affixes we add to words to change their syntactical or semantic function.
   b. innate grammatical rules.
   c. shortcuts for learning the meaning of abstract words.
   d. errors in underextension or overextension.

7. According to its proponents, the language acquisition device
   a. is found in the brains of most species of primates.
   b. is responsible for the defective, degenerate speech of adults.
   c. works best in people who speak several languages.
   d. makes reinforcement unnecessary for learning a language.

8. The most important piece of evidence against the existence of a language acquisition device is that
   a. adults speak differently to children than to other adults.
   b. adults, when properly reinforced, can learn a language as easily as children do.
   c. language universals are characteristics of the written, not spoken, language.
   d. the language centres in an adult's brain are similar to those in a child's brain.

9. The Gardners taught Washoe a manual language
   a. to eliminate confounding variables such as prosody, accent, and tone of voice.
   b. because chimpanzees cannot produce the variety of speech sounds that humans can.
   c. to provide some control over vocabulary.
   d. to reduce the possibility that researchers would demonstrate the meaning of a word with their hands.

10. Research such as Project Washoe is useful because it
    a. confirms Darwin's theory of language acquisition.
    b. demonstrates the uniqueness of human language abilities.
    c. confirms the existence of the language acquisition device.
    d. investigates the evolutionary continuity of the ability to communicate.

Answers for Self Tests

Lesson I

1. c	Obj. 10-1	2. b	Obj. 10-2	3. a	Obj. 10-2	4. a	Obj. 10-3	5. b	Obj. 10-3
6. d	Obj. 10-4	7. d	Obj. 10-5	8. d	Obj. 10-5	9. b	Obj. 10-5	10. a	Obj. 10-6

Lesson II

1. b	Obj. 10-7	2. b	Obj. 10-7	3. c	Obj. 10-7	4. d	Obj. 10-8	5. c	Obj. 10-8
6. a	Obj. 10-8	7. d	Obj. 10-9	8. a	Obj. 10-9	9. b	Obj. 10-10	10. d	Obj. 10-10

CHAPTER 11

Intelligence and Thinking

LESSON I

Read the interim summary on page 348 of your text to re-acquaint yourself with the material in this section.

11-1 Describe Spearman's two-factor theory of intelligence and the results of intelligence research using factor analysis.

Read pages 340-343 and answer the following questions.

1. State the definition of intelligence used by most psychologists.

2. a. Identify the three major approaches to the study of intelligence.

   1.

   2.

   3.

   b. Who was the most influential proponent of the developmental approach?

3. a. State the basic assumption of the differential approach to the study of the nature of intelligence.

   b. Explain two different positions concerning the basic nature of intelligence.

4. a. Spearman proposed that performance on a test of intellectual ability is determined by _____ factors: the _____ or _____ factor and the _____ or _____ factor.

   b. What, according to Spearman, are the three "qualitative principles of cognition" that comprise the g factor?

   c. Explain how analogy questions incorporate all three principles of cognition. (Sternberg, 1985)

   d. Intercorrelations among various tests of mental ability usually range from .30 to .70. How did Spearman interpret this fact?

5. If a researcher performs a factor analysis, what kind of information will be obtained?

6. a. What correlations did Birren and Morrison (1961) subject to factor analysis and how did they obtain their data? (Some typical questions from the subtests are presented in Table 11.5 in your text.)

   b. Study Table 11.1 in your text. What are the numbers in the three columns called? Define this term in your own words.

   c. Explain how an analysis of these factor loadings is useful in determining which abilities are represented by factors A, B, and C.

7. Discuss some of the limitations of factor analysis.

8. a. What data did Thurstone (1938) submit to factor analysis and how did he obtain the original data?

   b. What factors did he obtain from the analysis?

   c. What was revealed by a second factor analysis of Thurstone's data?

   d. What names did Horn and Cattell (1966) give to these factors? Briefly define them.

   e. Explain their differing views on the importance of learning and heredity on these two factors. (Horn, 1978)

   f. Study Table 11.2 in your text and describe the kind of tests that load heavily on fluid intelligence.

   g. Study Table 11.2 in your text and describe the kind of tests that load heavily on crystallized intelligence.

9. What then may account for individual performance on intellectual tasks?

Discuss Sternberg's information-processing approach to intelligence.

Read pages 343-345 and answer the following questions.

1. a. List and define the three aspects of intelligence that are addressed in the three parts of Sternberg's theory of intelligence.
    1.
    2.
    3.

   b. These three aspects contribute to what Sternberg calls _____ _____.

   c. Successful intelligence is the ability to
    1.
    2.
    3.

   d. According to Sternberg, what is a strong determinant of the degree of success that people achieve in life?

2. Now list and define the three functions served by the three aspects of analytic intelligence.

   1.

   2.

   3.

3. a. How does a person with good creative intelligence deal with novel situations? recurring situations?
   b. Explain why Sternberg believes the problem solving skills of people with good creative intelligence is related to Horn and Cattell's distinction between fluid and crystallized intelligence.
   c. What did Sternberg and Lubart (1996) say creative people were able to tolerate?

4. Finally, list and define the three forms of practical intelligence that Sternberg proposed.

   1.

   2.

   3.

5. According to Feldman (1982), why did some child prodigies who appeared on the "Quiz Kid" shows later have distinguished careers while others did not?

6. a. Briefly describe the experiences of the physician following serious damage to his frontal lobes.

b. What does his behaviour suggest about the importance of considering the practical uses of intelligence? the use of modern intelligence tests as a measure of overall intelligence?

7. To review: Compare your lists on the previous page with Table 11.3 in your text.

11-3 Describe Gardner's neuropsychological theory of intelligence.

Read pages 345-347 and answer the following questions.

1. Discuss Gardner's (1983, 1993, 1999) argument that intelligences are potentials.

2. Gardner believes that each of the intelligences he identifies are the result of _____, and have separate _____ underpinnings.

3. Briefly describe the eight categories of intelligence proposed by Gardener (1983) and explain the basis for his selection.

4. Explain why not all of the eight categories have traditionally been recognized as aspects of intelligence.

5. Explain an advantage of Gardner's approach.

6. Discuss work by other researchers who have drawn on Gardner's theory. (Salovey & Mayer, 1989–1990; Mayer & Salovey, 1993; Dawda & Hart, 2000)

11-4 Discuss evidence that the definitions of intelligence reflect cultural differences.

Read page 347 and answer the following questions.

1. a. Explain the three parts of a syllogism in your own words.

b. How is it used in tests of intelligence?

2. How well did members of two West African tribes solve syllogisms? (Scribner, 1977)

3. When unschooled people were tested using syllogisms that seemed relevant to their experience, how did a Kpelle tribesman respond? (Scribner, 1977) a Uzbekistanian woman? (Luria, 1977)

4. In Scribner's experience, how did unschooled people sometimes respond to her syllogisms?

5. What difficulties in intelligence testing and interpretation are suggested by these results?

Read the interim summary on page 354 of your text to re-acquaint yourself with the material in this section.

11–5 Describe Galton's contributions to intelligence testing.

Read pages 348-349 and answer the following questions.

1. Briefly explain why testing is one of the most important areas of applied psychology.

2. Describe how Charles Darwin influenced the work of his cousin Sir Francis Galton.

3. What observation convinced Galton to include tests of sensory discrimination in intelligence testing?

4. Describe Galton's contributions in the following areas:

   a. modern statistical testing.

   b. distribution pattern of human traits. (See Figure 11.1 in your text.)

   c. assessing the relationship between variables.

   d. assessing the heritability of human traits.

11–6 Describe the Binet-Simon Scale, the Stanford-Binet Scale, and Wechsler's tests.

Read pages 349-352 and answer the following questions.

1. a. What did Binet and Henri (1896) say about Galton's simple sensory tests?

   b. What was the original purpose of the Binet-Simon Scale?

   c. Define *norm* in your own words and explain its importance to intelligence testing.

d. Why are standardized testing procedures important?

e. Why did Binet revise the original test?

f. Describe the concept of mental age in your own words.

2. a. Briefly explain the kinds and grouping of tests on the Stanford-Binet Scale.

b. Explain the rationale of the intelligence quotient (IQ).

c. State the formula for computing the ratio IQ.

d. Explain how the deviation IQ differs from the ratio IQ. What is the standard deviation of the ratio IQ, and how is the deviation IQ expressed? (Study Figure 11.2 in your text.)

e. Calculate the ratio or deviation IQ (as appropriate) for the following students.

1. I.L., 11 years old, mental age of 13

2. S.M., 12 years old, mental age of 9

3. J.L.-T., 12 years old, score of 0.5 standard deviations above the mean for her age.

3. a. What do the acronyms WAIS, WAIS-R, WAIS-III, WISC, and WISC-III stand for?

b. See Table 11.5 in your text and describe some of the subtests and sample items from the WAIS-III.

c. Indicate two particular advantages of this test.

11-7 Explain reliability and validity in intelligence tests.

Read page 352 and answer the following questions.

1. a. What two procedures contribute to the reliability of a modern test of intellectual ability?

b. Define *criterion* in your own words and explain how it is related to the concept of validity.

2. Why is there no single criterion measure with which to assess the validity of intelligence tests?

3. a. Explain why IQ tests are considered a somewhat valid measure of academic success.

   b. What other influences beside IQ may affect success in school?

11-8 Discuss the use and abuse of intelligence tests.

Read pages 352-354 and answer the following questions.

1. What is it important to know that intelligence tests are valid and being used appropriately?

2. a. Explain how cultural bias may affect, and how cultural differences often affect, test performance.

   b. Discuss how the question Darou (1992) gave to a First Nations counselor was inappropriate.

3. a. Define self-fulfilling prophecy in your own words.

   b. Explain how low scores on an intelligence test may affect future educational opportunities and self-image.

4. Finally, explain how the use of intelligence tests may affect curriculum and teaching methods.

5. Identify several groups of children who may benefit from the general use of intelligence tests.

6. a. Define *mental retardation* in your own words.

   b. Discuss the double problem people with mental retardation face.

   c. What other terms may be more appropriate to use than mental retardation.

   d. Name and briefly describe the degrees of mental retardation.

   e. List other factors besides IQ that in part determine achievement and satisfaction in life for people with intellectual difficulties.

LESSON I SELF TEST

1. Scientists who study intelligence by trying to assess the kinds of cognitive abilities people use to think and solve problems are proponents of the
   a. differential approach.
   b. developmental approach.
   c. information-processing approach.
   d. intuitive approach.

2. A factor analysis can identify
   a. the best types of question to use to measure intelligence.
   b. groups of questions that accurately measure intelligence.
   c. groups of questions that seem to measure similar characteristics.
   d. the best type of test for a particular age group.

3. _____ is to analytic intelligence as _____ is to practical intelligence.
   a. metacomponent; performance component
   b. adaptation; performance component
   c. selection; shaping
   d. metacomponent; adaptation

4. An advantage of Gardner's neuropsychological theory of intelligence is that
   a. none of his types of intelligence had been previously identified.
   b. it minimizes the importance of verbal ability.
   c. it provides for non-Western views of intelligence.
   d. eight categories allow for greater distinctions than three categories.

5. The use of Western tests of intelligence in other cultures suggests
   a. the minimum level of formal education necessary for economic success.
   b. that intelligence can only be accurately assessed using a combination of written and ability tests.
   c. that the fluid intelligence of all human beings varies over the lifespan.
   d. the need for definitions of intelligence to reflect cultural differences.

6. Which is a lasting contribution Galton made to the field of intelligence?
   a. the use of the normal curve
   b. the invention of the correlation coefficient
   c. the discovery of a single criterion to measure overall intelligence
   d. the use of sensory discrimination tests to assess intelligence

7. The original purpose of the Binet-Simon Scale was
   a. to establish the correlation coefficients for factor analysis.
   b. to attempt to corroborate the notion of crystallized and fluid intelligence.
   c. to assess the intellectual abilities of normal children.
   d. to identify children who needed special instruction.

8. _____ is to the Binet-Simon Scale as _____ is to the Stanford-Binet Scale.
   a. ratio IQ; deviation IQ
   b. standard deviation; norms
   c. mental age; intelligence quotient
   d. sensory testing; verbal testing

9. Because the WAIS-R tests verbal and performance abilities separately it is useful in estimating the intelligence of people who
   a. have had few educational and cultural opportunities.
   b. are physically handicapped.
   c. have had little experience taking intelligence tests.
   d. experience test anxiety.

10. Modern intelligence tests
    a. should not be given to children from disadvantaged backgrounds.
    b. are less likely to contain questions that are culturally biased.
    c. often suggest needed changes in school curricula so that students will receive higher test scores.
    d. pose few problems because the potential for abuse is widely recognized.

LESSON II

Read the interim summary on pages 360-361 of your text to reacquaint yourself with the material in this section.

11-9 Discuss the meaning of heritability and describe the sources of environmental and genetic effects during development.

Read pages 355-357 and answer the following questions.

1. Define the concept of heritability in your own words and explain how this concept is often misinterpreted.

2. Keep your definition in mind and explain this statement: Even if hereditary factors do influence intelligence, the heritability of intellectual abilities must be considerably less than 1.0.

3. Carefully explain how any assessment of the heritability of intellectual abilities is influenced by the

   a. ancestral origin of the population.

   b. amount of environmental variability in the population.

   c. degree of interaction between genetic inheritance and the environment within the population.

4. Discuss the adverse effects on the development of a fetus if a pregnant woman

   a. contracts a disease such as Rubella early in her pregnancy.

   b. uses drugs such as cocaine, drinks alcoholic beverages, or smokes cigarettes. Be sure to mention fetal alcohol syndrome in your answer.

5. Review the effects of Down syndrome and phenylketonuria (PKU) on fetal brain development first discussed in Chapter 3.

6. a. Explain why Down syndrome is a genetic, but not hereditary, disorder.

   b. Now explain why all cases of familial mental retardation are not necessarily hereditary.

7. Summarize genetic and/or environmental factors that can affect intellectual development at or during

   a. conception

   b. prenatal development

   c. birth

   d. infancy

   e. later life

11-10 Discuss the results and implications of heritability studies of general intelligence and specific abilities.

Read pages 357-358 and answer the following questions.

1. a. If the heritability for a train is .5, what does this mean?
   b. What does a very high variability estimate mean?
   c. Environments are _____; some environments will promote the _____ expression of a _____ and some will _____ that expression.

2. a. Study Table 11.6 in your text, which summarizes the results of research to identify correlations in intelligence between people of varying kinship (Henderson, 1982). What is the correlation in intelligence between

   1. parent and child?   4. identical twins?

   2. adoptive parent and child?   5. fraternal twins?

   3. siblings?

   b. In general, how is the correlation in intelligence related to the percentage of genetic similarity?

3. a. What did Neisser et al. (1996) find concerning the heritability of IQ and age?

   b. What is a possible explanation for this finding? (Neisser et al., 1996; Sternberg & Grigorenko, 1999)

4. a. Describe how Scarr and Weinberg (1978) compared specific intellectual abilities of parents with their biological and adoptive children and that of children with their biological and adoptive siblings.

   b. Study Table 11.7 in your text and summarize the effect of kinship on specific abilities.

   c. How might we explain the fact that vocabulary scores were an exception to the general pattern?

11-11 Evaluate whether racial differences in intelligence are the result of heredity.

Read pages 359-360 and answer the following questions.

1. a. What is the average score on IQ tests for people identified as white? black? (Lynn, 1978; Jensen, 1985)

   b. What these means fails to tell us is that the variation of scores _____ each race is greater than the variation _____ races. That is, the IQ scores of the two races _____ more than they _____.

   c. What is the single, most widely accepted explanation for the difference between the two races?

2. Let's examine the evidence for some of the assertions about the meaning of racial differences in intelligence.

   a. What did Sternberg (1995) and Wahlsten (1997) conclude about the merit of assertions made in a controversial book *The Bell Curve* by Herrnstein and Murray (1994)?

   b. What three factors do people mention when asked the meaning of intelligence? (Sternberg et al., 1981)

   c. Why do people weight these factors differently? (Berry, 1984; Okagaki and Sternberg, 1993; Ruzgis & Grigorenko, 1994)

   d. If children are placed in special educational programs, what is the effect on their IQ scores? (Ramey, 1994)

   e. Compare the gain in general cognitive ability from university across the two races.

3. a. How do biologists define race?

   b. Why did early humans mate at first with a restricted group and why did mating patterns change?

   c. What was the result of greater human interbreeding and how does it affect attempts to classify people on the basis of race?

   d. Explain why skin pigmentation is not a valid criterion for classifying people by race by reviewing the selective advantage of different amounts of skin pigmentation. (Loomis, 1967)

4. a. Why is racial membership more of a cultural assignment than a biological one in North America?

   b. How may environmental differences, independent of hereditary differences, influence the IQ scores of people of different racial groups?

c. What were the results of a study by Scarr and Weinberg (1976) that tested black children adopted and raised in economically and educationally advantaged white families?

d. What do the results suggest about the influence of environmental factors on inherited intellectual ability?

5. Why does knowing a person's race tell us very little about his or her intelligence?

Read the interim summary on pages 370-371 of your text to re-acquaint yourself with the material in this section.

11-12 Describe research on concepts and their role in thinking.

Read pages 361-364 and answer the following questions.

1. We infer the existence of thinking from people's _____. Most of our thinking involves _____, but we also think in _____ and _____. Thinking can also involve some _____ mental processes that we are not always conscious of. In general, the purpose of thinking is to _____ _____.

2. a. Define *concept* in your own words.

b. Why is the ability to generalize a useful one?

c. Explain how formal concepts are defined.

3. a. Describe the Collins and Quillian (1969) model of the organization of a formally defined concept shown in Figure 11.3 in your text.

b. According to these researchers, why did subjects quickly answer questions about a specific characteristic of the concept but took longer to answer questions about a characteristic that was common to a more general concept?

c. Cite two studies that suggest people do *not* store concepts in an organized hierarchy. (Rips et al., 1973; Roth and Mervis, 1983)

4. a. Explain how the natural concepts we use in daily life differ in origin, precision, and use from those found in a dictionary. (Be sure to use the term *exemplars* in your answer. Rosch, 1975; Mervis and Rosch, 1981)

5. a. Study Figure 11.4 in your text, then fill in the blanks in Figure 1. Use examples of your own—something other than apples.

Level of Concept

Examples

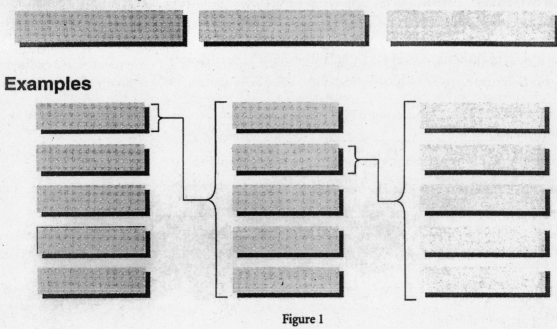

Figure 1

b. What level of concepts do we most commonly use? Cite research to support your answer. (Rosch et al., 1976)

6. a. When Goldstone, Medin and Gentner (1991) asked subjects which groups of figures, shown in Figure 11.5 in your text, were most similar to each other, how did they respond for the first group? the second group?

b. What do the results suggest about the nature of concepts?

11-13 Describe research on deductive and inductive reasoning.

Read pages 364-368 and answer the following questions.

1. Define *deductive reasoning* in your own words.

2. Summarize research on why skill in deductive reasoning involves mental models and spatial abilities.

a. Define the concept of mental models in your own words and explain how they may be used to solve problems involving logical deduction. (Johnson-Laird, 1995; Johnson-Laird et al., 1992)

b. Describe the skills that comprise spatial ability and discuss why such skills play a central role in Johnson-Laird's theory of mental models.

c. Study the hypothesized mental model in Figure 11.6 in your text and explain how it can be used to solve a comparison problem.

d. Now study two other hypothesized mental models shown in Figures 11.7 and 11.8 in your text and explain how they can be used to compare the height of four brothers (Just and Carpenter, 1987) or identify a family relationship.

3. a. Damage to the_____ _____ impairs spatial ability. (Luria, 1973)

b. How does this kind of damage appear to affect the use of mental models?

4. a. Before reading further think about the problem shown in Figure 11.11 in your text so that you can compare your reasoning with that of the subjects in this research by Wason and Johnson-Laird (1977) as you continue to read.

b. Did you ask to see card (a)? card (c)? Why?

c. Did you ask to see card (d) or overlook its importance? Why?

d. Why was card (b) uninformative?

e. Now try the slightly different version of this test shown in Figure 11.12 in your text and again compare your own reasoning with that of the subjects. (Griggs and Cox, 1982)

g. Describe the following explanations for the ease of the card problem in Figure 11.10 in your text over the problem shown in Figure 11.9 in your text.

1. mental models

2. pragmatic reasoning schemas. (Cheng & Holyoak, 1985)

5. a. Define *inductive reasoning* in your own words.

b. Explain how the cards shown in Figure 11.11 in your text are used to test inductive reasoning.

c. Why is training in inductive reasoning useful?

d. List two tendencies that may interfere with a person's ability to reason inductively.

6. a. Most people will conclude that if a high recovery rate follows the use of a drug, the drug is effective. What mistake are they making? (Stich, 1990)

   b. Refer to explicit and implicit memory to explain why this error occurs. (Reber, 1992)

   c. Under what circumstances do people consider information about the frequency of an event? (Holyoak and Spellman, 1993)

7. a. Explain the confirmation bias in your own words.

   b. Explain how it interferes with hypothesis testing using

      1. inductive reasoning. (Wason, 1968)

      2. deductive reasoning. (Johnson-Laird, 1985)

11–14 Describe the roles of spatial metaphors, algorithms, and heuristics in problem solving.

Read pages 369-370 and answer the following questions.

1. What is a *problem* and how is it often described? (Holyoak, 1990; Lakoff and Turner, 1989)

2. Explain the following steps of the problem-solving process noting any spatial metaphors that are appropriate. (Study Figure 11.12 in your text. Newell and Simon, 1972)

   a. initial state

   b. goal state

   c. operators

   d. problem space

   e. solution

3 a. Define *algorithm* in your own words.

   b. Now define *heuristics* in your own words.

   c. When there are no _____ to follow, we must use _____ to try to solve a problem.

4. Outline the four steps of means-ends analysis—a general heuristic method to solve any problem. (Newell and Simon, 1972; Holyoak, 1990)

1.

2.

3.

4.

5. What is the goal of all action at all times?

6. a. What are the characteristics of a good solution?

   b. Briefly explain some of the benefits of planning a solution to a problem.

LESSON II SELF TEST

1. Heritability is a statistical measure that expresses the extent to which
   a. observed variability in a trait results from genetic variability.
   b. genes are responsible for a particular trait.
   c. a particular trait has biological causes.
   d. observed variability in a trait results from environmental factors.

2. In which situation would the effects of environmental variability be larger than the effects of genetic variability?
   a. an isolated tribal society
   b. a medieval society in which only the rich or religious received any formal education
   c. an orphanage where all children receive the same care
   d. a Canadian suburb

3. Estimates of the contribution of environmental factors to the intelligence of children in the same family are _____ when the measurements are made during adulthood than when they are made during childhood because

   a. lower; fluid intelligence has stabilized.
   b. higher; the need to achieve is stronger in adults.
   c. lower; during adulthood environments are less similar.
   d. higher; crystallized intelligence is growing more rapidly.

4. We cannot conclude that observed racial differences in test scores are caused by hereditary factors because
   a. people of different races have different genetic backgrounds.
   b. testing conditions and experience taking tests can never be identical.
   c. environmental differences may affect people's scores.
   d. differences in test scores are not synonymous with racial differences.

5. Concepts are
   a. expressed in complete sentences.
   b. organized systematically in the brain.
   c. based on our own perceptions and interactions.
   d. nothing more than cultural inventions.

6. Basic-level concepts
   a. do not always differentiate clearly between a member and a nonmember.
   b. represent the most information stored in the most efficient manner.
   c. organize a small number of individual items and their characteristics.
   d. are based on differences rather than similarities between examples.

7. Inductive reasoning
   a. infers general principles from specific facts.
   b. ability is highly correlated with spatial ability.
   c. is just the opposite of reasoning following the scientific method.
   d. is based on the premise that information that confirms an hypothesis is conclusive.

8. The confirmation bias, a logical error in inductive reasoning, means people have failed
   a. to consider that the exception proves the rule.
   b. to use information from a control group.
   c. to select appropriate information needed to confirm a hypothesis.
   d. to seek information that might prove the hypothesis incorrect.

9. Heuristics are general rules
   a. for solving syllogisms.
   b. for constructing mental models.
   c. for identifying appropriate exemplars.
   d. useful in guiding an investigation.

10. Means-end analysis is a method
    a. that determines what kind of exemplar each obstacle represents.
    b. that identifies and reduces the differences between the current state and goal state.
    c. to evaluate the necessity of each new subgoal.
    d. to estimate the relative importance of cost and speed.

Answers for Self Tests

Lesson I

1. c Obj. 11-1	2. c Obj. 11-1	3. d Obj. 11-2	4. c Obj. 11-3	5. d Obj. 11-4
6. a Obj. 11-5	7. d Obj. 11-6	8. c Obj. 11-6	9. a Obj. 11-6	10. b Obj. 11-8

Lesson II

1. a Obj. 11-9	2. b Obj. 11-9	3. c Obj. 11-10	4. c Obj. 11-11	5. c Obj. 11-12
6. b Obj. 11-12	7. a Obj. 11-13	8. d Obj. 11-13	9. d Obj. 11-14	10. b Obj. 11-14

CHAPTER 12

Life-Span Development

LESSON I

Read the interim summary on page 378 of your text to re-acquaint yourself with the material in this section.

12-1 Describe the prenatal development of a human fetus and threats to normal development.

Read pages 374-377 and answer the following questions.

1. Study Table 12.1 in your text for an overview of life-span development and change.

2. What aspects of human development do developmental psychologists study?

3. List the three developmental stages of the prenatal period and their approximate duration.

   1.   2.   3.

4. a. Define *zygote* in your own words.

   b. Briefly describe the three layers of cells of the developing zygote and say what organs develop from them.

5. a. Outline the physical development of the embryo.

   b. What are teratogens, and how do they threaten embryonic development?

   c. Review how a person's sex is determined by referring to Figure 12.1 in your text.

   d. The gonads have the potential to develop into two different structures. Name them.

   e. What determines the direction in which the gonads develop?

   f. What is necessary for the development of male sex organs? female sex organs?

The development of male and female sex organs is shown in Figure 12.1 in your text.

6. Match these physical and behavioural changes with the month of the fetal stage in which they occur.

_____ regular sleeping and waking

_____ development of major organs complete

_____ possibility of survival

_____ shows some movement

_____ weight gain of about 250 gr per week

_____ mother feels movement

_____ fetus grows to more than 30 cm

a. Month 3

b. Month 4

c. Month 6

d. Month 7

e. Month 8 and 9

7. a. What may be the single most important factor that influences fetal development? Why?

   b. How may fetal development be affected if the mother is extremely malnourished?

8. Discuss the ways various teratogens can adversely affect fetal development
   a. How does tetracycline affect fetal development?

   b. What effect does the carbon monoxide in cigarettes have on the fetus? At what point in development is this particularly harmful?

   c. What physical effects result from maternal smoking? (Floyd et al., 1993) What other effects have also been found? (Franco et al., 2000, Chung et al., 2000)

   d. What effects have been found with maternal cocaine use? (Bard et al., 2000, Mayes, 1999, Porter et al., 2000) What is sometimes observed after the baby is born?

   e. Which drug use during pregnancy has been most widely studied?

   f. Describe fetal alcohol syndrome (FAS).

   g. If a child with FAS is raised in a healthy environment, what is still the result?

   h. What happens to animals as a result of prenatal alcohol exposure? (Ikonomidou, 2000)

   i. Drinking as little as _____ grams of alcohol a day early in pregnancy can produce some symptoms of FAS.

   j. What is the best advice concerning alcohol and pregnancy?

9. If a child with fetal alcohol syndrome is raised in a healthy environment, what is still the result?

Read the interim summary on pages 380-381 of your text to re-acquaint yourself with the material in this section.

12-2 Describe the physical and perceptual development of the human infant.

Read pages 378-380 and answer the following questions.

1. Define *reflex* in your own words and describe the rooting, sucking and swallowing reflexes of a human infant.

2. Now define *maturation* in your own words.

3. Study the milestones in a child's motor development shown in Figure 12.2 in your text. Name and explain the two necessary conditions for the development of motor skills. (Thelen, 1995)

4. Describe observations that indicate that the sensory systems of a newborn infant are functioning.

   a. audition

   b. vision

   c. touch

   d. balance

   e. taste preference

   f. odour recognition (Sullivan et al., 1991; Porter and Winberg, 1999; Porter et al., 1992)

5. a. Describe how infant pattern perception is studied using a scanning procedure and infrared light.

   b. Study Figure 12.3 in your text and describe the scanning patterns of one- and two-month-old infants looking at actual faces. (Salapatek, 1975)

   c. What do these results suggest about the perceptual ability of one- and two-month old infants?

   d. By the time infants are three months old, how has their perceptual ability changed? (Rosser, 1994) How has it changed by 4 or 5 months? (Fagan and Singer, 1979)

6. a. How do six-month-old infants usually react when placed on the glass and checkerboard platform called a visual cliff? (Gibson and Walk, 1960)

   b. What do their reactions suggest about their perception of space?

7. a. Define *stereopsis* in your own words and explain how it is related to development of depth perception. (Poggio and Poggio, 1984)

   b. Using the example of the development of normal stereoscopic vision, explain how the concept of a critical period applies to development in general. Cite research by Banks et al. (1975) to support your answer.

Read the interim summary on page 390 of your text to re-acquaint yourself with the material in this section.

12-3 Describe the importance of a responsive environment and describe and discuss the theories of cognitive development proposed by Piaget and Vygotsky.

Read pages 381-387 and answer the following questions.

1. What kind of environment is most effective in stimulating infant cognitive development?

2. Summarize research by Watson and Ramey (1972) on factors in cognitive development.
   a. Describe the testing conditions for the three groups of infants.

   b. Describe the results of a later retest and their implications for infant-rearing practices.

3. How did infants respond when they controlled the onset of a Sesame Set video? How did they respond when the contingency was broken? (Lewis et al, 1990)

4. How are these findings consistent with research conducted with adults?

5. Describe research by Dennis (1973) that underscores the importance of a stimulating environment. Be sure to refer again to critical periods.

6. a. What similarities in children's behaviour suggested to Piaget that development followed a sequence?

   b. Define *cognitive structure, schema,* and *concept* in your own words and give an example of each.

c. How, in general, do children learn about schemata and concepts?

d. Describe *assimilation* and *accommodation and give and an example of each.*

7. Summarize Piaget's four periods of cognitive development.

a. _____ Period

1. Duration

2. Carefully describe how a child's concept for objects changes throughout this period. Be sure to refer to *object permanence* in your answer. (See Figure 12.4 in your text.)

3. Name other cognitive structures that develop toward the end of this period.

b. _____ Period

1. Duration

2. What two abilities develop rapidly during this period?

3. Contrast the meaning of the terms *signifier* and *sign* and explain why Piaget believed the development of symbolism began in the sensorimotor period.

4. Describe the acquisition of the ability to perceive *conservation* of various characteristics of objects during this stage. (See Figures 12.5 and 12.6 in your text.)

5. Define *egocentrism* in your own words and give an example of egocentric behaviour characteristic of this stage.

c. Period of _____

1. Duration

2. What abilities develop during this stage?

3. What kind of reasoning is still difficult for children during this stage?

d. Period of _____

1. Duration

2. Describe reasoning skills of children at this stage.

3. What experience appears to influence the development of operational thinking?

4. Explain why this period may not be an inevitable stage of human development.

8. To review: Study Table 12.2 in your text, which summarizes Piaget's periods of cognitive development.

9. List some of the procedural objections to Piaget's work.

10. What did research by Gelman (1972) conclude about the age at which children are able to conserve various physical attributes?

11. Cite an observation that suggests Piaget overestimated children's egocentrism. (Flavell, 1992, Flavell et al., 1981)

12. According to Vygotsky, how may a child's cognitive development be influenced by the child's culture? (Rymer, 1992; Fuson and Kwon, 1992)

13. a. Carefully explain how Vygotsky's interpretation of why children talk to themselves differs from that of Piaget.

b. How do children's talks with themselves change around the age of seven?

c. What does Vygotsky call this speech and what does it represent?

14. How do the abilities of the people with whom children interact affect their cognitive skills? (Rogoff, et al., 1990)

15. Vygotsky stressed the importance of _____ _____ such as _____ and social _____ on a child's cognitive development.

12–4 Discuss the information processing model of cognitive development proposed by Case.

Read page 387 and answer the following questions.

1. Explain the structure and function of mental space or M-space proposed by Case and central to his theory of cognitive development.

2. Discuss the three variables that affect the expansion of M-space.

    a. What physical changes in the maturing brain contribute to more efficient information processing?

    b. What is the benefit of increased practice using schemata?

    c. How does the integration of schemata contribute to cognitive development? Be sure to mention central conceptual structures in your answer.

3. Discuss one important function of this model.

12-5 Describe and discuss research on the effects of television viewing of children's cognitive development.

Read pages 388-390 and answer the following questions.

1. In assessing the effects of watching television on children, what two issues must we consider?

    1.   2.

2. a. To illustrate the potential good that television can do, list some of the skills children have learned from watching *Sesame Street*. (Bogatz and Ball, 1972)

    b. What did research to determine the effects of watching *Sesame Street* on a large group of children from a wide range of socioeconomic backgrounds conclude? (Rice et al., 1990)

3. a. To illustrate the potential harm that television can do, what may children conclude about ways to solve problems as a result of watching programs containing violence?

    b. How do television sponsors attempt to influence the consumer behaviour of children? (McNeal, 1990; Taras et al., 1989)

    c. Which commercials do not appear to have had an influence? Why? (Lipsitz et al., 1993)

4. Summarize some of the criticisms of the medium of television on children's cognitive development. (Anderson and Collins, 1988)

5. a. Approximately how many hours a day do two-year-olds watch television (Hollenbeck, 1978)? older children (Neilsen, 1990)

b. Circle the group that tends to watch more television.   Boys   Girls

c. Children from which economic background watch more television? (Huston et al., 1990; Huston et al., 1989)

Let's examine research on some of these criticisms.

6. a. How did Anderson et al. (1985) objectively measure the amount of time children from ninety-nine families spent watching television?

b. How many hours per week did these children watch television?

c. What other activities do children also engage in while the television set is on? (Anderson and Collins, 1988)

7. a. When children are watching television, approximately how long do they look at the screen before looking away? How often do they look away each hour? (Anderson & Field, 1983)

b. What elements of a television program do children pay attention to? tend not to pay attention to? (Anderson & Lorch, 1983)

c. How do children appear to use auditory cues?

d. What does the documented selectivity of young viewers suggest about the ability of television to mesmerize them?

8. a. According to Moody (1980), how does television affect the brains of young children?

b. What does research suggest about this claim? (Anderson and Collins, 1988)

9. a. Why may watching television adversely affect children's cognitive development? (Singer 1993; Singer & Singer, 1990)

b. When television became available in remote towns, what kind of activities were displaced? (William & Boyes, 1986)

c. Television is most often the backdrop for homework in which subject? (Patton et al., 1983)

d. In general, how is the quality of homework done in front of the television affected?

10. a. How does television watching appear to affect the reading skills of young children (Corteen & Williams, 1986)? of older children?

b. And how serious were the effects?

11. What can we fairly conclude about the potential for good and harm of television programming?

Read the interim summary on page 396 of your text to re-acquaint yourself with the material in this section.

12-6 Describe the behaviours of infants that help establish the attachment between infant and caregiver.

Read pages 390-393 and answer the following questions.

1. a. Define *attachment* in your own words and then describe the mutually beneficial components of this relationship.

   b. What factors facilitate the development of attachment? (Bowlby, 1969)

2. What may be the benefit of nonnutritive sucking to an infant? Describe cultural differences in how the need for nonnutritive sucking is met. (Ainsworth, 1967)

3. a. Describe how Harlow (1974) raised infant monkeys using surrogate mothers.

   b. When did infant monkeys seek the wire-covered surrogate? the cuddly surrogate?

   c. Why may infant monkeys and young infants cuddle soft forms?

   d. When are children most likely to ask for a soft object?

4. Describe how Tronick et al. (1978) demonstrated the importance of looking behaviour.

   a. Describe how mothers and their infants usually interact together. What were mothers asked to do differently during the experiment?

   b. Study Figure 12.7 in your text and describe the infant's reaction to the new contingency. How did their mothers react?

   c. What do the results suggest?

5. a. What stimuli elicit smiles from an infant five weeks old? three months old?

 b. How do an infant's smiles strengthen the infant/caregiver attachment?

6. a. According to Wolff (1969), what three situations can an infant's cry signify?

 b. What event most effectively terminates crying?

 c. Explain the role of negative reinforcement in shaping this adult response.

 d. Describe Konner's (1972) observations with an African tribe that suggest that adults can distinguish the cry of pain from other cries.

 e. How does this observation differ from North American caregivers?

 f. What kind of needs do North American caregivers associate with the sudden onset of crying? the gradual onset? (Gustafson and Harris, 1990)

12-7 Describe the evaluation of the nature of attachment between caregiver and infant and discuss the importance of such attachment.

Read pages 393-395 and answer the following questions.

1. Attachment appears to be a _____ pattern necessary for _____
 _____. However, infants do not appear to have a natural inclination for attachment to a
 _____ adult and the object of attachment is usually the _____
 _____ An infant's caregiver provides a kind of _____ _____
 from which the infant can explore the world.

2. Compare and contrast stranger anxiety and separation anxiety.

	Stranger Anxiety	Separation Anxiety
Age of occurrence		
Behavioural responses		
Situations causing anxiety		
Situations reducing anxiety		

3. a. Describe the test of attachment called the Strange Situation and the following three patterns of attachment. (Ainsworth et al., 1978)

 b. What kinds of observations does this test allow?

2. Describe the following three patterns of attachment.

   a. secure attachment

   b. resistant attachment

   c. avoidant attachment

4. List two factors that affect the nature of an infant's attachment with the caregiver and indicate the more important. (Ainsworth et al., 1978; Pederson and Moran, 1996)

   1.   2.

5. a. Briefly describe caregiver behaviour that encourages

      a. secure attachment.

      b. resistant attachment.

      c. avoidant attachment.

   b. How did early patterns of attachment appear to affect social adjustment later in childhood? (Waters et al., 1979; Erickson et al., 1985; Waters et al., 2000)

6. If the mother is the primary caregiver, what is likely to be the role of the father? Cite research to support your answer. (Parke and Tinsley, 1981; Clarke-Stewart, 1978)

7. What kind of later relationships and experiences does early attachment appear to influence? (Feeney and Noller, 1991; Barnas et al., 1991)

8. Carefully summarize research to assess the effects of day care on infant attachment.

   a. Studies in the 1970s suggested that day care did not affect attachment. In evaluating this research, what factor must we keep in mind? (Field, 1994; Broberg et al., 1997; NICD, 1977))

   b. Why is it important to provide high-quality day care for all infants and children?

12-8 Describe how children's social development may be affected by their interaction with their peers, their parents' childrearing practices, and their family structure.

Read pages 395-396 and answer the following questions.

1. Summarize research by Harlow and his colleagues on the importance of peer interactions for young monkeys.

    a. How does an adolescent monkey, raised in isolation, react when introduced to normally reared peers?

    b. What kind of behaviours do young monkeys apparently learn through social interaction?

    c. Describe an effective procedure for introducing previously isolated monkeys to their peers. Be sure to use the term "therapist" monkey in your answer. (Novak & Harlow, 1975)

    d. How did Fuhrman et al. (1979) adapt the "therapist" technique for work with socially withdrawn children?

2. a. Briefly summarize the approaches of authoritarian, permissive, and authoritative parents in establishing and enforcing family rules.

    b. How do each of these approaches affect children's social development?

    c. What is an important factor in raising well-adjusted children?

LESSON I SELF TEST

1. During the _____ stage the developing infant _____.
    a. zygote; weighs about one ounce
    b. embryo; is most vulnerable to the harmful effects of chemicals
    c. zygote; fetal sex is determined
    d. embryo; has a detectable heartbeat

2. Research using harmless infrared light to study which parts of a stimulus an infant scans indicates that one-month-old infants
    a. gaze at the edges of the stimulus.
    b. shift their gaze between the centre and borders of the stimulus.
    c. scan the interior of a stimulus.

    d. scan the stimulus in a circular pattern.

3. Infant subjects who watched a stationary mobile
    a. kept trying to make it move.
    b. turned their heads to avoid looking at it.
    c. did not learn to control it when given the opportunity.
    d. were more easily frustrated by difficult problems later.

4. During the preoperational period, egocentric children
    a. insist on being the center of attention.
    b. believe that others see the world the way they do.

c. question authority.

d. believe their culture is superior.

5. Case suggests cognitive development relies on

   a. observation and imitation of others.

   b. critical periods for skill acquisition.

   c. brain maturation.

   d. a responsive environment.

6. When children watch television, they

   a. appear mesmerized by the moving light and sound.

   b. rarely look at the screen for more than a minute at a time.

   c. tend to pay more attention to visual stimuli than auditory ones.

   d. rarely engage in another activity at the same time.

7. Harlow's research with infant monkeys reared with surrogates suggests that

   a. these infant monkeys do not derive comfort from nonnutritive sucking.

   b. softness and warmth are inherently more reinforcing than the mother's characteristic body scent.

   c. physical contact with cuddly objects is a biological need.

   d. deprivation by contact with the mother is more serious than deprivation of contact with peers.

8. Infant human subjects whose mothers maintained masklike expressions

   a. resisted being picked up by their mothers at the end of the experiment.

   b. seemed undisturbed.

   c. tried to elicit a response from their mothers, but then turned away.

   d. cried when later retesting was attempted.

9. The most important factor in establishing a secure or insecure attachment between infant and mother is the

   a. infant's personality.

   b. infant's sleep and waking patterns.

   c. mother's personality.

   d. mother's behaviour.

10. Harlow's procedure for reintroducing previously isolated monkeys to their peers suggests that isolated monkeys should first be

   a. allowed to observe other monkeys from an adjacent cage.

   b. placed with a group of adult monkeys before peer monkeys are introduced.

   c. in a large monkey colony to provide them with some anonymity.

   d. with a younger, not-so-threatening monkey.

LESSON II

Read the interim summary on page 399 in your text to re-acquaint yourself with the material in this section.

12-9 Define gender identity, gender roles, and gender stereotypes and describe when and how they develop.

Read pages 396-399 and answer the following questions.

1. In your own words, define

   a. *gender identity.*

b. *gender role.*

c. *gender stereotype.*

2. When do children begin to perceive themselves as being a boy or a girl? (Berk, 1994)

3. a. What did Montemayor (1974) tell some of the boys and girls who played a marble toss game and how did the information affect their play?

b. What do their responses suggest about conformity to gender stereotypes?

4. a. How do parents tend to encourage conformity to gender stereotypes? (Fagot & Hagan, 1991; Dunn et al., 1987; Lytton & Romney, 1991)

b. If parents do not encourage stereotypical activities, how are their children's attitudes affected? (Weisner & Wilson-Mitchell, 1990)

5. Summarize Berk's (2000) conclusions about gender differences based on a review of recent research on gender differences.

6. Cite research to explain why gender, by itself, is not a good predictor of a person's behaviour or attributes. (Feingold, 1993; Deaux, 1985)

7. Summarize evidence that biology may influence the ready acceptance of gender role differences.

a. When the developing brains of laboratory animals are exposed to male sex hormones, what changes occur? (Carlson, 1995)

b. What may account for some gender differences observed in human brains? (Kolb & Stewart, 1995)

c. What did investigations using FMRI techniques demonstrate? (Gron et al., 2000)

d. Compare the verbal ability and spatial ability of girls and boys.

e. Carefully explain why these observed gender differences may have biological roots. (Kimura, 1987)

f. What kind of problems tied to reproduction may also have led to gender differences? (Buss, 19951)

8. Summarize evidence that socialization may influence the acceptance of gender differences.

    a. Review observations that our own gender expectations influence our behaviour toward infants and children.

    b. How did adult subjects characterize the crying of a baby boy? a baby girl? Why? (Condry & Condry, 1976)

    c. How do parents encourage their children to develop appropriate gender roles through play?

    d. After reviewing 172 studies, what did Lytton and Romney (1991) conclude about other significant inconsistencies in the way parents treat their sons and daughters?

    e. Carefully explain how parental expectations and encouragement may interact with a child's natural preferences to reinforce gender role differences. (Snow et al., 1983; Lytton & Romney, 1991)

9. Briefly describe the considerable influence of peers in the development of gender roles by

    a. comparing the degree to which knowledge of a baby's gender influences the behaviour of two-to-six year old children and adults. (Stern & Karraker, 1989)

    b. describing the kind of play that three-year-old children praise and criticize. (Langlois & Downs, 1980)

10. How do many parents indirectly encourage gender-stereotyped play? (Lewis et al., 1975)

Read the interim summary on pages 401-402 of your text to re-acquaint yourself with the material in this section.

12-10 Describe and discuss Piaget's and Kohlberg's theories of moral development.

Read pages 399-401 and answer the following questions.

1. Define the concept of moral behaviour in your own words.

2. Outline the two stages of Piaget's description of moral development.

    a. Stage I, or _____ _____

        1. Duration

        2. How does egocentrism influence a child's behaviour?

        3. What do young children think is the source and force of rules? What motivates children to follow them?

b. Stage II or _____ _____ _____

    1. How does the shift from egocentrism influence an older child's behaviour?

    2. How does increasing maturity influence the child's understanding of the source and force of rules?

3. What technique did Kohlberg use to assess children's moral beliefs? (Be sure to mention the story about Heinz.)

4. Study Table 12.3 in your text and fill in the blanks in Table 1 below.

5. State an objection to Piaget's assertion that young children consider only the magnitude and not the intent behind an event.

6. Explain these criticisms of Kohlberg's conclusions.

    a. the validity of Heinz' story as a measure of moral development (Sobesky, 1983)

    b. the level of moral reasoning in which people sometimes perform (Carpendale, 2000)

    c. the division of moral development into stages (Rest, 1979)

    d. the possibility the theory is gender-biased

        1. State Gilligan's (1982) objections.

        2. What has more recent research suggested? (Donenberg & Hoffman, 1988; Walker et al., 1994)

| Levels and Stages of Kohlberg's Theory of Moral Development ||
Level and Stage	Highlights
_____ Level	
Stage 1:	
Stage 2:	
_____ Level	
Stage 3:	
Stage 4:	
_____ Level	
Stage 5:	
Stage 6:	
Stage 7:	

Table 1

Read the interim summary on page 405 of your text to re-acquaint yourself with the material in this section.

12-11 Describe physical development during puberty and its behavioural effects.

Read pages 402-403 and answer the following questions.

1. a. _____, the period of sexual maturation, begins when the _____ stimulates the _____ _____ to secrete hormones that in turn stimulate the _____ to produce sex hormones.

    b. Explain the difference between primary and secondary sex characteristics.

    c. The most important _____ or female sex hormone is _____, which is secreted by a young woman's ovaries at puberty.

2. Trace the development of adult secondary sex characteristics.

	Boys	Girls
Approximate age of onset		
First visible change		
Subsequent physical changes		

3. What is the most important reason for the decline in the average age at the onset of puberty?

4. What are some of the concerns of adolescent boys and girls about their changing bodies?

5. What may account for adolescent self-consciousness?

6. What are some of the social consequences of early and late maturity in boys? (Jones and Bayley, 1950; Peterson, 1985; Brooks-Gunn, 1988) in girls? (Brooks-Gunn, 1989)

12-12 Describe social development during adolescence.

Read pages 403-405 and answer the following questions.

1. Study Erickson's eight stages of psychosocial development presented in Table 12.4 in your text. Be sure to notice how the time spent in a particular stage changes with age and the nature of the crises that cause changes.

2. Briefly explain Erickson's concept of the identity crisis. How do adolescents resolve this crisis successfully and unsuccessfully?

3. a. Name and define the two components of identity development proposed by Marcia (1980, 1994, 1998).

   1.   2.

   b. List and explain Marcia's four identity statuses summarized in Figure 12.8 in your text.

   1.

   2.

   3.

   4.

   c. In what two ways has Marcia's research contributed to a better understanding of adolescence?

4. What does Gilligan (1982) assert about the social nature of searching for a personal identity?

5. Briefly summarize how self-concept changes throughout childhood and adolescence. (Berk, 1993; Damon and Hart, 1992)

6. a. What is the most important function of a girl's childhood friendships?

   b. How does the function of girls' friendships change around age 14? Why?

   c. What are some of the personal concerns of adolescent boys and how do they affect friendship?

7. a. If adolescents and their parents regard important issues in the same way (Youniss and Smollar, 1985), what then tends to provoke conflicts?

   b. When do these conflicts generally begin? (Paikoff and Brooks-Gunn, 1991)

Read the interim summary on page 411 of your text to re-acquaint yourself with the material in this section.

12-13 Describe the physical changes that occur late in adult life and their consequences.

Read page 406 and answer the following questions.

1. List several reasons why it is more difficult to outline changes in adult development.

2. a. When do our physical abilities peak and what steps can we take to remain physically fit?

   b. Nevertheless, what kinds of physical abilities begin to decline as adults age?

3. a. By age 70, how much has muscular strength declined in both men and women? (Young et al., 1984) Why?

   b. How does aging affect endurance and how can these changes be offset? (Spirduso and MacRae, 1990)

4. Summarize some of the functional changes that accompany old age.

   a. Explain why older people show very little functional change in their sensory abilities.

   b. How are functional changes in highly developed skills affected by old age? Cite research to support your answer. (Salthouse, 1984, 1988)

12-14 Discuss the nature of cognitive changes in late adulthood and the variables that affect them.

Read pages 406-409 and answer the following questions.

1. a. Name the most common form of dementia. Approximately what percent of the population is affected?

   b. Discuss the three subgroups of Alzheimers patients (Fisher et al., 1999)

   c. Describe some of the early and later symptoms and eventual outcome. (Terry and Davies, 1980; Khachaturian and Blass, 1992)

   d. What is the cause of at least one kind of Alzheimer's disease? (Gottfries, 1985; Selkoe, 1989)

e. Compare the brains of normal people and people with Alzheimer's disease shown in Figure 12.9 in your text and describe the physical changes in the brain resulting from the disease.

2. Explain how depression can contribute to mental deterioration in some older people.

3. Summarize research to identify how aging affects intellectual abilities.

   a. What do the results of the Seattle Longitudinal Study indicate is the pattern of change in people's scores on five tests of intellectual abilities over several decades? (Schaie, 1990)

   b. Describe the decline more precisely by studying the graph shown in Figure 12.10 in your text, and describe how test scores of most people on specific ability tests changed over a seven-year period.

   c. Now study Figure 12.11 in your text and contrast changes in the ability of adult subjects to recognize and recall words. (Schaie, 1980)

   d. What kind of cues found in recognition tasks may benefit older people? (Schaie and Willis, 1991)

   e. How accurately did younger and older subjects estimate distances from watching slides shown in logical order? shown in scrambled order? (Kirasic and Bernicki, 1990)

   f. What may account for the performance of older subjects in the scrambled order presentation?

   g. Explain the difference between a cross-sectional study and a longitudinal study.

   h. Compare the results of research to determine performance on a test of verbal abilities as a function of age using both approaches. (Study Figure 12.12 in your text. Schaie and Struther, 1968)

   i. What accounts for these differences and which approach gives a more accurate assessment of cognitive abilities over time?

4. a. Define and explain the difference between crystallized intelligence and fluid intelligence in your own words.

   b. Which of these appears to decline with age? (Baltes and Schaie, 1974; Horn, 1982)

   c. What kind of intellectual pursuits are best suited to people who excel in crystallized intelligence? fluid intelligence?

5. a. How does age affect the response speed of older people? What kind of situation impairs their responses?

   b. If time restraints are removed, how do response rates change? (Arenberg, 1973; Botwinick and Storandt, 1974)

   c. What are two reasons that may explain an age-related decline in speed?

   1.   2.

6. How do some cultures try to benefit from the natural caution of older people?

7. a. Describe the different conditions under which two groups of older subjects were paid. (Leech and Witte, 1971)

   b. Which payment condition resulted in an increase in speed? Why?

12-15 Describe the nature of social development in adulthood.

Read pages 409-411 and answer the following questions.

1. a. List the three sources of data Levinson and his colleagues (Levinson et al., 1978) based their hypothesized pattern of adult development.

   b. Briefly describe the common pattern they believe most men experience.

   c. When do the most important crises occur? Why?

   d. During the mid-life crisis, how do men who have not yet succeeded react? men who have succeeded?

   e. What realization affects all men at this time?

2. a. Using the "Midlife Crisis Scale," what did Costa and McCrae (1980) discover about the pattern of the lives of 548 men?

   b. And what was the conclusion of a study of 60 women? (Reinke et al., 1985)

   c. What can we conclude about the notion of a mid-life crisis?

3. According to many developmental psychologists, what are the two most important aspects of life?

4. a. Trace the effects of having children on marital happiness. (Daniels and Weingarten, 1982; Cavanaugh, 1990)

   b. How does the life of a couple change once the youngest child has left home? (Deutscher, 1968; Neugarten, 1974)

5. Briefly summarize some of the advantages and disadvantages of dual-earner marriages for the partners and children. (Crosby, 1991; Schaie and Willis, 1992)

6. How do old people feel when they contemplate their own death? Why? (Kalish, 1976)

7. a. List and describe the five stages of dying proposed by Kubler-Ross (1969, 1981)

   b. On what grounds has her theory been criticized?

   c. How has her theory, nevertheless, contributed to the study of dying and death?

LESSON II SELF TEST

1. If parents encourage or reward "gender appropriate" behaviour, they
   a. contribute to the development of gender-stereotypes.
   b. recognize and accept biological gender differences.
   c. will increase their children's emotional stability.
   d. encourage submissive behaviour.

2. Knowing a baby's gender influences the behaviour of
   a. adults more than children.
   b. children more than adults.
   c. boys more than girls.
   d. women more than men.

3. With respect to moral development, an egocentric child
   a. believes that his or her cultural norms are superior.
   b. can imagine other people's feelings.
   c. can evaluate whether punishment is appropriate for the offense.
   d. evaluates events in terms of personal consequences.

4. Gilligan asserted that Kohlberg's conclusions were gender-biased because he suggested that
   a. men and women base their moral judgments on different values.
   b. his female subjects were not representative of the population as a whole.

c. justice is a stronger consideration for men than women when making moral judgments.

d. reproductive roles influence moral judgments.

5. Early-maturing boys are more likely _____ than late-maturing boys.

a. to engage in negative attention-getting behaviour

b. to score better on tests of intellectual ability

c. to be perceived as leaders by their peers

d. to accept gender stereotypes

6. The differences that adolescents have with their parents

a. confirm the assumption of a generation gap.

b. are more frequent between mothers and their offspring.

c. confirm that most adolescents are unhappy most of the time.

d. are usually over relatively minor events.

7. According to Erickson, an adolescent's psychosocial development

a. consists of two components: crisis and commitment.

b. is shaped by the way he or she resolves the crises encountered in social relations with others.

c. is preparation for the decision to marry, or remain single.

d. culminates in the formation of new self-perceptions to replace older ones formed in childhood.

8. Advancing age affects

a. both the physical and functional capabilities of the sensory systems.

b. muscular strength more than endurance.

c. physical appearance more than physical ability.

d. highly developed skills that cannot be compensated for by alternate strategies.

9. _____ people excel in _____ which is based on _____.

a. Older; fluid intelligence; knowledge and experience

b. Older; fluid intelligence; the capacity for abstract reasoning

c. Older; crystallized intelligence; knowledge and experience

d. Young; crystallized intelligence; the capacity for abstract reasoning

10. Research on the mid-life crisis using the Midlife Crisis Scale found

a. that only slightly more than half the population undergoes a mid-life crisis.

b. that an increasing number of women are reporting mid-life crises.

c. that men living alone were more likely to undergo a mid-life crisis.

d. no evidence for a mid-life crisis.

Answers for Self Tests

Lesson I

1. b	Obj. 12-1	2. a	Obj. 12-2	3. c	Obj. 12-3	4. b	Obj. 12-3	5. c	Obj. 12-4
6. b	Obj. 12-5	7. c	Obj. 12-6	8. c	Obj. 12-6	9. d	Obj. 12-7	10. d	Obj. 12-8

Lesson II

1. a	Obj. 12-9	2. b	Obj. 12-9	3. d	Obj. 12-10	4. a	Obj. 12-10	5. c	Obj. 12-11
6. d	Obj. 12-12	7. b	Obj. 12-12	8. b	Obj. 12-13	9. c	Obj. 12-14	10. d	Obj. 12-15

CHAPTER 13

Motivation and Emotion

LESSON I

Read the interim summary on pages 421-422 of your text to re-acquaint yourself with the material in this section.

13-1 Explain the terms motivation and drive, describe the physiology of reinforcement, and describe and evaluate the drive reduction hypothesis and the optimum-level hypothesis.

Read pages 416-419 and answer the following questions.

1. a. Define *motivation* in your own words.

   b. Motivation can affect the _____, the _____, and the _____ of an organism's behaviour.

   c. Explain the two types of phenomena characteristic of motivation and give an original example of each.

   d. Motivation cannot be separated from _____ and _____ Explain this statement.

2. a. Define *homeostasis* in your own words and explain its importance.

   b. Explain how deficits or imbalances in homeostasis affect

      1. regulatory behaviours.

      2. motivation.

3. List and explain the functions of the four essential features of a regulatory system.

   1.   3.

   2.   4.

4. Study the example of a regulatory system in Figure 13.1 in your text. Using the example of a room thermostat, explain the process of negative feedback, an essential characteristic of all regulatory systems.

5. a. Define *drive* in your own words and give an example of a biological need and a nonbiological drive.

   b. Study Figure 13.2 in your text and explain the drive reduction hypothesis of motivation and reinforcement.

   c. Outline the primary difficulties with this hypothesis.

6. a. Explain why electrical brain stimulation has the same effect on the organism as natural reinforcers do.

   b. Study Figure 13.3 in your text and now explain the normal function of the reinforcement system and how electrical stimulation changes it.

   c. What is the common effect of all reinforcing stimuli? (See Figure 13.4 in your text)

7. a. The _____-_____ hypothesis is an attempt to find a common explanation for both _____ and _____ reinforcement.

   b. Summarize the optimum-level hypothesis of reinforcement and punishment.

   c. Name and describe the two kinds of exploration hypothesized by Berlyne.

   d. Discuss the optimum–level hypothesis proposed by Hebb (1955).

   e. What problem applies to the optimum-level hypothesis as well as the drive-reduction hypothesis?

13–2 Discuss how intermittent reinforcement, unnecessary reinforcement, and learned helplessness affect perseverance.

Read pages 420-421 and answer the following questions.

1. a. Define *perseverance* in your own words.

   b. How quickly does extinction occur if a behaviour has previously been reinforced regularly? reinforced intermittently?

   c. In other words, intermittent reinforcement leads to _____.

2. Define intrinsic and extrinsic rewards and give an example of each.

3. a. What is the general idea behind the overjustification hypothesis? (Deci & Ryan, 1987; Lepper et al., 1973; Vallerand, 1997)

   b. According to this theory, what happens after the shift from intrinsic to extrinsic motivation has taken place and extrinsic rewards are taken away? What does this occur?

4. Discuss research conducted by Lepper et al. (1973) that provides support for the overjustification hypothesis.

   a. What was carefully documented prior to the experimental manipulation?

   b. Describe the three conditions used in this experiment.

   c. What did the researchers observe when they returned again?

   d. What did these findings reveal?

5. What characteristics of extrinsic rewards can lean to an increase in intrinsic motivation?

6. What conclusions can be made concerning extrinsic rewards? When are they most useful? When do educators and parents need to be careful?

7. Define *learned helplessness* in your own words and explain how it differs from other forms of learning.

8. Describe how Overmeier and Seligman (1967) demonstrated learned helplessness in dogs.

9. According to Seligman (1975), how do experiences that lead to learned helplessness affect

   a. mood and motivation?

   b. personality?

10.Match the term with the correct definition.

_____ rewards that originate outside oneself

_____ continued performance in the absence of regular reinforcement

_____ the optimum value of a system variable

_____ an increase in the frequency of a response that is followed by an appetitive stimulus

_____ rewards that originate inside oneself

_____ a process of detection and correction to maintain physiological systems at their optimum value

_____ the effect of a stimulus that increases the probability of a behaviour

_____ a collective term for the factors that influence the nature, strength, and persistence of a behaviour

_____ an increase in the frequency of a response that is followed by the removal of an aversive stimulus

Choices:

a. extrinsic rewards

b. drive

c. intrinsic rewards

d. negative reinforcement

e. set point

f. motivation

g. positive reinforcement

h. perseverance

i. homeostasis

Read the interim summary on pages 427-428 of your text to re-acquaint yourself with the material in this section.

13-3 Discuss the physiological mechanisms that begin a meal and cultural and social influences on eating

Read pages 422-424 and answer the following questions.

1. Briefly explain the empty stomach theory of hunger (Cannon and Washburn, 1912) and cite research that refutes this theory (Inglefinger, 1944).

2. a. What is a more likely cause of hunger?

   b. List the two primary fuels for the body and their composition.

c. Summarize information on the body's nutrient reservoirs in the table below

	Short-Term Reservoir	Long-Term Reservoir
Location		
Form of stored fuel		
Fuel converted from		

d. How do the fat cells of an obese person differ from those of a person with normal weight?

3. Study Figure 13.5 in your text and explain how the body is nourished when there is

a. food in the digestive system.

b. no food in the digestive system.

4. Explain the glucostatic hypothesis proposed by Mayer (1955a). Be sure to use the term *glucostats* in your answer.

5. a. What has subsequent research suggested about the number of nutrient detectors? (Langhans, 1996) Where are these nutrient detectors located?

b. Where do these detectors send their information?

c. Researchers have concluded that this type of hunger is limited to what kind of situation?

6. In general, cultural and social factors influence _____ and _____ we eat. Our immediate environment also affects our _____ and we eat more in the presence of _____ who are _____.

13-4 Discuss the physiological mechanisms that end a meal and the possible causes of obesity and anorexia nervosa.

Read pages 424-427 and answer the following questions.

1. Explain why a meal does not stop when the body's supply of nutrients is replenished.

2. a. The primary cause of satiety seems to be a _____ _____.

   b. Describe how Davis and Campbell (1973) demonstrated that the stomach contains receptors that respond to food quantity to support your last answer.

   c. Cite research demonstrating the stomach also contains receptors that respond to food quality.

      1. Explain the rationale and procedure used by Deutsch et al. (1978).

      2. Which group of rats ate less?

      3. What do the results confirm about the location of detectors for food content?

3. a. Detectors in the stomach contribute only to the _____-_____ control of eating.

   b. List several long-term factors that contribute to the control of eating.

4. a. Describe the ob mouse—the subject of years of laboratory research on the control of food intake.

   b. Carefully explain why these mice become obese. (Campfield et al., 1995; Halaas et al., 1995; Pelleymounter et al., 1995)

   c. What physiological changes occur in ob mice that are given daily injections of leptin? (See Figure 13.6 in your text.)

   d. State the findings of research on leptin and human obesity conducted by Maffei et al. (1995)

5. a. What percentage of Canadians between the ages of 20 and 64 are obese? (Statistics Canada, 1995)

   b. List the physical problems associated with obesity. How much money per year is spent treating such health problems/

6. a. After a review of the literature, what did Rodin and her colleagues conclude about psychological variables as a cause of obesity? (Rodin et al., 1989)

   b. How do psychological variables appear to affect the obese instead?

7. How do mealtime experiences early in life influence later eating habits?

8. Summarize research to explain obesity beginning with the relationship between metabolism and obesity. What did Rose and Williams (1961) conclude about the effects of metabolic rate after studying paired subjects?

9. a. Why do obese people overeat and fail to loose weight if their fat cells secrete high levels of leptin? (Tartaglia et al., 1995)

   b. What are some reasons why we are not using leptin to treat obesity?

10. a. What is the basic proposition of models speculating evolutionary forces in obesity? (Assanand et al., 1998).

    b. Outline one version of this approach that emphasizes variability in the environments of our ancestors. (James & Tryhurn, 1981)

    c. Discuss the second version of the evolutionary approach that emphasizes a human trait to avoid energy deficits. (Pinel et al., 2000)

11. a. What is the chief characteristic of anorexia nervosa?

    b. What percentage of individuals with this disorder are males? females? How is this pattern changing? (Stoutjesdyk & Jevne, 1993)

    c. Why is the evidence about hereditary factors inconsistent? (Fairburn et al., 1999)

    d. Why do most psychologists believe that it may be a result of social influences?

    e. Discuss one theory's position on what happens if an individual responds to these social pressures. (Epling & Pierce, 1991; Pierce & Epling, 1997)

    f. List some of the serious health consequences of this disorder.
       1. death rate

       2. bone density

       3. effects on menstruation

       4. effects on the brain (Artmann et al., 1985; Lankenau et al., 1985)

12. a. What is the chief characteristic of bulimia?

    b. How do cycles of binging and purging affect
       1. mood? (Mawson, 1974; Halmi, 1978)

       2. the nutrient intake and body weight of sufferers? (Weltzin et al., 1991)

11. What is the relation between the endocrine system and anorexia?. (Wade and Gray, 1979; Halmi, 1978)

Read the interim summary on page 430 of your text to re-acquaint yourself with the material in this section.

13-5 Describe the motivational effects of sex hormones.

Read pages 428-429 and answer the following questions.

1. Explain the statement "Sex hormones do not cause behaviour."

2. The prenatal effect of sex hormones are called _____ effects and these effects are _____. The effects of sex hormones on an already developed system that occur during adulthood are called _____ effects.

3. a. Explain how Davidson et al. (1979) demonstrated the activational effects of testosterone on male sexual behaviour.

4. What physiological factor had the strongest influence on the sexual activity of married couples? (Persky et al., 1978)

5. a. What is the primary difference between the menstrual cycle of primates and the estrous cycle of other female mammals?

   b. At what time during the estrous cycle do females of nonprimate species permit copulation? Why?

   c. How does sexual receptivity of a female rate change if her ovaries are removed? if she is later given replacement hormones?

6. a. How are women and other female primates unique among mammals?

   b. In higher primates the ability to mate is not controlled by _____ and _____.

   c. What have most studies reported concerning the effect of estradiol and progesterone on a woman's sexual interest? (Kelly & Byrne, 1992; Meyers et al., 1990)

   d. What is one explanation for this phenomenon?

13–6 Discuss the factors that may influence sexual orientation.

Read pages 429-430 and answer the following questions.

1. How does human homosexuality appear to differ from the homosexuality of members of other species?

2. How does recent research refute traditional theories that homosexuality is

    a. a disorder?

    b. an emotional disturbance caused by faulty child rearing?

3. Summarize the findings of a survey of a large number of male and female homosexuals reported by Bell, Weinberg, and Hammersmith (1981).

    a. What is the single most important predictor of adult homosexuality?

    b. What is the relationship between gender nonconformity and later homosexuality?

    c. What do all of these finding suggest about the importance of biological factors in the development of homosexuality?

4. Now summarize some research on possible hormonal factors in the development of homosexuality.

    a. Cite research to refute the suggestion that male homosexuals have insufficient blood levels of testosterone. (Garnets & Kimmel, 1991)

    b. How does stress affect a pregnant female rat and subsequently her male offspring? (Ward, 1972; Anderson et al., 1980)

    c. What anatomical differences were observed in the brains of deceased heterosexual and homosexual males? (Swaab and Hofman, 1990; LeVay, 1991; Allen and Gorski, 1992)

    d. What limited conclusion can we draw from these differences?

5. How may exposure to high levels of androgens during development affect the sexual orientation of females? (Meyer-Bahlberg et al., 1995; Money et al., 1984)

6. a. Explain the rationale for studying the incidence of homosexuality in twins.

   b. Compare the concordance rate for homosexuality for pairs of male and female fraternal and identical twins. (Bailey and Pillard, 1991; Bailey et al., 1993)

7. a. In conclusion, what two biological factors likely affect a person's sexual orientation?

   b. These findings contradict suggestions that sexual orientation is what kind of an issue?

LESSON I SELF TEST

1. Drives
   a. have behavioural effects opposite to those of reinforcement.
   b. are only produced by homeostatic imbalances.
   c. cannot be directly measured.
   d. are involved in reinforcement, but not in punishment.

2. The drive-reduction and optimum-level hypotheses share the common problem that researchers do not
   a. agree whether reinforcement is caused by events that decreases or increases drive.
   b. agree on how many drives there are.
   c. know how to measure an organism's drive or arousal.
   d. agree that all drives are unpleasant, aversive conditions.

3. What is the best way to encourage a person to persevere at a long, difficult task?
   a. Reinforce work on all components of the task.
   b. Never reinforce work on any of the components of the task.
   c. Intermittently reinforce work on components of the task.
   d. Apply an aversive stimulus if the person stops working.

4. A likely cause of hunger is
   a. a rise in metabolic rate.
   b. an empty stomach.
   c. contraction of the muscles of the stomach.
   d. depletion of the body's store of nutrients.

5. The two primary nutrients are _____ and _____. The brain lives primarily on _____ and the rest of the body lives on _____.
   a. glucose; fatty acids; glucose; glucose or fatty acids
   b. unsaturated fats; complex carbohydrates; complex carbohydrates; unsaturated fats
   c. glycerol; glycogen: glycerol; glycogen
   d. fatty acids; complex carbohydrates; complex carbohydrates; glucose or fatty acids

6. A likely cause of satiety is
   a. an increase in metabolic rate.
   b. a stomach full of food.
   c. the cessation of contraction of the muscles of the stomach.
   d. replenished stores of nutrients.

7. People with an inefficient metabolism
   a. have difficulty maintaining a normal body weight.
   b. have difficulty matching food intake to physical activity.
   c. must eat less food in order to keep from gaining weight.
   d. can eat large meals without gaining weight.

8. The organizational effects of sex hormones
   a. affect prenatal development.
   b. occur at the time of puberty.
   c. decrease with age in women, but not men.
   d. increase with sexual experience.

9. During the portion of the estrous cycle when the levels of estradiol and progesterone are high
   a. sexual receptivity peaks.
   b. the lining of the uterus builds up and then sloughs off.
   c. a woman ovulates.
   d. pregnancy cannot occur.

10. The most important single predictor of adult homosexuality is
    a. insufficient blood levels of testosterone.
    b. little or no adolescent heterosexual activity.
    c. faulty child-rearing practices.
    d. a self-report of homosexual feelings.

LESSON II

Read the interim summary on page 433 of your text to re-acquaint yourself with the material in this section.

13-7 Discuss the biological significance and physiological basis of aggressive behaviour and the environmental factors that affect it.

Read pages 430-433 and answer the following questions.

1. What do ethologists study?

2. Define these terms in your own words.

   a. *intraspecific aggression*

   b. *threat gesture*

   c. *appeasement gestures*

3. a. Discuss two ways that intraspecific aggression may promote the survival of a species of animals.

   b. Explain how ritualized threat gestures and appeasement gestures reduce overt aggression.

   c. For which species are these gestures especially important? (Lorenz, 1966; Eibl-Eibesfeld, 1980)

4. a. Study Figure 13.7 in your text and describe how adult aggression is affected if a male mouse, castrated immediately after birth, receives an injection of

    1. a placebo and then an injection of testosterone when fully grown?

    2. testosterone following castration and again when fully grown?

   b. Carefully explain why the mice respond differently by referring to the organizational and activational effects of testosterone.

5. Summarize research on the role of hormones in human aggression.

   a. Offer two observations that suggest testosterone may also influence human aggressive behaviour.

   b. Some cases of human aggression such as sexual assault are treated with drug therapy. Explain

    1. the treatment rationale.

    2. its efficacy. (Bain, 1987)

6. a. Compare the testosterone levels of male and female prison inmates who engaged in violent behaviour. (Dabbs et al., 1987, 1995; Dabbs et al., 1988, 1997)

   b. Carefully explain why we cannot conclude that high testosterone levels caused increased aggressive behaviour. (Jeffcoate et al., 1986)

7. a. Compare the aggressiveness of male weight lifters who were taking anabolic steroids with those who were not. (Yates et al., 1992)

   b. Why does it remain uncertain whether anabolic steroids increase aggressiveness?

8. a. If children are physically punished frequently by their caregivers, what might these children conclude about ways to solve problems?

   b. How do victims of extreme child abuse often treat their own children? However, what is true of most adults who were physically abused as children?

9. a. On average, how many violent acts have North American children witnessed on television before the age of 18 years? Half of these acts have been viewed before what age? (Plagens et al., 1991)

b. What conclusions can be made from the investigations on media violence? (Wood et al., 1991)

c. Explain what this conclusion does not does not mean.

d. What approach to dealing with television violence seems prudent?

Read the interim summary on pages 437-438 of your text to re-acquaint yourself with the material in this section.

13-8 Discuss the acquisition and control of conditioned emotional responses and the neural control of emotional behaviour.

Read pages 433-436 and answer the following questions.

1. a. Define *emotion* in your own words.

b. What is the reason for the existence of emotions?

2. Name and describe the three components of an emotional response.

3. a. Explain how a conditioned emotional response develops.

b. What is the name for the initial defensive reflex? the responses controlled by the autonomic nervous system?

4. Describe the conditioned emotional response involving the electric mixer. Make sure you identify the specific response, and the nonspecific emotional responses.

5. a. Refer to Figure 4.32 and review the location of the amygdala. What role does it play in the expression of conditioned emotional responses? (Kapp et al., 1982; LeDoux, 1995)

b. What is the effect on conditioned emotional responses if the amygdala is

    1. destroyed? (Coover et al., 1992; Davis, 1992b; LeDoux, 1992)

    2. stimulated? (Davis, 1992b)

    3. long term stimulation?

c. What do these observations suggest about the causes of stress?

6. Refer to Figure 13.8 and review the location of orbitofrontal cortex. List several areas from which it receives information and to which it sends information.

7. Summarize early case histories that suggested the role of the orbitofrontal cortex in emotional behaviour.

a. What part of Phineas Gage's brain was largely destroyed as a result of his accident and how did his injury affect his behaviour? (See Figure 13.9 in your text.)

b. Describe the performance of Becky the chimpanzee on a behavioural task before and after surgery to remove the frontal lobes. (Jacobsen et al., 1935)

c. How did the medically necessary removal of the frontal lobes of a human appear to affect the patient? (Brickner, 1936)

d. What human application did these last two cases suggest to Egas Moniz?

e. Following prefrontal lobotomy, what emotional changes were observed in patients?

f. What were some of the unexpected side effects of this surgery?

g. Why was this procedure eventually abandoned? (Jasper, 1995; Pressman, 1998; Valenstein, 1986)

8. a. How well did a patient who had had surgery for the removal of a brain tumor of the orbitofrontal cortex asses hypothetical situations? (Eslinger and Damasio, 1985)

b. How well did this same patient conduct his personal affairs following surgery?

c. What does this clinical evidence suggest about the role of the orbitofrontal cortex in making judgments and conclusions?

13-9 Discuss the use of polygraph tests in criminal investigations.

Read pages 436-437 and answer the following questions.

1. What kind of physiological reactions are measured by a polygraph during the questioning of subjects under investigation? Why?

2. a. Polygraphers use two general methods of questioning: the control question test and the guilty knowledge test. What does the polygrapher hope to accomplish using the control question test?

   b. Describe some of the preliminary questions.

   c. If this method is to succeed, how must the subject react? What belief will strengthen this reaction?

   d. How do innocent people also react during polygraph testing? (Lykken, 1988, 1998)

   e. What did Lykken (1988, 1998) conclude about the validity of polygraph testing based on a literature review? Be sure to refer to false positives in your answer.

3. a. What kind of information are subjects questioned about when the guilty knowledge method is used?

   b. If questioned about a hat found at the scene of a robbery, what are the chances a subject who knows nothing about the hat will show a strong reaction on any one of three sets of questions? on all three sets? (Lykken 1988)

   c. What kinds of questions are asked in the guilty knowledge test (Lykken, 1981)

   d. To avoid the possibility the examiner will accidentally or deliberately affect the results, what steps should be taken?

   e. Explain why the guilty knowledge test method cannot be used in every criminal investigation.

   f. How accurate is the guilty knowledge test in identifying guilty suspects? What is the misidentification rate? (Bradley, et al., 1996)

Read the interim summary on page 442 of your text to re-acquaint yourself with the material in this section.

13–10 Describe research, including cross-cultural studies, on human expression and recognition of emotion.

Read pages 438-442 and answer the following questions.

1. a. List the three situations in which Kraut and Johnston (1979) observed the emotional reactions of their subjects.

    1.

    2.

    3.

  b. When did subjects show the greatest reactions?

2. Give some original examples to illustrate that human emotions can be elicited by stimuli that

  a. you remember or imagine.

  b. involve your cognitive processes.

3. In what way is human emotional expression similar to that of other animals? different from other animals?

4. Briefly explain why judgments about the significance of stimuli determine a person's emotional response.

5. a. State Darwin's hypothesis concerning the origin of human facial expression of emotion.

  b. Briefly explain why he believed facial expressions, especially of people from isolated cultures, supported his hypothesis.

6. Describe modern research by Ekman and Friesen (Ekman, 1980) that supported Darwin's hypothesis.

  a. Who were the subjects?

  b. Describe the testing procedure, and explain why the researchers decided to tell little stories.

  c. How accurately did members of this isolated new Guinea tribe recognize the facial expressions of Westerners described in the stories and shown in Figure 13.10 in your text?

d. And how accurately did university students identify the expressions of the Fore people shown in Figure 13.11 in your text?

7. a. Explain why young blind and sighted children, but not blind and sighted adults, are the most appropriate subjects for studies of innate facial expressions.

   b. As blind children grow older how do their facial expressions change and what does this change suggest? (Woodworth and Schlosberg, 1954; Izard, 1971)

   c. Taken together, what do these studies suggest about the basis of human emotional expression?

8. What is the explanation for the finding that people can notice more quickly an angry face in a happy crowd than a happy face in an angry crowd? (Hansen & Hansen, 1988)

9. Explain these three ways we can alter our emotional display.

   a. masking

   b. modulation

   c. simulation

10. Explain cultural display rules in your own words. According to Ekman and Friesen (1975), how do display rules affect emotional expression?

11. a. Compare the facial expressions of Japanese and American students filmed while they watched a film about a gruesome rite alone and in the company of others.

   b. Why were the results consistent with the researchers' expectations? (Ekman et al., 1972; Friesen, 1972)

12. a. Explain leakage and how Ekman and Friesen (1974) studied this phenomenon among nursing students.

   b. State the findings and what they suggest about attempts to mask displays of emotion.

13. a. How successful are people in detecting deceit from facial expressions? (DePaulo, 1994; Ekman & O'Sullivan, 1991)

   b. What is the exception to this rule? (Eckman et al., 1999)

Read the interim summary on page 445 to re-acquaint yourself with the material in this section.

13-11 Describe and evaluate the James-Lange theory of emotion and research on the role of cognition and automatic responses on feelings of emotions.

Read pages 442-445 and answer the following questions.

1. State the James-Lange theory of emotion in your own words.

2. Study Figure 13.12 in your text and fill in the blank boxes in Figure 1 on the next page.

3. a. What kind of injury was common to all the subjects Hohman questioned? (Hohman, 1966)

   b. Why did he ask them about the intensity of their emotional feelings?

   c. Describe the results and explain how they support the James-Lange theory. (See Figure 13.13 in your text.)

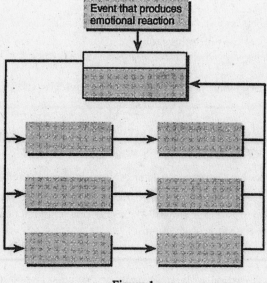

Figure 1

4. Outline a current controversy in the field of emotion.

5. What is one of the difficulties of evaluating this controversy noted by Lazarus?

6. Describe Schachter's hypothesis of emotion. (Schachter, 1964)

7. a. What were subjects told was the purpose of the experiment? (Schachter and Singer, 1962).

   b. Some subjects were given saline injections, but others received another drug. What was the drug and what are its physiological effects?

   c. Describe the two testing situations.

   d. What additional information was given to some subjects?

   e. How did the researchers predict this additional information would affect subjects' reactions?

   f. Compare the emotional states of subjects who received injections of adrenaline or a placebo and were told to expect side effects with subjects who received the same kinds of injections and were not told about side effects?

   g. Therefore, what was the only factor that influenced the intensity of emotional feelings?

   h. What do these results suggest about the way we respond to our physiological states?

8. a. All subjects in a study by Nisbett and Schachter (1966) were given a placebo pill. What were some of the subjects told about the effects of the pill? others told?

   b. Compare the tolerance to pain of subjects who did and did not perceive their reactions as drug-induced.

   c. Explain what these results suggest about the effect of cognition on judgments about emotional states.

   d. What did the subjects say when the experimenters later explained the results to them? (Nisbett and Wilson, 1977)

9. What did Schachter contribute to the study of emotion?

10. What should we conclude about the basis of our own emotions?

LESSON II SELF TEST

1. Threat gestures
   a. are a response made by the subordinate animal.
   b. help reduce overt aggression.
   c. are a response to appeasement gestures.
   d. are invariably followed by an attack.

2. Field studies of long-term viewing of violence on television suggest that
   a. it would be prudent to have children who watch television violence engage in vigorous physical activity to discharge their feelings.
   b. the more closely violent television situations resemble the child's actual environment the greater their effect will be.
   c. young children are more vulnerable than older children to the effects of television violence.
   d. long-term viewing appears to increase aggressive behaviour, but the evidence is not conclusive.

3. _____is produced by a neutral stimulus that has been paired with an emotional stimulus.
   a. A conditioned emotional response.
   b. A coping response.
   c. An offensive emotional response.
   d. A defensive emotional response.

4. People such as Phineas Gage, who have suffered damage to the orbitofrontal cortex,
   a. suffer from compulsive behaviours.
   b. are especially timid in social situations.
   c. respond appropriately to hypothetical social situations, but not when these situations apply to them.
   d. show a tendency to express emotional feelings with gestures and facial expressions rather than with words.

5. In most countries, the results of polygraph examinations are not admissible in court because
   a. not every criminal investigation can use this technique.
   b. the sensitivity of polygraph equipment is not uniform.

   c. these tests will often identify innocent people as being guilty.
   d. any interruption in questioning may alter the validity of the results.

6. Emotions
   a. do not occur spontaneously.
   b. are elicited by neutral stimuli.
   c. always occur immediately after the stimuli that elicit them.
   d. are independent of cognitive processes.

7. Darwin's assertion that emotional expressions are innate unlearned patterns of movement, especially of facial muscles, is believed to be correct because
   a. all languages have words to express emotion.
   b. facial expressions of emotion are different in isolated cultures.
   c. although they can be affected by cultural display rules, facial expressions are universal.
   d. blind children must be taught to smile.

8. The James-Lange theory states that
   a. emotion-producing situations elicit an appropriate set of physiological and behavioural responses.
   b. emotions are determined jointly by perception of physiological response and cognitive assessment of a situation.
   c. outward manifestations of emotion are accurate reflections of inner physiological responses.
   d. emotions are behaviours.

9. Schachter hypothesized that
   a. emotion-producing situations elicit an appropriate set of physiological responses.
   b. emotions are determined jointly by perception of physiological responses and cognitive assessment of a situation.
   c. emotions are determined jointly by cognitive assessment of a situation and internal feedback about other people's expressions.
   d. emotions are self-reports based on self-analysis of internal physiological responses.

10. After Nisbett and Schachter (1966) explained the design and rationale of the placebo/electric shock experiment to the subjects, the subjects
    a. recognized that they had gone through the process the researchers had explained.
    b. insisted they had not experienced the process the researchers had explained.
    c. were skeptical that any subjects would go through the process the researchers had explained.
    d. urged the researchers to repeat the study with other subjects because they had not experienced the process the researchers had explained.

Answers to Self Tests

Lesson I

1. c	Obj. 13-1	2. c	Obj. 13-1	3. c	Obj. 13-2	4. d	Obj. 13-3	5. a	Obj. 13-3
6. b	Obj. 13-4	7. d	Obj. 13-4	8. a	Obj. 13-5	9. a	Obj. 13-5	10. d	Obj. 13-6

Lesson II

1. b	Obj. 13-7	2. d	Obj. 13-7	3. a	Obj. 13-8	4. c	Obj. 13-8	5. c	Obj. 13-9
6. a	Obj. 13-10	7. c	Obj. 13-10	8. a	Obj. 13-11	9. b	Obj. 13-11	10. b	Obj. 13-11

Personality

LESSON I

Read the interim summary on pages 455-456 of your text to re-acquaint yourself with the material in this section.

14–1 Distinguish between personality types and traits, and summarize research to identify personality traits by Allport, Cattell, Eysenck, and the five-factor model.

Read pages 450-455 and answer the following questions.

1. Define *personality* in your own words.

2. a. What do psychologists who study personality hope to discover?

   b. What are two developments resulting from research on personality?

   c. What two kinds of efforts are required to study human personality? (Buss, 1995)

3. a. The _____ _____ was the earliest explanation of individual _____.

   b. See Figure 14.1 in your text and complete this table summarizing the humoural theory of personality.

Personality Type	Predominant Humour	Behavioural Characteristics

4. a. Define and distinguish between *personality types* and *personality traits*. (See Figure 14.2 in your text.)

   b. Why do most researchers prefer a classification system based on personality traits rather than personality types?

   c. Explain why it is unlikely that genes for specific personality types are passed from generation to generation.

d. If learning affects personality traits, where must any change take place?

5. a. Explain why categorization must precede scientific explanation.

   b. Briefly describe Allport's efforts to identify the traits necessary to describe personality. (Allport and Odbert, 1936)

   c. Define cardinal, central, and secondary traits and provide an example of each.

   d. How did Allport's research influence other psychologists?

6. a. Describe Cattell's use of the method of factor analysis to identify personality factors or traits.

   b. How many traits did he identify and what did he call them? Why? (See Figure 14.3 in your text)

7. a. Name and define the three factors that Eysenck identified through factor analysis. Make sure you identify both ends of each dimension. (Eysenck, 1970; Eysenck and Eysenck, 1985)

   b. See Table 14.1 in your text and give some examples of questions that a neurotic individual would answer yes. What are some other likely characteristics of this individual?

   c. According to Eysenck, how do these factors influence the development of a person's temperament? (See Figure 14.4 in your text.)

   d. Why have Eysenck's three factors been widely accepted?

8. a. Name the five personality factors of the *five-factor model* identified through a factor analysis of words related to personality. (Tupes and Christal, 1961; Norman, 1963; Costa & McCrae, 1998a ; McCrae and Costa, 1985; 1997)

   b. Describe the NEO-PI which measures these factors.

c. What were the results of an attempt to validate the five factors using a factor analysis of adjectives from the California Q-Set? (McCrae, Costa, & Busch, 1986)

d. What have the five factors been found to predict? (DeNeve & Cooper, 1998; Vollrath, 2000; Barrick & Mount, 1991)

e. Discuss the two distinct dimensions of conscientiousness. (Jackson et al., 1996)

Read the interim summary on page 459 of your text to re-acquaint yourself with the material in this section.

14–2 Describe the psychobiological approach to personality: the effects of heredity and environment and the brain mechanisms that may be responsible for differences in personality traits.

Read pages 456-459 answer the following questions.

1. a. What was the conclusion of eleven studies designed to determine the similarity of pairs of identical and fraternal twins on each of Eysenck's three personality dimensions? (Figure 14.5 in your text. Zuckerman, 1991)

b. Approximately what percentage of the variability of these three dimensions may be attributed to heredity? to the common environment?

2. Are the personality characteristics of identical twins raised apart less similar than those raised together (Zuckerman, 1991)? What does this imply about the effects of family environment on personality?

3. a. What is the major source of the interaction between heredity and environment? (Plomin and Bergeman, 1991)

b. Compare the ratings of family environments made by pairs of identical and fraternal twins and shown in Figure 14.6 in your text.

c. Outline two possible explanations for these results. Which explanation appears to be correct? (Loehlin, 1992)

d. What aspect of family life appears to play the largest role in shaping personality? Cite research to support your answer. (Plomin and Bergeman, 1991)

e. Can we necessarily apply these findings to other cultures? Explain your answer.

f. What personality characteristics appear to be influenced by family environment and not heredity? (Loehlin and Nichols, 1976; Rose, 1988)

4. Describe two kinds of confirming evidence that brain mechanisms are involved in personality traits.

5. Complete the table below, which illustrates the behavioural traits of the major personality dimensions and the biological characteristics that may be responsible for them. (See Table 14.2 in your text.)

Personality Trait	Behavioural Characteristics	Biological Characteristics

6. Summarize research on a possible biological basis of timidity.

   a. When "timid" cats encounter a novel situation, what part of the brain becomes more active? Adamec and Stark-Adamec, 1986)

   b. Which personality dimensions may be related to childhood shyness? (Briggs, 1988)

   c. On what basis did Kagan et al. (1988) place young children in experimental groups for continued study?

   d. How long did testing continue?

   e. Describe the behavioural and physiological responses of both groups in test situations.

   f. What do these results suggest about the basis of shyness?

Read the interim summary on page 464 of your text to re-acquaint yourself with the material in this section.

14–3 Describe the social learning approach to personality.

Read pages 459-463 and answer the following questions.

1. According to social learning theory what two factors determine personality?

2. a. According to Skinner, what single factor explains both consistency and change in behaviour?

   b. How did his ideas influence social learning research?

3. Define *expectancy* in your own words and go on to explain how expectancies change as a result of reward and punishment and observational learning.

4. Define observational learning. Be sure to use the word model in your answer.

5. a. Define *reciprocal determinism* in your own words.

   b. Explain the patterns of interaction in reciprocal determinism suggested by Bandura. (See Figure 14.7 in your text.)

   c. Now define *self-efficacy* in your own words.

   d. How is the frequency and quality of behaviour-environment interactions affected by high self-efficacy? low self-efficacy?

   e. What kind of people are more likely to succeed in spite of adversity? (Seligman and Schulman, 1986)

6. a. On what points concerning personality and behaviour do Bandura and Mischel agree?

   b. How does Mischel explain individual differences in personality? What does he call these influences?

7. List Mischel's five person variables.

   1.   4.

   2.   5.

   3.

8. What is the relation between these variables and perceptions, goals, and behaviour?

9. a. Finally, define *locus of control* in your own words.

   b. Compare an internal versus an external focus of control. (Study Figure 14.8 in your text.)

10. a. Briefly explain how the I-E Scale, devised by Rotter, assesses the degree to which a person attributes the consequences of behaviour to internal or external factors.

    b. State the conclusions of research using the I-E Scale to study

1. willingness to work hard to obtain a goal.

2. health practices.

3. failure. (Lefcourt, 1966, 1992)

14-4 Evaluate the controversy about the relative importance of personality traits and environmental situations in predicting behaviour.

Read pages 463-464 and answer the following questions.

1. What is Mischel's (1968, 1976) view of the predictive value of stable personality traits? Be sure to mention his supporting example.

2. a. Describe the subjects, the personality traits that were assessed, and some of the experimental situations in research to determine the stability of personality traits conducted by Hartsborne and May (1928),

   b. In general, how did the children behave?

   c. What did the authors conclude about these particular traits?

3. And what did Mischel (1968) conclude after reviewing later studies?

4. a. Outline Epstein's (1979, 1986) position on the stability and importance of personality traits.

   b. Who were the subjects in his studies, and what did he ask them to do?

   c. What did he find when he correlated behaviour on any two days? across many days?

5. Explain how Mischel (1977, 1979) has modified his views on the predictive value of personality traits and situations. Be sure to mention powerful and weak situations.

6. a. Mischel and Shoda (1995, 1998) propose a _____ of the train and social learning approaches.

   b. Discuss the CAPS approach. Which influences would have to be recognized in this approach?

7. What conclusions can be made concerning the interaction between personality and situations?

LESSON I SELF TEST

1. Extraversion is an example of
   a. a personality type.
   b. a personality trait.
   c. temperament.
   d. a personality stage.

2. Eysenck's personality theory includes these three factors:
   a. self-praise, self-criticism, and self-control.
   b. stimuli, responses, and reinforcement.
   c. extraversion, neuroticism, and psychoticism.
   d. heredity, environment, and experience.

3. The five-factor model is based on
   a. the theoretical framework of the Greeks' four original temperaments.
   b. the cross-situational consistency of word use.
   c. a factor analysis of adjectives appearing in the California Q-Set.
   d. an analysis of the words used to describe differences in personality.

4. Most studies of the personality traits of identical twins found
   a. a correlation of about 50 percent or higher for the heritability of the traits of neuroticism, extraversion, and psychoticism.
   b. a high correlation only if the twins had been reared together.
   c. that all personality characteristics are influenced to a high degree by heredity.
   d. that personality traits could not be accurately assessed until adolescence.

5. Zuckerman suggests that people who score high on psychoticism have a deficient _____ system.
   a. arousal
   b. reinforcement
   c. punishment
   d. anxiety

6. The results of a study that attempted to assess the biological basis of shyness found that
   a. children outgrow their shyness around 7.5 years of age.
   b. no correlation exists between physiological responses and behavioural responses
   c. shyness is an enduring personality trait.
   d. there are structural differences in the brains of the shy and nonshy children.

7. Social learning theorists believe that
   a. personality is determine by the consequences of behaviour and the individual's beliefs about those consequences.
   b. behaviours acquired through observational learning are not enduring because direct reinforcement is never experienced.
   c. innate personality traits have a stronger influence on behaviour than environment.
   d. self-discovery is the most important learning experience.

8. When compared to people with an external locus of control, people with an internal locus of control are more likely to
   a. give up before obtaining a goal.
   b. exercise regularly and quit smoking.
   c. attribute failure to bad luck.
   d. blame others for setbacks.

9. Epstein demonstrated that the cross-situational consistency of most personality traits is higher when
   a. only two situations are measured.
   b. multiple observations across several days are made.
   c. responses on alternate days are measured.
   d. laboratory observations are correlated with personal journal entries.

10. The fact that people prefer to choose the situations they enter suggests that personality traits
    a. have a stronger predictive value than situations.
    b. and situations are independent variables.
    c. interact with situations.
    d. develop through social interactions and reinforcement.

LESSON II

Read the interim summary on page 472 of your text to re-acquaint yourself with the material in this section.

14-5 Describe the historical background that led to Freud's psychodynamic theory of personality, and explain his hypothetical mental structures and defense mechanisms.

Read pages 464-468 and answer the following questions.

1. Explain the psychodynamic struggle conceived of by Freud.

2. Explain how Freud's early training with

   a. von Brücke influenced his approach to research.

   b. Charcot influenced his thinking about the sources of problems of the mind.

3. a. Briefly summarize the case of Anna O. as it was originally presented by Freud and Breuer and the new evidence that challenges their description. (Ellenberger, 1972) Does this information invalidate psychoanalysis?

   b. What did Freud conclude from the case of Anna O. and his own clinical practice about the

      1. motivation for human behaviour?

      2. source of psychic energy?

      3. need for equilibrium?

      4. cause of psychological disturbances?

      5. events that trigger instinctual drives?

4. Explain Freud's belief that personality is shaped by both conscious and unconscious powers. Be sure to mention repression in your answer.

5. Name and define the three kinds of elements Freud believed were present in the mind.

   1.

2.

3.

6. Outline the structures and functions of the mind, according to Freud.

   a. What are the names and functions of the major structures of the mind? (See Figure 14.9 in your text.)

      1.

      2.

      3.

   b. What is the function of the libido? the pleasure principle?

   c. How do the reality principle and defence mechanisms affect the functioning of the ego?

   d. What are the names and functions of the divisions of the superego?

   e. What are the two primary drives? What holds them in check?

   f. What conflict is resolved through compromise formation? Be sure to mention Freudian slips in your answer.

7. a. What did Freud believe was the source of dreams; and, therefore, what could be learned by analyzing them?

   b. Compare the manifest content of a dream with its latent content. What purpose do these separate forms serve?

8. Explain how Freud used free association, a method of analysis he developed, to uncover the unconsciousness.

9. Summarize the Freudian defense mechanisms.

   a. Which structure of the mind contains the defence mechanisms? When are they needed?

   b. Briefly explain each of these defense mechanisms. (See Table 14.3 in your text.)

      1. repression

      2. reaction formation

3. projection

4. sublimation

5. rationalization

6. conversion

14-6 Explain Freud's psychosexual theory of personality, and explain how it influenced the theories of Jung, Adler, Horney, and Erikson.

Read pages 468-472 and answer the following questions.

1. Explain the development of a fixation in your own words.

2. Outline the stages hypothesized by Freud in his psychosexual theory of personality development.

    a. Oral stage   Age:

       1. Source of gratification:

       2. Causes of fixation:

       3. Results of fixation:

    b. Anal stage   Age:

       1. Source of gratification:

       2. Causes of fixation.

       3. Results of fixation:

    c. Phallic stage   Age:

       1. Source of gratification:

       2. characterize the complexes that occur during this stage.

       3. Describe the Oedipus complex. Be sure to explain the source of this conflict

       4. Describe penis envy and the Electra complex.

       5. How is the conflict for both boys and girls resolved? What is the process called?

       6. Discuss how this process is also the initial source of superego development.

    d. Latency period   Age:

    e. Genital stage   Age:

       1. Source of gratification:

3. Discuss how psychosexual development is the basis of personality traits.

4. In general, which of Freud's ideas did neo-Freudians accept? reject?

5. a. In what ways did Jung disagree with Freud's views?

   b. What kind of information is stored in the collective unconscious?

   c. Explain why Jung believed archetypes to be "forms without content."

6. a. According to Adler, how do feelings of inferiority influence children's behaviour and lead to a striving for superiority?

   b. What other interest motivates behaviour?

7. a. In what ways did Horney agree and disagree with Freud's views on personality development?

   b. What did she believe is the source of basic anxiety?

   c. Outline Horney's three strategies for coping with basic anxiety as well as their corresponding basic orientations.

   d. According to Horney, how does basic anxiety and the accompanying strategies and orientations influence personality development?

8. a. In what ways did Erikson disagree with Freud's views on the motivation and timing of personality development?

   b. According to Erikson, what are life crises and how do they influence psychosocial development?

9. Why have the writings of Freud received little scientific support?

Read the interim summary on pages 475-476 of your text to re-acquaint yourself with the material in this section.

14-7 Discuss the humanistic approach to the study of personality and the contributions of Maslow and Rogers.

Read pages 472-475 and answer the following questions.

1. a. Describe the humanistic approach to the study of personality—its emphasis and beliefs about people.

   b. Who were the two most influential humanistic psychologists?

2. In what ways did Freud and Maslow agree and disagree about the importance and nature of human motivation?

3. a. Describe Maslow's hierarchy of needs shown in Figure 14.10 in your text.

   b. In order to progress to the next higher level, what must a person do?

   c. Why did Maslow examine the lives of historical figures such as Albert Einstein?

4. a. According to Rogers, how does a person's self-concept and the need for positive regard interact to shape personality development?

   b. Explain why Rogers believed that the positive regard of others is often conditional. Be sure to refer to *conditions of worth* in your answer.

   c. If a person spends too much time trying to obtain the positive regard of others, how will self-actualization be affected?

   d. To eliminate this possibility, how must the conditions for obtaining positive regard change?

5. a. How did Rogers believe an atmosphere of unconditional positive regard would facilitate progress during therapy?

   b. Describe the Q sort and explain how Rogers used it to guage a client's progress.

6. Discuss two criticisms of the humanistic approach.

7. To review: Study the summary of major personality theories shown in Table 14.4 in your text.

Read the interim summary on pages 480-481 of your text to re-acquaint yourself with the material in this section.

14-8 Describe and evaluate an objective test of personality, the Minnesota Multiphasic Personality Inventory (MMPI).

Read pages 476-477 and answer the following questions.

1. What is the underlying assumption of all personality tests?

2. What are some of the characteristics of an objective test?

3. a. What was the purpose of the first MMPI?

   b. Describe how test questions were originally selected. Be sure to describe the control group.

   c. Describe the format of the current revised MMPI-2.

4. a. What is the general purpose of the MMPI validity scales?

   b. Explain what each of the validity scales indicates about a person who receives a high score.

      1. ? scale

      2. L scale

      3. F scale

      4. K scale

5. What are some of the ways the MMPI is used?

6. Why do advocates of the five-factor model object to the MMPI? (Johnson et al., 1984)

14-9 Explain the rationale of projective tests of personality, and describe and evaluate the Rorschach Inkblot Test and the Thematic Apperception.

Read pages 477-478 and answer the following questions.

1. Why are projective tests designed to be ambiguous?

2. a. See Figure 14.11 in your text and describe the Rorschach inkblots and their use.

   b. Describe two methods of interpreting a person's descriptions of the inkblots and their features.

3. a. Why did Murray and Morgan develop the Thematic Apperception Test (TAT).

   b. Describe the kind of pictures that are a part of the TAT and explain how they used during testing.

   c. Why are the results often difficult to interpret?

4. Summarize research on the reliability and validity of projective tests.

   a. What were the results of a comparison of the scores of people in mental hospitals and university students? (Eron, 1950)

   b. What aspects of test administration appear to lower the validity of TAT results? (Lundy, 1984, 1988)

   c. What emotional circumstances may also affect results? (Masling, 1960)

   d. What gender related criticism of the TAT has been suggested? (Worchel et al., 1990)

   e. What were the results of a comparison of Rorschach test scores and scores on objective tests of personality? (Greenwald, 1990)

5. a. Why are these tests still used?

   b. What do their proponents assert about their usefulness? (Watkins, 1991)

14–10 Describe gender differences in personality and identify some of their biological and cultural causes.

Read pages 479–480 and answer the following questions.

1. a. Define *stereotype* in your own words.

   b. What has been the general conclusion of research to confirm these stereotypes?

   c. List some personality variables that differ and do not differ significantly between the sexes. (Snow and Weinstock, 1990; Jones, 1991; Poole et al., 1991)

2. Summarize research on gender differences related to social behaviour.

   a. Compare the level of aggression exhibited by

      1. young boys and young girls during play (Fabes and Eisenberg, 1992).

      2. elementary and high school students. (Woodall and Matthews, 1993). How did patterns of aggression differ?

      3. American and Israeli preschool girls. Israeli girls and American boys. (Lauer, cited in Bower, 1991)

   b. Offer an explanation based on cultural experience that may explain the more aggressive behaviour of Israeli children.

   c. How are girl gang members expected to behave in some cultures and subcultures? (Bower, 1991)

   d. Under what circumstances do males emerges as leaders? females? (Eagly and Karau, 1991)

   c. Under what circumstances are males more likely to offer assistance? females? (Eisenberg et al., 1991

   f. How do males tend to behave in their relationships? females? (Buss, 1995)

3. What did Rose (1995) conclude from a review of research about the influence of heredity on personality differences?

4. Now summarize research on the biological and cultural causes of these gender differences in personality.

   a. What is the most likely cause of evolved personality differences between the sexes? (Loehlin, 1992; Tooby and Cosmides, 1990)

   b. What kind of personality traits may have developed in females and males that resulted from their biological differences? (Buss, 1995)

   c. What aspects of a culture tend to influence gender differences in personality? (Wade and Tavris, 1994)

   d. Identify two technological advances that have influenced notions of gender-appropriate traits for males and females in western cultures in the 20th century.

LESSON II SELF TEST

1. Freud divided the mind into three structures:
   a. the ego, the superego, and the ego-ideal.
   b. the ego, the ego-ideal, and the conscience.
   c. the id, the ego, and the superego.
   d. the id, the ego, and the libido.

2. What are internalized prohibitions?
   a. guilt feelings
   b. forbidden sexual fantasies
   c. rules of behaviour learned in childhood
   d. Freudian slips

3. During the latency period the sexual instinctual drive
   a. is almost completely submerged.
   b. finds an outlet in heterosexual activity.
   c. is directed toward the parent of the other sex.
   d. emerges.

4. Erikson believed that personality development
   a. is a struggle between the personal and collective unconscious.
   b. continues throughout life.
   c. is motivated not only by sexual desires but also by religious and spiritual concerns.

   d. is a striving for perfection.

5. Which of the following is not one of the three options for dealing with anxiety in Horney's theory?
   a. moving toward others
   b. moving against others
   c. moving with others
   d. moving away from others

6. According to _____, positive personality development results from _____.
   a. Rogers; replacing a striving for superiority with regard for the common good
   b. Horney; experiencing unconditional positive regard
   c. Maslow; satisfying successive levels of his hypothesized hierarchy of needs
   d. Jung; integrating his hypothesized basic orientations and strategies

7. A high score on the K scale of the MMPI indicates the person may be
   a. lying.
   b. careless.
   c. defensive.
   d. evasive.

8. Projective personality tests
   a. measure the degree to which a subject agrees or disagrees with the examiner's interpretation of an ambiguous situation.
   b. are based on the assumption that an ambiguous situation will elicit the subject's true feelings.
   c. are not as difficult to score as empirical tests.
   d. require that subject responses be realistic.

9. One social behaviour that appears to reflect large gender differences in personality is
   a. aggression.
   b. friendship patterns.
   c. sportsmanship.
   d. religious practices.

10. The evolutionary origins of gender differences in personality
    a. are easier to identify in societies with a patriarchal or matriarchal form of social organization.
    b. seem likely to have evolved from divisions of labour resulting from sexual reproduction roles.
    c. are less subject to interpretation than cultural origins.
    d. are more difficult to identify in nomadic societies.

Answers to Self Tests

Lesson I

1 .b	Obj. 14-1	2. c	Obj. 14-1	3. d	Obj. 14-1	4. a	Obj. 14-2	5. c	Obj. 14-2
6. c	Obj. 14-2	7. a	Obj. 14-3	8. b	Obj. 14-3	9. b	Obj. 14-4	10. c	Obj. 14-4

Lesson II

1. c	Obj. 14-5	2. c	Obj. 14-5	3. a	Obj. 14-6	4. b	Obj. 14-6	5. c	Obj. 14-6
6. c	Obj. 14-7	7. c	Obj. 14-8	8. b	Obj. 14-9	9. a	Obj. 14-10	10. b	Obj. 14-10

CHAPTER 15

Social Psychology

LESSON I

Read the interim summary on page 494 of your text to re-acquaint yourself with the material in this section.

15-1 Describe schemata and explain how they guide our interpretation of people's behaviour, including our own.

Read pages 486-489 and answer the following questions.

1. In your own words, define

   a. *social psychology.*

   b. *social cognition.*

   c. *impression formation.*

   d. *schema.*

2. Briefly explain how we make use of impressions and schemata in our daily lives.

3. a. Asch (1946) presented two groups of subjects nearly identical lists of traits that described a hypothetical person. What was the only way the lists differed?

   b. How were subjects' impressions of the hypothetical person affected when that person was described as

      1. warm or cold?

      2. polite or blunt?

   c. What do the results suggest about the

      1. importance of particular central traits?

      2. relationship between schemata and central traits?

4. a. Asch (1946) also presented two groups of subjects other nearly identical lists of traits for the purpose of studying first impressions. What was the only way these lists differed?

b. How did word order affect subjects' impressions?

c. What do the results suggest about the importance of first impressions?

d. What is the name of this effect?

e. What does this effect appear to reflect?

5. A _____-_____ is a(n) _____ structure for organizing the knowledge, feelings and ideas that make up our _____-_____ Our self-concept is _____ and changes through _____.

6. Describe some of the experiences and events that shape self-concept and change self-concept (Markus & Naurius, 1986; Ruvolo & Markus, 1992).

7. Briefly outline the model proposed by Markus and Kitayama (1991) to explain the influence of culture on the formation of a self-concept.

15-2 Discuss the use of external and internal factors to determine the causes of behaviour and discuss Kelley's theory of attribution.

Read pages 489-490 and answer the following questions.

1. a. Discuss a benefit and a drawback of our ability, to learn what to expect from particular people in particular situations.

b. Define *attribution* in your own words and explain its role in our daily lives.

2. a. Define *external factors* and *internal factors* in your own words.

b. Suppose that as you are standing in the check-out line of a crowded grocery store you notice that a woman in the next line looks ill. She says to the man in front of her, "I'm not feeling very well, would you mind if I went ahead of you?" "Of course not," the man replies. Would you attribute the man's behaviour to internal factors? Explain your answer.

c. What if the man had said, "I'm sorry, but I want to get home and watch the football game"?

3. Research suggests that we decide whether the behaviour of other people is due to external, or
_____ causes or internal, or _____ causes on the basis of
_____, _____, and _____. (Kelley, 1967)

4. a. Carefully explain the standards of consensual behaviour, consistency and distinctiveness and how they are used to determine whether behaviour is caused by external or internal causes. (See Table 15.1 in your text.)

b. Would you attribute the behaviour of the people in the following situations to external or internal factors? Explain the basis-consensus, consistency or distinctiveness-of your decision.

   1. William's violin teacher was not surprised that he was unprepared for his weekly lesson, because he is usually ill-prepared.

   2. Nicholas looked nervously at all the cutlery around his plate. When everyone else picked up a small fork to use for the first course, he did so, too.

   3. "I've noticed that lately Peter has been driving carelessly." Mrs. Lindsey told her husband. "He never drove like that until he started carpooling."

   4. "Marcy, you have been never been late to work before, but this month you have already been late four times. Can you tell me what's going on?" the supervisor asked.

15-3 Describe the common attributional biases and discuss research on their causes.

Read pages 490-492 and answer the following questions.

1. When the fundamental attributional error affects our judgments about the behaviour of others, what factors do we tend to overestimate? underestimate?

2. Discuss research on the fundamental attribution error. (Jones & Harris, 1967)

   a. Describe how the essays for the two groups differed.

   b. Now describe the additional manipulation the researchers made.

   c. What were the students asked to estimate?

   d. What results did they find?

   e. What conclusions were made?

3. a. Explain another attributional error—the belief in a just world. (Lerner, 1980)

   b. What is the unfair consequence of this error?

   c. Why do people make this error?

   d. How does belief in a just world motivate people to persist at achieving their goals? (Hafer, 2000b)

   e. Discuss the research to support this position.

   f. Who is especially susceptible to this belief? (Furnham, 1992)

4. How do we tend to explain our own behaviour and that of others when the actor-observer effect influences our judgments? (Sande et al., 1988) Support your answer by citing research on college-age couples by Orvis et al., (1976).

5. Carefully outline two explanations for the fact that we make the fundamental attributional error when we observe the behaviour of others and not when we view our own behaviour. (Jones and Nisbett, 1971)

6. a. In explaining our own behaviour, we tend to attribute our failures to _____ causes and our successes to _____ causes, illustrating the _____-_____ bias. (Miller & Ross, 1975)

   b. Why may we commit this error? (Brown and Rogers, 1991)

   c What is this attribution error called?

7. a. Explain the error of false consensus in your own words.

   b. What did psychology students asked to choose from two unpleasant experiments believe about the choices of the majority of other subjects? (McFarland & Miller, 1990)

   c. Outline two possible explanations for the error of false consensus. (Ross, 1977)

15-4 Explain the use of heuristics in social cognition and discuss the fallacies associated with them.

Read pages 492-494 and answer the following questions.

1. a. What are heuristics and when do we use them?

   b. When these shortcuts fail, what do we call the failures?

   c. What are the two most important kinds of heuristics?

     1.   2.

2. Explain the representativeness heuristic (Lupfer et al., 1990) and the associated failure called the base-rate fallacy.

3. Define base-rate fallacy in your own words.

4. a. Reread the example of the athletic psychology professor and then make up an example of your own that might fool other people.

   b. Use the concepts of the representativeness heuristic and base-rate fallacy to explain why people would tend to be fooled.

5. Explain the availability heuristic in your own words.

6. Summarize research on the variables that can affect the availability of an event or concept and negatively influence decision making.

   a. Explain how Tversky and Kahneman (1982) demonstrated the influence of this heuristic on the answer to a question about the position of the letter k in English words.

   b. Do the exercise in Table 15.2 in your text. How did you respond? Why do people tend to answer that there are more of one than the other?

   c. Describe the priming phenomenon. How can this phenomenon explain the medical stude syndrome?

   d. Explain why personal encounters are given disproportionate weight in decision making and provide an example to support your answer. (Borgida and Nisbett, 1977)

Read the interim summary on page 500 of your text to re-acquaint yourself with the material in this section.

15-5 Describe the formation of the affective, cognitive, and behavioural components of attitudes and discuss the use of persuasion to change attitudes.

Read pages 494-497 and answer the following questions.

1. Briefly define these components of attitude. (See Figure 15.1 in your text.)

   a. affective component

   b. cognitive component

   c. behavioural component

2. Explain two means by which affective components of attitude develop and are transmitted. (Rajecki, 1990)

   1.

   2.

3. Briefly summarize research that demonstrated that attitudes can be influenced by mere exposure to a stimulus. (Zajonc, 1968; Murphy, Monoham, & Zajonc, 1995)

4. The mere exposure effect is limited to what kind of stimuli? What happens with repeated exposure to stimuli that we do not like?

5. Explain how children acquire the cognitive components of attitudes.

6. a. How many times were LaPiere and a Chinese couple refused service on a cross-country trip? How did responses to a later letter contradict their experiences? (LaPiere, 1934)

   b. What did this study seem to indicate about the relation between the cognitive and behavioural components of an attitude? What does more recent research suggest?

7. Summarize research on the variables that affect the behavioural components of attitudes.

   a. How does the degree of specificity affect predictions about behaviour?

b. Study Table 15.3 in your text and identify the best predictor of membership or volunteer service in the Sierra Club and explain why. (Weigel et al., 1974)

c. Describe research by Sivacek and Crano (1982) that demonstrated the importance of motivational relevance.

d. Most parents agreed it would be thoughtful to do something for the teachers at the end of the school year. However, few volunteered to serve on a committee to sponsor an appreciation luncheon. Offer two explanations, one based on the degree of specificity and the other on the motivational relevance, to explain the behaviour of the parents.

e. "A variable that affects the relation between attitude and behaviour is whether or not the attitude is activated in the context where behavioural consistency is an issue." (page 498 in your text) Discuss this statement and provide an example.

f. Briefly explain how circumstances may affect the performance of a behaviour that someone rates as desirable.

8. Decide whether the following situations illustrate an (A) affective, (B) behavioural, or (C) cognitive component of attitude.

_____ Meg recently told a friend, "When I was little I always thought Mrs. Zinn was abrupt and unfriendly. Later I learned she was in almost constant pain from arthritis, but I still don't like to be the one to answer the phone if she is calling."

_____ "I never quite believed people who complained about how hard it was to get a job until I started looking for one myself."

_____ "Our teacher has been telling us a lot about what its like to be vegetarian. He thinks its much healthier than eating meat. I've been thinking a lot about becoming a vegetarian, too," thirteen-year-old Mario told his mother.

_____ "We'll be moving away this summer, so I don't think we'll get involved in building the new playground, even though we certainly think it is a worthwhile project."

9. List two aspects of the persuasion process.

1.   2.

10. Now list two characteristics of the source of the message that tend to increase its persuasiveness. Cite research to support your answer. (Hovland and Weiss, 1951; Chaiken, 1979; Roskos-Ewoldsen & Fazio, 1992)

1.   2.

11. Under what circumstances is it preferable to present a one-sided argument? a two-sided argument? (McAlister et al., 1980)

12. a. How effective was the New Jersey program "Scared Straight" in deterring youthful offenders from resuming delinquent activities? (Hagan, 1982)

    b. When are scare tactics most effective in changing attitudes.? (Gliecher & Petty, 1992)

13. a. Summarize the elaboration likelihood model of attitude change through persuasion shown in Figure 15.2 in your text. (Cacioppo et al., 1993; Petty & Wegener, 1999)

    b. Indicate whether the argument illustrates the central or peripheral route of persuasion by writing a *C* or a *P* in the space.

    _____ In an effort to convince voters to support an addition to the high school, the building committee prepared careful comparisons of the advantages and disadvantages of building an addition, renting portable classrooms, and implementing a system of shifts.

    _____ "Professional knives, copper cookware, and six volumes on international cuisine are not going to make me an outstanding cook," Tanya said as she skimmed the ads in the magazine she was reading.

    _____ During the weekend, Tong discussed with his family everything his boss had told him about the increased responsibilities, the people he would be working with, and the financial benefits of the promotion he was being offered.

15-6 Describe Festinger's theory of cognitive dissonance and Bem's self-perception theory.

Read pages 497-500 and answer the following questions.

1. a. Festinger's theory of _____ _____ is an attempt to explain the effect of discrepancies between attitudes, behaviours, and self-image on _____ formation.

    b. Explain the feeling produced by cognitive dissonance in your own words. Describe some of the situations that can produce it.

    c. Explain why dissonance reduction serves as a negative reinforcer.

    d. Explain how people can achieve dissonance reduction. Be sure to mention consonant elements in your answer.

        1.

        2.

        3.

2. Which strategy is the candidate in the following examples using to reduce the dissonance between his self-image and his election loss?

    a. "We just weren't able to raise as much money as my opponent."

    b. "It doesn't really matter that much. There are a lot of other ways to be active in municipal government."

    c. "I think if we start earlier and work harder to get out the vote on election day, we can win next time."

3. a. According to dissonance theory, how does induced compliance affect attitudes? Provide an example.

    b. List some variable that can influence the degree of dissonance a person feels.

4. a. Study Figure 15.3 in your text and using dissonance theory, explain why poorly paid subjects rated working with spools on a tray a more interesting task than well paid subjects? (Festinger and Carlsmith, 1959)

    b. What is the explanation for this finding?

    c. Briefly summarize the two examples provided in your text concerning how compliance can change one's attitude (the executive versus the salesperson).

5. a. Why is the finding that induced compliance produces arousal important to dissonance theory.

    b. Describe the task Croyle and Cooper (1983) used to produce various levels of cognitive dissonance. Then study Figure 15.4 in your text and describe and explain the results.

6. According to dissonance theory, which items do we tend to value most highly, designer running shoes or discount running shoes? Why?

7. a. Restate Bem's (1972) self-perception theory in your own words.

    b. How do people make judgments about their own or someone else's behaviour or attitudes?

8. How does the self-perception theory explain the task ratings of poorly paid subjects?

9. What is an advantage of the self-perception theory?

Read the interim summary on pages 503-544 of your text to re-acquaint yourself with the material in this section.

15-7 Discuss research on the origins of prejudice, some of its damaging consequences, and the reasons we have hope for change.

Read pages 500-503 and answer the following questions.

1. a. Define and carefully distinguish between a *prejudice* and a *stereotype*.

   b. Next define *discrimination* in your own words and carefully distinguish between discrimination and prejudice.

   c. Explain how these perceptions, whether they are held by individuals, groups or even nations, can lead to serious consequences.

2. a. Briefly recount the experiences of the Rattlers and the Eagles. What do the findings of this experiment suggest is an important factor in the development of prejudice? (Sherif et al., 1961)

   b. Describe how Meindl and Lerner (1985) manipulated the self-esteem of subjects. How did English-speaking Canadians whose self-esteem had been threatened then rate French-speaking Canadians?

   c. Should we assume that these results would be obtained in other cultures? (Feather & McKee, 1993)

3. Explain how the use of heuristics and stereotypes may contribute to prejudice.

4. a. Give some examples of where people learn stereotypes.

   b. When are stereotypes more extreme? (Thompson et al., 2000)

   c. Why is the media a particularly dangerous source?

   d. When people are given evidence against their stereotypes, how do they respond? (Kunda & Oleson, 1997)

5. a. Why do people overestimate the number of violent crimes and the number of those crimes committed by members of visible minority groups?

   b. Define illusory correlation and discuss this concept in terms of crimes and visible minorities.

6. a. Define the *illusion of outgroup homogeneity* and discuss how it contributes to the formation of stereotypes.

b. Mrs. Devlin, who lived near the university, was frequently disturbed by loud music coming from the student residences. She was often heard to comment, "University students are all so thoughtless." Explain why her attitude as an example of this illusion.

7. a. Discuss the basis of the evolutionary explanation for ingroup biases toward outgroups (Krebs & Denton, 1997).

b. What were the evolutionary advantages to categorizing individuals as belonging to one's own group or to another group?

c. Why do these once adaptive processes lead to difficulties in contemporary societies.

8. Explain a self-fulfilling prophecy in your own words.

9. a. After listening to the recorded voices of female subjects who had been conversing with male subjects who had been led to believe the women were either attractive or unattractive, independent observers rated the women. Which group received positive ratings? (Snyder et al., 1977)

b. Explain the results as an example of the self-fulfilling prophecy.

10. a. Explain how prejudices perpetuate exploitation of one group by another. Why is this kind of prejudice especially resistant to change?

b. What is the best way to minimize prejudice that results from inadvertent stereotypes and preconceptions.

c. In what specific ways did school children, who had received training about some of the difficulties of the handicapped, show changes in their attitudes. (Langer et al., 1985)

LESSON I SELF TEST

1. Schemata are
   a. unbiased assessments of the causes of behaviour.
   b. based on group consensus.
   c. mental frameworks that organizes information about people, places, or things.
   d. reinforced by first impressions.

2. We attribute the behaviour of other people to external or internal causes on the basis of three components:
   a. dispositional, intuitional, and situational.
   b. consensus, consistency, and distinctiveness.
   c. affective, behavioural, and cognitive.
   d. appetitive stimuli, aversive stimuli, and neutral stimuli.

3. We make the fundamental attributional error
   a. most often when we explain the causes of our own behaviour.
   b. when we overestimate the significance of dispositional factors and underestimate situational factors.
   c. when we underestimate the importance of distinctive behaviour.
   d. when we rely more on the observations of others and less on our own.

4. The actor-observer effect suggests that we tend to attribute our own behaviour to
   _____and the behaviour of others to
   _____.
   a. the situation; personal disposition
   b. personal disposition; vicarious classical conditioning
   c. social cognition; reliance on heuristics
   d. intuition; group consensus

5. The first time she visited a friend's home, they walked around his vegetable garden and Rosa noted the many varieties of tomatoes he grew. She was surprised to learn later that he did not like to eat fresh tomatoes. Her surprise was the result of the
   a. representativeness heuristic.
   b. availability heuristic.
   c. base-rate fallacy.
   d. false consensus.

6. Attitudes consist of three different components:
   a. affective, behavioural, and cognitive.
   b. arousal, interaction, and reaction.
   c. consensus, consistency, and distinctiveness.
   d. dispositional, intuitional, and situational.

7. Cognitive dissonance theory predicts that
   a. dissonance reduction is motivated by an aversive drive.

   b. self-confident people experience the least dissonance.
   c. people habituate to mild physiological arousal.
   d. attitudes, but not behaviours, are resistant to coercion.

8. Results of research based on student essays on alcohol use at Princeton University support cognitive dissonance theory because
   a. subjects showed a preference for obtaining group consensus before writing the essay.
   b. researchers obtained evidence of physiological arousal.
   c. the greater the motivational relevance of the issue the more compelling the essays.
   d. subjects who were paid the least showed the greatest change of attitude.

9. An advantage of Bem's self-perception theory is that
   a. all attributions about behaviour are based on situational rather than dispositional factors.
   b. it is based on principles of classical conditioning.
   c. it does not depend on a motivating aversive drive.
   d. it offers the best explanation of inconsistent behaviour.

10. Which is the most accurate statement about prejudice?
    a. Healthy competition with members of other groups serves as a outlet to discharge prejudicial feelings.
    b. The tendency to affiliate with a group is accompanied by the tendency to be suspicious of others.
    c. The increased use of heuristics would decrease errors in judgment about other people.
    d. We are more likely to form prejudices against people who are similar to ourselves.

LESSON II

Read the interim summary on pages 512-513 of your text to re-acquaint yourself with the material in this section.

15-8 Describe research on the nature and effects of conformity and the conditions that facilitate or inhibit bystander intervention.

Read pages 504-507 and answer the following questions.

1. The most powerful social influences on our behaviour and attitudes may be the _____ of other people.

2. Give several examples of beneficial social conventions.

3. Compare social norms and group norms.

4. a. Describe the perceptual illusion, the autokinetic effect, used by Sherif (1936).

   b. After questioning subjects individually about the movement of the light, what did he ask them to do?

   c. How did the behaviour of the subjects change when they were again asked about the movement of the light? Be sure to use the term *collective frame of reference* in your answer.

   d. How long did the collective decision influence individual behaviour? Offer a possible explanation.

5. Define *conformity* in your own words.

6. Outline research by Asch (1951, 1952, 1955) on group conformity.

   a. Briefly describe the

      1. task. (See Figure 15.5 in your text.)

2. group composition.

3. seating arrangement and its significance.

4. results.

5. subjects' reasons for their responses.

b. What do the results suggest about the strength of the tendency to conform (the Asch effect)?

7. According to Baron et al. (1996), what are the two primary reasons for conformity?

8. a. Following the death of Kitty Genovese, what explanation was given for the indifference of the bystanders?

b. Define *bystander intervention* in your own words.

c. Briefly describe how Darley and Latané (1968) used a staged seizure to study bystander intervention.

d. Study Figure 15.6 in your text and identify the circumstances in which subjects responded and failed to respond to the "seizure?"

e. From talking with subjects who did not respond, what did the researchers conclude were some of the reasons for the subjects' behaviour?

9. Summarize the four steps that lead up to a decision to intervene proposed by Latané and Darley (1970).

10. Explain these obstacles to intervention.

a. diffusion of responsibility

b. bystander competence (Shotland and Heinold, 1985)

15-9 Discuss research on social facilitation and social loafing and the conditions under which each occurs.

Read pages 507-508 and answer the following questions.

1. Define *social facilitation* in your own words.

2. Compare the results of research by Triplett (1897) with that of other early investigators.

3. Summarize Zajonc's (1965) explanation of social facilitation. Be sure to refer to arousal and dominant response in your answer.

4. Describe the task and the results of research by Martens (1969), which tested Zajonc's explanation.

5. Discuss the level of arousal and "performance" of burglars who work in groups. (Cromwell et al., 1991)

6. Define *social loafing* in your own words.

7. Now use this concept to explain why a tug-of-war team made a smaller combined effort than the simple combination of individual efforts. (Ringelmann, cited by Dashiell, 1935)

8. Summarize research on the factors that determine whether social facilitation or social loafing will occur.

   a. What information did some subjects in a study using a shouting format receive? Describe the results. (Williams et al., 1981)

   b. Explain why identifiability deters social loafing.

   c. What are two variables that affect social loafing?

   d. Compare cohesive and non-cohesive groups in social loafing. (Karau & Hart, 1998)

   e. Which testing condition encouraged subjects to take the most responsibility for identifying a moving dot? (Harkins & Petty, 1982)

   f. Explain why responsibility deters social loafing.

9. a. What did Karau and Williams (1995) conclude are two factors that moderate social loafing?

   b. How do they explain their conclusion?

15-10 Describe research on the effects of making a commitment.

Read page 508 and answer the following questions.

1. How did making a bet on a horse affect a person's confidence in his or her choice? (Knox & Inkster, 1968)

2. Over 55 percent of homeowners, who had previously accepted a small sign, later agreed to display a huge sign in front of their homes. However, less than 20 percent of homeowners who had not been previously contacted agreed to display the huge sign. Refer to the foot-in-the-door technique to explain the response of each group. (Freedman & Fraser, 1966)

3. How do salespeople using the low-balling technique get people to make a commitment?

4. In terms of self-image, how does making a commitment strengthen compliance?

5. What concepts are illustrated by the following situations?

   _____ "Here, try some of our new baked potato chips."

   _____ Everyone thought he was drunk, and he died on the sidewalk.

   _____ "Mom, please don't put tofu in my lunch anymore. No one brings that kind of food to school."

   _____ "I could hardly believe it. While I was standing on the corner with my map out trying to figure out where I was, two different people stopped to help me," Maggie reported about her attempts to find her away around the city.

   _____ "You three working together should have finished raking the leaves long ago. Why isn't it done?" their father asked.

   _____ "I don't really want to go to the party tonight, but I said I would go, so I'll go."

   Choices:

   a. conformity   b. diffusion of responsibility

   c. commitment   d. bystander intervention

   e. social loafing

15-11 Discuss research on compliance with the requests of attractive people and authority figures.

Read pages 509-510 and answer the following questions.

1. How did mock jury awards to attractive plaintiffs compare with awards to unattractive plaintiffs? (Kulka & Kessler, 1978)

2. a. Explain how classical conditioning may account for the effects of attractiveness.

   b. Explain why it easier for attractive people to get others to comply with a request.

3. In general, how do we respond to the request of authority figures? When is this obedience approved by societies?

4. a. Describe the experimental procedure Milgram (1963) used to study obedience to authority.

   b. Now study Figure 15.7 in your text and state the percentage of subjects who delivered what they believed to be a 450-volt shock to the "learner."

   c. How was the experimental procedure changed in later research? Under these conditions, what percentage of subjects shocked the learner? (Milgram, 1974)

   d. What do these results suggest about the tendency to obey authority figures?

   e. Explain why most people find these results surprising. (Ross, 1977)

   f. Discuss the negative information the experiment revealed to the participants.

   g. In his defence, what did Milgram do to inform subjects about the true nature of the experiment as the end of each experimental session and then later on?

15–12 Explain how decision making is affected by group polarization and the tendency to avoid dissent and discuss ways to resist social influences.

Read pages 510-512 and answer the following questions.

1. a. How does the position of a group trying to reach a joint decision change if the initial position is risky? conservative?

   b. What is the name of this phenomenon?

2. a. List three kinds of influences present during group discussion that may explain group decision making.

   1.   2.

   b. How is the position of group members influenced by any new information that may be presented?

   c. How does repeated exposure to the issues influence group attitudes? (Brauer et al., 1995)

   d. Describe how social reinforcement contributes to making a group decision regardless of the merit of that position.

3. Define *groupthink* in your own words. (Janis, 1972, 1982)

4. Study Figure 15.8 in your text and then fill in the blanks in the table below.

Antecedent Conditions				
Symptoms				
Decision-Making Outcomes				

5. Briefly summarize some precautions to avoid groupthink.

6. a. Why does our species generally benefit from accepting social influences? (Cialdini, 1993)

b. What is the best way to protect ourselves from the unscrupulous use of social influence?

Read the interim summary on page 518 of your text to re-acquaint yourself with the material in this section.

15-13 Describe research on the effects of positive evaluation, familiarity, similarity, and physical appearance on interpersonal attraction.

Read pages 513-515 and answer the following questions.

1. Define *interpersonal attraction* in your own words.

2. Discuss the factors that influence interpersonal attraction.

   a. Humans like to be evaluated _____. That is, we like people who treat us _____ and do not like those who _____ us.

   b. The more _____ we are exposed to someone, the more _____ our attitude is towards them.

   c. How has the effect of exposure been documented by research on friendship patterns in apartments? (Festinger et al., 1950)

   d. Study Figure 15.9 in your text and summarize the results of research by Saegert et al. (1973) on how the number of interactions among subjects during an experiment affected their attraction for each other.

3. a. Couples are often similar in attractiveness. Why do we make this choice?

   b. When couples are mismatched in attractiveness, what sometimes occurs? (White, 1980)

   c. List two reasons why couples and friends tend to hold similar opinions.

   d. What other factors tend to strengthen interpersonal attraction?

4. a. List some of the stereotypes favouring attractive people. (Eagly et al., 1991)

   b. Discuss some of the similarities and differences between North American and Koreans in beauty stereotypes. (Wheeler & Kim, 1997)

   c. Explain how differences in the emphasis placed on interconnectedness across cultures can account for some of the differences in beauty stereotypes.

d. Briefly describe the experimental procedure and results of research by Walster et al.(1966) on the effects of physical appearance.

5. a. Explain possible reasons why we do not dwell on physical attractiveness when discussing factors that are important to us.

   b. Discuss the research that supports these explanations. (Hadjistavropoulos & Genest, 1994)

6. Are the beauty stereotypes correct? (Feingold, 1992)

15-14 Describe research on the role of anxiety and reinforcement on interpersonal attraction and the development of different kinds of love for others.

Read pages 515-516 and answer the following questions.

1. a. Describe the two conditions in which male university students were interviewed by an attractive female. (Dutton & Aron, 1974)

   b. Compare the responses of the men interviewed on the suspension bridge with those of the men interviewed on the conventional bridge.

   c. How do the researchers explain their results? Be sure to refer to attribution theory in your answer. Cite other research that supports their explanation. (McClanahan et al., 1990; Rubin, 1973)

2. a. Carefully distinguish between these three kinds of affection for others: liking, loving, and romantic or passionate love.

   b. Summarize the five elements of romantic love.

3. a. How does the passionate love a couple has for each other appear to change in long lasting relationships?

   b. Why may this change occur?

   c. What is the name of this kind of love?

4. a. List the three elements that Sternberg believes combine to produce liking and forms of love.

   1.   2.   3.

   b. Study Table 15.4 and describe some of the possible combinations of these factors and the resulting relationships.

5. Briefly discuss the possible evolutionary functions of love.

15-15 Discuss how the reproductive roles of men and women may influence their choice of a mate.

Read pages 517-518 and answer the following questions.

1. Review why the costs of sexual behaviour and reproduction are higher for women than for men.

2. As a result of their reproductive roles, what kind of mating strategy should men follow? women follow? (Buss, 1989; 1992; Symons, 1979)

3. What characteristics of a potential mate may be preferred by men? by women? (Buss, 1992; Kendrick et al., 1994)

4. a. In a survey of people representing 37 different cultures, how did men and women rate the importance of physical attractiveness? socioeconomic status? (Buss, 1990)

   b. What, therefore, is a good predictor of the socioeconomic status of a woman's husband? the gender of the older spouse at the time of marriage?

   c. How may these preferences influence the way men and women seek to attract each other? (Buss & Schmitt, 1993; Schmitt & Buss, 1996)

5. a. What task did Kendrick and his colleagues ask nearly 400 university students in heterosexual relationships to perform?

   b. What did they tell the students was the purpose of the experiment and what was the real purpose?

   c. What were the characteristics of the photographed men and women that influenced male and female subjects when they later rated their current dating partners? (See Figure 15.10 in your text.)

LESSON II SELF TEST

1. Subjects who were asked to estimate the length of lines went along with the group decision despite some doubts, which suggests
   a. that group pressure affects perceptions as well as behaviour.
   b. that the subjects found the other members of the group to be attractive.
   c. how strong the pressure to conform can be.
   d. that group pressure increases self-esteem.

2. A common reason why people fail to intervene in an emergency is that they
   a. may not feel competent to intervene.
   b. are indifferent.
   c. prefer anonymity.
   d. fear bystander disapproval.

3. Social facilitation suggests that the presence of others when a task is being performed
   a. increases arousal
   b. inhibits the dominant response.
   c. makes a simple task more difficult.
   d. makes a difficult task easier.

4. Social loafing occurs
   a. only when the task require physical effort.
   b. when people choose or are required to work alone.
   c. most often when the expectation of a reciprocal gesture is low.
   d. when individual contributions to the group effort are anonymous.

5. The reason most people find the results of Milgram's studies in which subjects "shocked" learners for incorrect responses surprising is because of the tendency to
   a. believe that most people do not wish to harm others.
   b. overestimate empathy for others.
   c. underestimate bystander indifference.
   d. make the fundamental attributional error.

6. _____ often causes group members to develop attitudes that are even stronger than their initial ones about a particular subject.
   a. Groupthink
   b. Social loafing
   c. Group polarization
   d. Social facilitation

7. People tend to choose
   a. partners who are about as physically attractive as they are.
   b. the most attractive partner they can.
   c. a less attractive partner to reduce the likelihood of rejection.
   d. a less attractive partner because they tend to have more interesting personalities.

8. According to Sternberg, which is the highest form of love?
   a. companionate
   b. passionate
   c. fatuous
   d. consummate

9. A good explanation for the responses of men interviewed on a suspension bridge and a conventional bridge is that the woman
   a. became a conditioned reinforcer because the presence of another person can reduce aversive arousal.
   b. was a source of heightened arousal.
   c. modelled acceptable behaviour in times of stress.
   d. became an aversive stimulus that threatened their self-esteem.

10. Research suggests that when evaluating a potential mate, men tend to emphasize _____, while women emphasize _____.
    a. socioeconomic status; intelligence
    b. physical attractiveness; socioeconomic status
    c. submissiveness; dominance
    d. willingness to work hard, youth

Answers to Self Tests

Lesson I

1. c   Obj. 15-1   2. b   Obj. 15-2   3. b   Obj. 15-3   4. a   Obj. 15-3   5. a   Obj. 15-4
6. a   Obj. 15-5   7. a   Obj. 15-6   8. b   Obj. 15-6   9. c   Obj. 15-6   10. b   Obj. 15-7

Lesson II

1. c   Obj. 15-8   2. a   Obj. 15-8   3. a   Obj. 15-9   4. d   Obj. 15-9   5. d   Obj. 15-11
6. c   Obj. 15-12   7. a   Obj. 15-13   8. d   Obj. 15-14   9. a   Obj. 15-14   10. b   Obj. 15-15

Life-Style, Stress, and Health

LESSON I

Read the interim summary on page 526 of your text to re-acquaint yourself with the material in this section.

16–1 Describe how cultural evolution influences life-style choices.

Read pages 524-526 and answer the following questions.

1. Cultural evolution is

   a. an adaptive change to

   b. driven by

   c. a product of

   d. a force behind

2. Explain

   a. some of the components of life-style.

   b. why there is no predominant modern life-style.

   c. some of the consequences of a healthy and an unhealthy life-style

3. a. How are unhealthy life-styles with their obvious negative biological consequences acquired and maintained?

   b. Why are the genes that contribute to this choice largely unaffected by the process of natural selection?

4. a. State the law of effect.

   b. Carefully explain how the reinforcing effects of unhealthy life-styles ultimately makes the law of effect work to our disadvantage?

Read the interim summary on page 535 of your text to re-acquaint yourself with the material in this section.

16-2 Describe the effects of nutrition and physical fitness on health.

Read pages 526-529 and answer the following questions.

1. Today, we consume considerably _____ fiber and considerably _____ fat than our ancestors did about 100 years ago. These dietary changes appear to contribute to the incidence of _____ _____ _____, the leading cause of death among people living in Western nations, and _____.

2. a. Where is serum cholesterol found naturally and what is its function?

   b. List the two forms of serum cholesterol.

      1.   2.

   c. Which one do we refer to as "good"? as "bad"? Why?

   d. How are LDL cholesterol levels affected by dietary fiber?

3. Study Figure 16.1 in your text and state the relationship between intake of fat and incidence of breast cancer. (Cohen, 1987)

4. Although we know which foods are healthy choices, why do we continue to eat too many that may be unhealthy? (Information on wise food choices is shown in Figure 16.2 in you text.)

5. Summarize some of the numerous health risks resulting from the lack of exercise. (Peters et al., 1983; Powell et al., 1987; Brown, 1991)

6. List the health risks that can be avoided by being physically fit. (Kaplan, 2000)

7. What general conclusion about exercise and health can be made from a sample of the results of a long-term longitudinal study of the lifestyles of Harvard University alumni? (Paffenbarger et al., 1986)

8. a. How is the body affected during aerobic exercise? as a result of regular aerobic exercise?

   b. How did regular aerobic exercise appear to affect the response to mental stress of a group of college students? (Kubitz and Landers, 1993)

16–3 Discuss research on the health effects of cigarette smoking and describe treatment programs for treating addiction to nicotine.

Read pages 529-531 and answer the following questions.

1. Summarize some of the documented health risks of smoking to smokers.

2. a. Discuss the health risks associated with passive smoking. Document research to support your answer. (Hirayama, 1981; He et al., 1999; Steenland et al., 1997; Benniger, 1999)

   b. Which group is particularly at risk of the consequences of second hand smoke? Discuss the health problems these individuals often demonstrate. (Adair-Gischoff & Sauve, 1998; Li et al., 1999)

3. a. Briefly summarize the patterns of tobacco use shown in Table 16.1 in your text.

   b. What has been the trend in tobacco use over the past decade? What, however, continues to be high?

4. Discuss reasons why adolescents being smoking (Barber et al., 1999; Biglan et al., 1995; Aloise-Young et al., 1984)

5. a. What do cigarette manufacturers capitalize on when advertising cigarettes?

   b. How do the companies typically portray cigarette smokers?

   c. Discuss the research relating smoking to advertising. (Pierce et al., 1998; Pierce & Gilpin, 1995)

   d. Are adolescents who smoke more likely to smoke as adults? Cite research to support your answer (Chassin et al., 1990)

6. Track the patterns in regulating tobacco advertising from 1988. What are some future regulations predicted to be?

7. a. What does it mean to be addicted to a drug such as nicotine? Be sure to use the terms tolerance, physical dependance, and psychological dependance in your answer.

   b. What are the physiological effects of nicotine on the heart and central nervous system?

8. Explain the role of positive and negative reinforcement in acquiring and maintaining an addiction.

9. Why is switching to low-nicotine cigarettes usually an unsuccessful way of decreasing the health risks of smoking?

10. a. Describe the transdermal patch and explain how it is used to help people who are trying to stop smoking.

    b. Compare the success rates of this treatment program with the success rates of other treatment programs. (Pomerleau, 1992)

    c. To underscore the importance of treatment and prevention programs, study the immediate and long-term benefits of not smoking shown in Table 16.2 in your text.

    d. Briefly outline the steps of the Waterloo Smoking Prevention Project. (Flay et al., 1985)

    e. How successful has this program been in the short-run? the long-run? (Muray et al., 1989)

    f. What can be done to improve the effectiveness of this program in the long run?

16-4 Describe research on the health effects of alcohol abuse and describe treatment programs for treating alcoholism.

Read pages 531-533 and answer the following questions.

1. Alcoholics are addicted to _____ the _____ substance in alcohol which affects the functioning of the _____ and _____ _____ _____. Within the population of _____ alcoholics in Canada today, males outnumber females by a ratio of _____ to _____ .

2. Summarize some of the serious consequences of alcohol abuse shown in Table 16.3 in your text.

3. a. Why is alcohol distributed so quickly throughout the body?

   b. Discuss how blood-levels of alcohol are affected by

      1. body weight and muscularity.

      2. stomach contents.

      3. alcohol metabolism by the liver.

4. Summarize the dangerous consequences of mixing alcohol with other drugs shown in Table 16.4 in your text.

5. Describe the withdrawal symptoms that alcoholics experience if they suddenly stop drinking.

6. a. If the children of alcoholic parents are raised by nonalcoholic adoptive parents, how likely are these children later to become alcoholics? (Vaillant and Milofsky, 1982; Cloninger, 1987)

   b. What do these findings suggest about the causes of alcoholism?

7. Compare the reasons why people start drinking with those for why they start smoking.

8. a. Outline some of the skills psychologists who work in drug abuse treatment programs attempt to teach their clients.

   b. How effective are abuse prevention programs? (Pomerleau, 1992)

16-5 Describe ways to reduce the spread of sexually transmitted diseases such as AIDS, discuss factors that contribute to a fear of people infected with AIDS.

Read pages 533-535 and answer the following questions.

1. Summarize some of the personal consequences of contracting a sexually-transmitted disease (STD) shown in Table 16.5 in your text.

2. a. List three ways that the human immunodeficiency virus (HIV) which eventually causes acquired immune deficiency syndrome (AIDS) is spread.

   1.   2.   3.

   b. Wahat percentage of HIV infections were transmitted by each?

   c. According to the World Health Organization, how many people were infected with HIV at the beginning of 2000?

3. Why do people such as intravenous drug users or couples about to engage in sex sometimes fail to follow practices that would reduce or prevent the transmission of HIV?

4. a. What are the goals of prevention programs to teach safer behaviour?

   b. What kind of personal or cultural beliefs reduce the effectiveness of these programs?

5. a. Explain how fear of contagion affects behaviour toward people who are sick.

   b. List the four conditions, all of which apply to the AIDS epidemic, that must exist for this phenomenon to occur.

      1.   3.

      2.   4.

6. Discuss the persistent belief that HIV can be acquired through casual contact. (Bishop, 1991a, 1991b)

Read the interim summary on page 537 of your text to re-acquaint yourself with the material in this section.

16-6 Describe how unhealthy life-styles can be changed by means of self control.

Read pages 536-537 and answer the following questions.

1. Once again state the two factors that influence behaviour.

2. Explain the exercise of self-control in terms of short-term and long-term reward.

3. Study Figure 16.3 in your text and explain why the value of a short-term reward sometimes outweighs the value of a long-term one and we make an unhealthy choice.

4. Explain how we can maintain the greater value of the long-term reward. Be sure to mention the *moment of decision* in your answer.

5. What is the goal of health psychologists?

LESSON I SELF TEST

1. The genes of individuals with unhealthy life-styles continue to be transmitted to succeeding generations because
   a. there is no dominant unhealthy life-style.
   b. biological evolution is not as powerful a force when population numbers in the millions as it does today.
   c. the consequences of unhealthy life-styles usually appear after the individual has already reproduced.
   d. advances in medicine can often reduce the consequences of an unhealthy life-style.

2. What is the leading cause of death of people living in Western countries?
   a. cancer
   b. car accidents
   c. CHD
   d. AIDS

3. _____ levels of _____ or cholesterol are associated with _____ rates of coronary heart disease.
   a. Low; low-density lipoprotein; "bad"; low
   b. High; low-density lipoprotein; "good" high
   c. High; high-density lipoprotein; "bad"; high
   d. Low; high-density lipoprotein; "good"; low

4. Research suggests that the incidence of breast cancer is highest in cultures where people eat large amounts of
   a. fibre.
   b. fat.
   c. protein.
   d. food grown using chemical fertilizers.

5. Like all reinforcers, nicotine stimulates the brain to secrete
   a. serotonin.
   b. dopamine.
   c. acetylcholine.
   d. endogenous opiates.

6. Blood alcohol levels are affected by a person's
   a. age.
   b. disposition.
   c. experience drinking alcohol.
   d. body weight.

7. Alcohol is metabolized by the liver
   a. at a slower rate in men than in women.
   b. at a higher rate in the presence of caffeine.
   c. at a rate that is related to the alcoholic content of the beverage.
   d. at a constant rate regardless of how much alcohol is consumed.

8. If fear of contagion is to occur the disease must _____
   a. be crippling but not fatal.
   b. incubate slowly.
   c. appear suddenly.
   d. mutate unexpectedly.

9. When you must choose between a short-term reward and a larger long-term reward, you are likely to choose the
   a. long term reward.
   b. long-term reward only in the presence of others.
   c. short-term reward.
   d. short-term reward only if others will not know.

10. The best way to exercise self control
    a. is to join a support group.
    b. to follow a program of behaviour modification.
    c. try to lead a healthy life-style which will eliminate taking steps to change an unhealthy one.
    d. make a prior commitment to a course of action that eliminates having to make a difficult choice.

LESSON II

Read the interim summary on pages 548-549 in your text to re-acquaint yourself with the material in this section.

16-7 Discuss the stress response and its physiological basis.

Read pages 538-540 and then answer the following questions.

1. Define *stress* and *stressor* in your own words.

2. a. Why was stress a useful behavioural adaptation for our ancestors that was selected for during biological evolution and why is it useful to us today? (Linsky et al., 1995)

   b. When does stress become harmful? (Selye, 1991)

3. a. In response to a stressor, the _____ signals the _____ gland and the _____ nervous system and changes begin to occur throughout the body.

   b. Carefully explain these resulting physiological changes.

      1. heart, blood flow, and blood sugar

      2. respiration

      3. digestion

      4. adrenal glands

   c. When do these responses become maladaptive?

4. List the three stages of response to stress of the general adaptation syndrome (GAS). Next to each stage note some of the physiological changes that occur.(See Figure 16.4 in your text. Selye, 1956)

   1.

   2.

   3.

5. Explain why long-term stress has harmful effects on health. Be sure to use the phrase *fight or flight response* in your answer.

6. How do the health histories of concentration camp survivors and air traffic controllers tend to confirm the explanation you have just given? (See Figure 16.5 in your text. Cohen, 1953; Cobb and Rose, 1973)

7. Which of the three components of emotion are responsible for the harmful effects of stress on health? How do they affect the body's energy resources?

8. Describe the hormonal response to stress. (See Figure 16.6 in your text.)

   a. List the hormones secreted by the adrenal glands when the body is under stress.

   b. How does epinephrine affect the body's energy supply?

   c. How do epinephrine and norepinephrine together affect the body and eventually contribute to cardiovascular disease?

   d. Explain why cortisol is referred to a glucocorticoid by describing its affects on the body.

9. a. What may be the consequence of subjecting a rat whose adrenal glands have been removed to stress?

   b. What precaution do physicians take when treating humans whose adrenal glands have been damaged or removed? (Tyrell and Baxter, 1981)

10. a. According to Selye (1976), what causes the harmful effects of stress?

    b. Summarize some of the short-term and long-term effects on health of prolonged stress.

11. a. What eventually happened to low status monkeys in a vervet monkey colony who were subjected to continuous stress by the others?

    b. Describe the physiological signs of chronic stress in the deceased monkeys. (Uno et al., 1989)

    c. Cite evidence that stress may cause brain degeneration in humans, as well. (Jensen et al., 1982)

16-8 Discuss the variables that affect stress reactions and explain how personality factors can influence the effects of stress on the development of cardiovascular disease and posttraumatic stress disorder.

Read pages 540-543 and answer the following questions.

1. a. What does Lazarus suggest is an important factor in determining the amount of stress we experience? (Lazarus & Folkman, 1984)

   b. Identify and describe the two steps in the cognitive appraisal of a particular stressor.

   c. What determines the level of stress we experience?

2. a. What research finding prompted Kobasa to analyze the psychological inventories of business executives who served as subjects? (Kobasa, 1979)

   b. What attitudes were characteristic of subjects who showed little, if any, risk for stress induced illness?

   c. What term does Kobasa use to refer to these individuals?

   d. What factors may be important in developing this trait? (Kobasa & Maddi, 1991)

3. List some serious health problems that may result from stressful life-styles.

4. a. List the two most important risk factors for CHD.

   b. What psychological factor may determine the likelihood of developing this disease?

   c. Briefly describe the cold pressor test.

   d. What did Wood et al. (1984) find when they checked the blood pressure of adults who had once participated in a cold pressor test.

   e. What do their findings suggest about the interaction between individual reaction to stress and cardiovascular disease?

5. a. What criterion did Manuck and his colleagues use to identify individual differences in reactivity to stress in monkeys who had been fed a high-cholesterol diet? (Manuck et al., 1983, 1986)

b. Which monkeys later had the highest rates of coronary heart disease?

c. What is a possible explanation of the results?

6. a. List some of the traits of the personality patterns identified by Friedman and Rosenman (1959, 1974).

Type A Pattern   Type B Pattern

b. Which group appears to be most susceptible to cardiovascular disease? (Rosenman et al., 1975; Review Panel, 1981)

c. What does other research suggest about personality type and CHD? (Pitts & Phillips, 1998)

7. Summarize research to identify personality variables that might affect the likelihood of developing cardiovascular heart disease.

How does type A behaviour appear to affect

1. smoking habits? (Howard et al., 1976; Lombardo & Carreno, 1987)

2. blood pressure and blood levels of cholesterol? (Howard et al., 1976; Irvine et al., 1991; Weidner et al., 1987)

8. a. Explain the cause and describe some of the symptoms of posttraumatic stress disorder.

b. What additional symptoms do children sometimes experience?

c. Describe the work of mental health professionals with victims of natural disasters and violent events.

d. Explain why people with PTSD often abuse alcohol.

16-9 Discuss how stress affects the immune system and contributes to the development of infectious diseases.

Read pages 543-546 and answer the following questions.

1. Define *psychoneuroimmunology* in your own words.

2. a. Let's construct an overview of the functions of the immune system. The white blood cells of the immune system develop in the _____ _____, and in the _____ _____. Some of these cells circulate in the _____, _____ _____ or _____ and others reside permanently in _____. _____.

    b. List the two types of specific immune reactions.

       1.   2.

    c. Briefly explain the chemically mediated reaction by explaining the relationship between

       1. antigens and antibodies.

       2. B-lymphocytes and immunoglobulins.

       3. immunoglobulins and antigens.

    d. Now briefly explain cell-mediated reaction. Be sure to explain where antibodies produced by T-lymphocytes are found.

To review these reactions study Figure 16.7 in your text.

3. What is the function of natural killer cells?

4. Describe two harmful immune system responses: allergic reactions and autoimmune diseases.

5. Outline a possible explanation of the neural control of the immune system by describing

    a. the effect of stress on the secretion of glucocorticoids.

    b. the role of the brain in glucocorticoid secretion.

    c. the effects of glucocorticoids on the immune system.

    d. the role of glucocorticoid receptors. (Solomon, 1987)

6. a. When rats were subjected to inescapable shock, what immune response occurred? Keller et al., 1983)?

b. Indicate what procedure abolished this response and explain why this result appears to confirm the effect of stress on glucocorticoids release. (Study Figure 16.8a in your text.)

c. What immune response was *not* abolished by the removal of the adrenal glands? What does this finding suggest about the way the effects of stress on the immune system are mediated? (Study Figure 16.8b in your text.)

7. a. Describe two effects of intermittent inescapable shock. (Shavit et al., 1984)

b. What evidence indicates that these effects are mediated by endogenous opiods?

c. Where in the body do these opiates appear to exert their effect on natural killer cells? (Shavit et al., 1986)

8. What stress-related responses sometimes occur

a. when a spouse dies?

b. during final examinations? (Glaser et al., 1987)

c. to patients with rheumatoid arthritis? (Feigenbaum et al., 1979)

d. when rats are handled or exposed to a cat? (Rogers et al., 1980)

9. a. State the hypothesis tested by Stone et al. (1987) in their study of the development of upper respiratory, diseases. (Stone et al., 1987)

b. Describe the set of records that volunteers were asked to keep.

c. Study Figure 16.9 in your text and describe the results.

d. Outline the explanation of the effect of mood on health suggested by the researchers. Be sure to use the term *immunoglobulin* in your answer.

10. Describe the effects of stress on the immune system of

   a. relatives of an Alzheimer's patient. (Kiecolt-Glaser et al., 1987)

   b. men before and after their wives died of breast cancer. (See Figure 16.10 in your text. Schleifer et al., 1983)

16-10 Discuss evidence concerning the existence of a cancer-prone personality.

Read pages 546-548 and answer the following questions.

1. a. What are some of the characteristics of type C personality—a concept introduced in the 1980s. (Morris, 1980; Temoshok et al., 1985)

   b. Why and how may these characteristics affect susceptibility to cancer? (Temoshok, 1987; Eysenck, 1988, 1994)

2. In a study of cancer patients, what two personality variables were related to the thickness of cancer tumours? (Temoshok et al., 1985)

3. In a large scale study of healthy people,

   a. who were the subjects and how long were they studied?

   b. what kind of tests and questionnaires were administered?

   c. which subjects were most likely to develop lung cancer? (Grossarth-Maticek et al., 1985)

4. a. Who are the subjects in an ongoing follow-up study? (Grossarth-Maticek & Eysenck, 1990)

   b. What kind of tests were administered?

   c. What are some of the initial findings?

5. Why are the results of studies of subjects who already have cancer difficult to interpret? (Borysenko, 1982; Shakin & Holland, 1988)

6. What other factor might also affect susceptibility to cancer?

7. a. If personality variables do suppress the immune system, what aspect of cancer is most likely affected?

   b. Why are most studies of stress and cancer in animals not relevant to cancer in humans? (Justice, 1987)

   c. What bodily mechanism is the most important defense against cancer in humans?

8. What can we conclude and what is still unknown about the role of personality variables in the development of cancer?

9. a. Why was a group of women with advanced breast cancer given psychotherapy in addition to standard medical treatment for their disease? (Spiegel et al., 1982)

   b. What were some of the benefits of the psychotherapy?

   c. Why did the researchers examine the medical records of their subjects years later? (Spiegel et al., 1989)

   d. What relation between psychotherapy and survival rate did they discover?

   e. What other factors could also account for prolonged survival?

10. Carefully explain why believing that positive or negative thinking alters the course of disease may be harmful.

Read the interim summary on page 554 of your text to re-acquaint yourself with the material in this section.

16–11 Discuss the sources of daily stress and describe some effective strategies for dealing with stress.

Read pages 549-554 and answer the following questions.

1. Why do some people who experience a series of stressors over a short period of time have a higher risk of illness while others who have similar experiences do not? (Holmes and Rahe, 1967; Rahe and Arthur, 1978; DuPue and Monroe, 1986)

2. Give an original example of these stressful situations

   a. an approach-approach conflict.

   b. an approach-avoidance conflict.

c. an avoidance-avoidance conflict.

3. a. What is the assumption of the Social Readjustment Rating Scale (SRRS)? (Holmes and Rahe, 1967)

   b. What are some life changes people taking the test were asked to rate and what unit was used to report their responses?

   c. What problems are associated with high scores? (Monroe et al., 1992)

4. a. Describe the kind of personal records that are used to compute a person's score on The Daily Hassles and Uplifts Scale.

   b. What kind of event is the best predictor of physical illness and adjustment problems? (DeLongis et al., 1988; Garret? et al., 1991)

5. a. Define *coping strategy* in your own words.

   b. What kind of responses are appropriate if a person follows a problem-focused coping strategy,? an emotion-focused coping strategy? (Lazarus & Folkman, 1984; Folkman & Lazarus, 1991)

Let's look at some strategies for coping with the stress of everyday life.

6. a. Who were the subjects in research to evaluate the role of aerobic exercise in stress reduction? (McCann and Holmes, 1984)

   b. What were subjects in each of the three testing groups asked to do?

   c. Which test group reported the greatest change in depression level?

   d. What kind of physiological changes may account for the benefits of aerobic exercise? psychological attitudes?

7. a. State the rationale for cognitive reappraisal

   b. Looking for a job is usually a stressful experience. How could cognitive reappraisal strategy be used to reduce stress.

   c. Discuss two benefits of this approach to stress reduction.

8. Outline the three steps of the progressive relaxation technique.

9. a. Define *social support* in your own words and explain why this coping strategy continues throughout life.

   b. List two benefits of turning to other people at stressful times.

10. a. What is the premise of stress inoculation training? (Meichenbaum, 1985, 1993)

    b. Where does training in this technique usually occur?

11. Let's look more closely at the procedure. Begin by listing the three phases of training and summarizing the goals of each.

Phase	Summary of Goals
1.	
2.	
3.	

12. a. Explain the transactional nature of stress and coping to be learned in Goal 1.

    b. Explain how keeping a diary of stressful events contributes to meeting Goal 2.

13. Describe how a plan and skills to cope with stress emerges by meeting Goals 3, 4, and 5.

14. a. Explain why imagery rehearsal is stressed in Goal 6.

    b. According to Goal 7, how can expected and unexpected stressors be handled?

To review: Table 16.6 in your text outlines the phases and goals of stress inoculation training.

LESSON II SELF TEST

1. The three stages of the general adaptation syndrome are
   a. avoidance, approach, and acceptance.
   b. denial, resistance, and resignation.
   c. appraisal, adjustment, acceptance.
   d. alarm, resistance, and exhaustion

2. Stress
   a. may accelerate the aging process.
   b. does not affect the elderly more than the young as long as the elderly remain in good health.
   c. does not affect the elderly as much as the young because the elderly have developed and practiced more coping responses.
   d. often causes brain damage in elderly, but not the young.

3. Most of the harmful effects of stress may be caused by
   a. the prolonged secretion of glucocorticoids.
   b. the prolonged interruption of glucocorticoid secretion.
   c. too few glucocorticoid receptors.
   d. understimulated glucocorticoid receptors.

4. People with Type A pattern are
   a. less likely to smoke.
   b. more likely to speak rapidly.
   c. more tolerant.
   d. less likely to suffer from CHD.

5. The immune system develops _____through exposure to _____.
   a. antibodies; antigens
   b. interferon; antibodies
   c. antigens; antibodies
   d. antibodies; B-lymphocytes

6. Research has shown that
   a. cell-mediated, but not chemically mediated immune reactions can be triggered by stressful situations.
   b. undesirable events can trigger illness by affecting the production of IgA.
   c. glucocorticoid receptors are destroyed by stress hormones.
   d. respiratory infections can be caused by a fall in blood levels of glucocorticoids.

7. For the results of research to determine whether personality variables affect the development of cancer to be valid
   a. subjects should be healthy at the beginning of the study.
   b. subjects should include both healthy people and those with cancer.
   c. only some of the subjects should later develop cancer.
   d. subjects with cancer should be tested before the disease affects their emotions and personality.

8. If personality variables increase the likelihood of developing cancer because of their effects on the immune system, these variables probably affect the
   a. particular type of cancer that develops.
   b. formation of tumours not their growth.
   c. growth of tumours, not their formation.
   d. success of chemotherapy and radiation treatments.

9. One of the benefits of coping with stress through a network of social support is that we can
   a. benefit from the experience of others.
   b. shift some personal responsibility to others.
   c. develop an emotion-focused coping strategy which is often more effective than problem-focused coping.
   d. reduce our reliance on personal cognitive reappraisal by listening to what others say.

10. Stress inoculation training
    a. usually takes place in a clinical setting.
    b. is most beneficial when the stressors are constant and inescapable.
    c. is ineffective if the stressors we later encounter are catastrophic.
    d. reduces encounters with avoidance/avoidance conflicts.

Answers to Self Tests

Lesson I

1. c	Obj. 16-1	2. c	Obj. 16-2	3. a	Obj. 16-2	4. b	Obj. 16-2	5. b	Obj. 16-3
6. d	Obj. 16-4	7. d	Obj. 16-4	8. c	Obj. 16-5	9. c	Obj. 16-6	10. d	Obj. 16-6

Lesson II

1. d	Obj. 16-7	2. a	Obj. 16-7	3. a	Obj. 16-7	4. b	Obj. 16-8	5. a	Obj. 16-9
6. b	Obj. 16-9	7. a	Obj. 16-10	8. c	Obj. 16-10	9. a	Obj. 16-11	10. a	Obj. 16-11

CHAPTER 17

The Nature and Causes of Mental Disorders

LESSON I

Read the interim summary on page 569 of your text to re-acquaint yourself with the material in this section.

17-1 Describe how the behaviour of people with mental illness is maladaptive and outline some current perspectives on the causes of mental illness.

Read pages 560-564 and answer the following questions.

1. a. Mental disorders are characterized by abnormal _____, _____, and _____.

    b. What is the most important features of a mental disorder?

2. In general, mental disorders are caused by interactions among what three factors?

3. a. According to the psychodynamic perspective, mental disorders originate from _____ _____ produced by the struggle between the three constructs of the mind hypothesized by _____: the _____, the _____, and the _____.

    b. When the mind's defence mechanisms are overwhelmed by this conflict, what symptoms may develop?

4. The _____ perspective is a major influence in the treatment of mental disorders today. Treatment is based on the premise that mental disorders are caused by specific _____ in the _____ and _____.

5. a. According to the cognitive-behavioural perspective, why does a person develop a mental disorder?

    b. What, then, should be the goal of treatment?

6. a. According to the humanistic perspective, what is the importance of unconditional positive regard for proper personality development and mental health?

    b. What does humanistic therapy urge people to achieve?

7. a. The_____ in which people live may play a significant role in the development of _____.

   b. How may sociocultural factors influence the interpretation of behaviour?

   c. Define culture-bound syndromes in your own words.

8. a. According to the diathesis-stress model, what combination of factors may predispose a person to develop a mental disorder?

   b. If a person has a predisposition toward a mental disorder, what factors may prevent it from developing?

17-2 Describe the Diagnostic and Statistical Manual IV (DSM-IV), some difficulties with this classification system and explain the importance of classifying mental disorders.

Read pages 564-566 and answer the following questions.

1. What is the name of the classification system for mental disorders most commonly used in North America?

2. a. Briefly explain how the five axes or criteria are used to make a diagnosis. A portion of these axes is shown in Table 17.1 in your text. Be sure to mention the GAF scale in your answer to number 5.

   1.

   2.

   3.

   4.

   5.

3. a. Why is diagnosis and treatment based on the DSM-IV consistent with the medical perspective?

   b. What other perspectives may, therefore, be overlooked?

4. Why is the diagnosis of mental disorders so difficult even when following the guidelines of the DSM-IV?

5. a. Explain how classifying a person's mental disorder may have serious consequences for the patient.

b. Briefly describe how Langer and Abelson (1974) demonstrated the prejudicial effect that labelling can have on clinical judgments. (See Figure 17.1 in your text.)

6. Why does Szasz (1960, 1993) argue against diagnosing and classifying mental disorders?

7. Describe the benefits of classifying mental disorders.

8. Which mental disorders appear to occur most frequently? (Study Table 17.2 in your text. Bland et al., 1988)

17-3 Describe the nature of clinical and actuarial diagnosis, and discuss research on their reliability and validity.

Read pages 567-568 and answer the following questions.

1. a. What are the two steps in the process of making clinical predictions about behaviour?

   b. What are some of the sources of data about individuals available to mental health professionals?

   c. Name the two methods of interpreting the data.

   d. What is the basis of clinical judgments made by mental health professionals? of actuarial judgments?

2. What must be done to make a fair comparison between these two methods of prediction? (Meehl, 1954)

3. a. What procedure did Goldberg (1970) devise to compare the accuracy of clinical and actuarial judgments?

   b. Compare the accuracy of the diagnoses made by clinicians drawing on their own experience and those made by following Goldberg's actuarial rule.

4. Compare the accuracy in diagnosing Alzheimer's disease using clinical and actuarial methods. (Leli and Filskov, 1984)

5. What is the consistent conclusion of over 100 studies comparing the accuracy of clinical and actuarial judgments in the social sciences? (Dawes et al, 1989)

6. Explain why actuarial judgments are usually more accurate.

    a. Why is the reliability of the actuarial method always higher than that of a clinical judgment? (Fries et al., 1986)

    b. List several other reasons that may account for inaccuracies in clinical judgment. (Greenwald et al., 1986)

7. How has modern technology made it easier for mental health professionals to use actuarial methods?

8. Why do many practitioners prefer using the clinical method and even avoid actuarial methods? (Guilmette et al., 1989; Dawes et al., 1989)

9. Because actuarial judgments are consistently more accurate, in what ways should mental health professionals redirect their professional activity?

Read the interim summary on page 579 of your text to re-acquaint yourself with the material in this section.

17-4 Describe the symptoms and possible causes of the major anxiety disorders: panic disorder, phobic disorders, and obsessive-compulsive disorder.

Read pages 569-574 and answer the following questions.

1. a. Define *neurosis in* your own words.

    b. Complete these sentences.

        1. Neurotics do not

        2. Neurotics almost always

    c. Describe how neuroses can disrupt a normal daily life.

    d. Define *anxiety* in your own words.

2. a. Briefly describe a panic attack, a characteristic of panic disorder.

   b. People with panic disorder often suffer from _____ _____ between panic attacks. Explain why they do.

   c. Explain how panic attacks may cause phobias. Be sure to refer to classical conditioning in your answer.

3. Discuss evidence that panic disorder may be a medical problem rather than a mental one.

   a. evidence for heritable trait (Knowles et al., 1999; Torgerson, 1983; Crowe et al., 1983)

   b. physiological response patterns that are biologically controlled (Ley, 1985; Stein et al., 1995)

   c. artificially induced attacks (Biber & Alkin, 1999; Crowley and Arana, 1990; Woods et al., 1988)

   d. sensitivity to bodily sensations

4. Explain how the expectation of facing and being overwhelmed by stressors may trigger an attack. (Mogg et al., 1993; Telch et al., 1989)

5. Define and distinguish between a specific fear and a phobic disorder. (See Table 17.3 in your text.)

6. Describe the following forms of phobic disorders recognized by the DSM-IV. Be sure to mention the incidence either in the general population or between the sexes, age of onset of symptoms, and then explain how severely they disrupt daily life.

   a. agoraphobia

   b. social phobia

   c. specific phobia

7. a. How does psychoanalytic theory explain phobias?

   b. What explanation for the way phobias develop is widely accepted by clinical psychologists and behaviourists?

   c. Discuss several observations that suggest that learning through classical conditioning is not a complete explanation for the origin of phobias.

8. Discuss the biological basis of phobias.

   a. Describe the stimuli and experimental procedure used by Ohman & Soares (1998) to investigate a possible biological explanation for phobias.

   b. Which stimuli were more resistant to extinction?

   c. What evidence suggests that these responses occur without awareness?

   d. What do the results suggest?

9. Define the two components of obsessive-compulsive disorder in your own words.

10. State the incidence of obsessive-compulsive disorder in the general population and between the sexes, age of onset of symptoms, and how it disrupts daily life. (Robbins and Regier, 1991; Sturgis, 1993; Turner et al., 1985)

11. a. List the two principal kinds of obsessions and give an example of each.

    b. List the four categories of compulsions and give an example of each.

12. a. Explain how a normal behaviour such as thinking about other things can develop into an obsession. Be sure to mention the role of reinforcement in your answer.

    b. Explain the kind of behaviour and competencies people with obsessive-compulsive disorder believe they should exhibit and how this belief may explain their checking behaviour? (Sarason and Sarason, 1993)

13. a. Discuss the evidence suggesting that obsessive-compulsive disorder may have genetic causes. (Pauls & Alsobrook, 1999; Nestadt et al., 2000)

    b. Describe Tourette's syndrome and explain how it may be associated with obsessive-compulsive disorder. (Pauls & Leckman, 1986; Alsobrook & Pauls, 1997; Cath et al., 2000)

c. What are several nongenetic causes of obsessive-compulsive disorder? (Hollander et al., 1990)

17-5 Describe the symptoms and possible causes of somatization disorder and conversion disorder.

Read pages 574-576 and answer the following questions.

1. a. List the two most important somatoform disorders.

   1.   2.

   b. Describe somatization disorder, its incidence in men and women, and the criteria set by the DSM-IV for this diagnosis. (Reiger et al., 1988)

   c. Describe hypochondriasis and explain how it differs from somatization disorder.

2. Describe the following evidence that suggests that somatization disorder may be hereditary.

   a. incidence among first degree female relatives of people with the disorder (Coryell, 1980)

   b. evidence of association with other serious behaviour problems (Guze et al, 1967; Woerner and Guze, 1968)

3. Describe conversion disorder and the criteria set by the DSM-IV for this diagnosis.

4. Describe the case of the new father, Mr. L., in order to explain the origins and symptoms of conversion disorder. (Hofling, 1963)

5. Define *malingering* in your own words.

6. Briefly explain how to distinguish between conversion disorder and

   a. malingering.

   b. somatization disorder.

c. Explain how the physical symptoms of people with conversion disorder change with the times. (See Figure 17-2 in your text)

7. According to psychoanalytic theory, what is the primary cause of conversion disorders?

8. a. Describe two conditions that support the suggestion of behaviourists that conversion disorders may be learned. (Ullman and Krasner, 1969)

   b. Now describe the case of the soldier with an eye injury that illustrates how both of these conditions contribute to the problem. (Brady and Lind, 1961)

17-6 Describe the symptoms and possible causes of the major dissociative disorders and culture-bound syndromes.

Read pages 576-578 and answer the following questions.

1. How do dissociative disorders differ from somatoform disorders?

2. Define dissociative amnesia. What kinds of events may lead to this disorder?

3. What are the distinguishing characteristics of dissociative fugue and dissociative identity disorder?

4. What tragic childhood experience have the majority of persons with dissociative identity disorder endured?

5. a. How did Spanos (1996) explain multiple personality disorder?

   b. Briefly describe research with normal subjects to test their ability to assume several personalities. (Spanos et al., 1985)

   c. What do the results suggest is the best way to approach a diagnosis of multiple personality disorder?

6. a. In general, what kind of conflict may cause a person to develop a dissociative disorder?

   b. What advantage does each of the three principal forms of dissociative disorder offer a person?

7. Define *culture-bound syndrome* in your own words and give several examples.

8. Discuss some of the difficulties in trying to determine the causes of culture-bound syndromes.

9. What observations suggests that some culture-bound syndromes are learned responses to environmental events or situations?

LESSON I SELF TEST

1. The _____ perspective states that mental disorders _____.
   a. cognitive-behavioural; are a result of our evolutionary history
   b. medical; are learned maladaptive behaviour patterns
   c. humanistic; are labeled and treated according to sociocultural variables
   d. psychodynamic; arise from intrapsychic conflict

2. The Diagnostic and Statistical Manual IV diagnostic criteria
   a. discourage treatment of hopeless cases.
   b. facilitate research on the causes and treatments of mental disorders.
   c. are cross-indexed to accepted treatments.
   d. eliminates the possibility of multiple diagnoses.

3. An advantage of a classification system for mental disorders is that
   a. it provides a completely reliable basis for diagnosis.
   b. diagnosing a mental disorder explains its causes.
   c. the search for beneficial treatments is facilitated.
   d. medical professionals, rather than patients, assume responsibility for their care.

4. _____ judgments are more accurate than _____ judgments because _____.
   a. Clinical; actuarial; there is no substitute for professional experience
   b. Clinical; actuarial; professionals follow heuristic rules in making diagnoses
   c. Actuarial; clinical; more data can be organized and retrieved by using a computer or a formula
   d. Actuarial; clinical; actuarial formulas can account for inaccurate or evasive responses from patients

5. Panic attacks
   a. are immediately followed by anticipatory anxiety.
   b. may be mistaken for a heart attack.
   c. can be successfully controlled with injections of lactic acid.
   d. may result from an inherited tendency to overreact to unusual bodily sensations.

6. People with obsessive-compulsive disorder
   a. fail to recognize how their compulsive behaviour controls their lives.
   b. obtain pleasure from performance of their compulsive behaviours.
   c. realize that their thoughts and behaviours are senseless.
   d. are especially susceptible to acquiring phobias through classical conditioning.

7. People with somatization disorder
   a. have an excessive fear of becoming ill.
   b. complain of symptoms that have no physiological cause.
   c. have a real illness that is made worse by physiological problems.
   d. have a neurological problem with a psychological rather than a physical cause.

8. People with conversion disorders
   a. are almost always women.
   b. do not appear to be upset by their symptoms.
   c. are reluctant to talk about their symptoms.
   d. are usually malingering.

9. A disorder in which the person temporarily forgets who they are and may relocate and adopt a new identity defines
   a. dissociative amnesia.
   b. dissociative fugue.
   c. dissociative identity disorder.
   d. malingering.

10. People with dissociative identity disorder
    a. tend to resist being hypnotized.
    b. often have a high number of convictions for child abuse.
    c. may be simulating their condition and should be regarded with skepticism.
    d. follow consistent behavioural patterns regardless of which personality dominates at a particular time.

L E S S O N I I

Read the interim summary on page 582 of your text to re-acquaint yourself with the material in this section.

17-7 Describe the symptoms and possible causes of antisocial personality disorder.

Read pages 579-582 and answer the following questions.

1. What is a personality disorder? (See Table 17.4 in your text for descriptions of various personality disorders.)

2. a. Outline some of the diagnostic criteria set by the DSM-IV for antisocial personality disorder.

   b. What is the approximate incidence in men? in women?

   c. What are some of prominent personality characteristics of psychopaths, as identified by Cleckley (1976) and shown in Table 17.5 in your text?

3. Refer to both the diagnostic criteria and Cleckley's list and describe the life-style of a psychopath.

4. What are some typical reasons provided by criminal psychopaths for why they commit crimes? (Hare, 1999; Hare et al., 1988)

5. a. What did Cleckley (1976) suggest is the defect that characterizes the psychopath?

   b. What do some investigators believe to be the cause of their inability to experience normal emotions?

6. Summarize research on the emotional responses of psychopaths.

   a. Describe the procedure and results of research by Hare (1965) and Williamson et al. (1991) on anticipatory, fear responses of psychopaths.

   b. Now describe the procedure and results of research by Schmauk (1970) on the degree to which psychopaths respond to various forms of aversive stimuli.

7. What were the conclusions of research by Mednick et al., 1983 on the effect of being the biological son of a convicted criminal being raised in an adoptive family? (See Figure 17.3 in your text.)

8. Describe how antisocial personality disorder may arise from

   a. parental lack of supervision and attention.

   b. a child's perceptions of the social environment.

Read the interim summary on page 584 of your text to re-acquaint yourself with the material in this section.

17-8 Describe the symptoms and possible causes of psychoactive substance abuse disorders.

Read pages 582-584 and answer the following questions.

1. List two psychoactive substance use disorders recognized by the DSM-IV.

   1.   2.

2. Explain how the reinforcing effects of certain drugs contribute to their abuse.

3. Restate the only two possible sources of individual differences.

4. Why has most research on the effects of heredity on addiction focused on alcohol rather than other drugs?

5. In Canada, approximately _____ percent of the population has problems associated with alcohol.

6. Study Table 17.6 in your text and then fill in the blanks in the table below.

7. a. Compare the incidence of steady drinking among the adopted biological sons of fathers who were steady drinkers with the biological sons of fathers who did not abuse alcohol. (Cloninger et al., 1985)

   b. What influence, if any, did the adoptive family environment have on the drinking habits of their adoptive sons?

   c. How did having a biological father who was a steady drinker affect daughters?

Feature	Types of Alcoholism	
Usual age of onset (years)		
Spontaneous alcohol seeking (inability to abstain)		
Fighting and arrests when drinking		
Psychological dependence (loss of control)		
Guild and fear about alcohol dependence		
Novelty seeking		
Harm avoidance		
Reward dependence		

8. Briefly explain how heredity and environment interact to influence binge drinking in males and females.

9. What are some of the ways heredity could influence a susceptibility to alcohol? What effect do researchers believe is most likely responsible?

10. Summarize research on the behaviour of steady and binge drinkers that suggests biological brain differences.

    a. Briefly describe and compare some strong personality tendencies observed in steady drinkers and binge drinkers. (Cloninger, 1987)

b. What does little slow alpha activity in the EEGs of binge drinkers suggest about their arousal levels? (Propping et al., 1981)

c. What do these binge drinkers report they feel when they are drinking? (Propping et al., 1980)

d. How might the behaviour of steady drinkers be affected by an undersensitive punishment mechanism? an undersensitive reinforcement system?

e. How might the behaviour of binge drinkers be affected by an oversensitive punishment system?

11. a. How does alcohol affect the brains of alcohol-preferring rats? alcohol-nonpreferring rats? (Fadda et al., 1990)

b. Which animals may sustain a stronger reinforcing effect from alcohol?

12. a. What kind of perceived personal shortcomings may lead to alcohol use?

b. Explain how alcohol use may lead to alcohol abuse through negative reinforcement.

Read the interim summary on page 590 of your text to re-acquaint yourself with the material in this section.

17-9 Describe the characteristic symptoms of schizophrenia and the major types of schizophrenic disorders.

Read pages 584-586 and answer the following questions.

1. Explain the controversy that surrounds the study of schizophrenia.

2. Approximately what percentage of the Canadian population is afflicted with schizophrenia? (Bland et al., 1988)

3. How is the term *schizophrenia* often misused?

4. List the two categories of symptoms of schizophrenia and distinguish between them.

1.   2.

5. Discuss some of the positive symptoms.

   a. Identify and describe the most important positive symptom of schizophrenia.

   b. Define delusion in your own words and explain the following types of delusions.

      1. delusions of persecution

      2. delusions of grandeur

      3. delusions of control

   c. Define *hallucination* in your own words and describe some of the kinds of hallucinations that schizophrenics experience.

6. Identify some of the negative symptoms.

7. What may be the physiological basis of the positive symptoms? the negative symptoms?

8. Define *undifferentiated schizophrenia* in your own words. When is it an appropriate diagnosis?

9. Describe the catatonic postures and waxy flexibility characteristic of catatonic schizophrenia.

10. a. What are the most important symptoms of paranoid schizophrenia?

    b. Why are the delusions of paranoid schizophrenics often rich in detail?

11. Describe the prominent symptoms of disorganized schizophrenia. Be sure to use the term *word salad* in your answer. (Snyder, 1974)

17-10 Discuss and evaluate research on the early predictors of schizophrenia and the role of heredity in the development of this disorder.

Read pages 586-587 and answer the following questions.

1. Define and distinguish between *reactive* and *process schizophrenia* first suggested by Bleuler.

2. Why is it important to identify the early signs of schizophrenia?

3. a. When viewers watched home movies taken during the childhood of people with adult-onset schizophrenia, what did they observe? (Walker & Lewine, 1990)

   b. In what ways did the children who later became schizophrenics differ from normal children? What do their observations suggest about the possibility of identifying early predictors?

4. State the predominant view of the causes of schizophrenia.

5. a. Compare the concordance rates for the heritability of a tendency toward schizophrenia for identical and fraternal twins and the children of schizophrenic parents even if they have been adopted. (Gottesman & Moldin, 1998; Gottesman & Shields, 1982; Gottesman, 1991)

   b. Now study Table 17.7 in your text and describe how the incidence of schizophrenia varies with the relation to a person identified as schizophrenic.

6. a. Carefully explain how most investigators believe heredity and environment interact to cause schizophrenia.

   b. Explain what it means for a set of twins to be discordant for schizophrenia.

   c. Study Figure 17.4 in your text and describe the findings of research to determine the number of schizophrenic children of fraternal and identical twins discordant for schizophrenia. (Gottesman & Bertelsen, 1989)

   d. Explain how the results support the notion that schizophrenia, while heritable, is probably triggered by environmental factors.

17-11 Discuss research on the physiological causes of schizophrenia.

Read pages 587-589 and answer the following questions.

1. a. What is the pharmacological effect of cocaine and amphetamine and the antipsychotic drugs?

    b. What is the effect of these drugs on the symptoms of schizophrenia?

    c. Outline the dopamine hypothesis of schizophrenia that was suggested by the effects of these drugs.

2. Now use what you learned in Chapter 4 about synapses and transmitter substances to explain the effects of cocaine, amphetamines, and the antipsychotic drugs in the brain.

3. What symptoms of schizophrenia are alleviated by antipsychotic drugs? What symptoms are not alleviated? (Angrist et al., 1980)

4. Describe brain damage discovered in the brains of schizophrenics that may account for the negative symptoms of this disease. (Pfefferbaum et al., 1988; Sullivan et al., 1998; Zipursky et al., 1998)

5. When researchers compared the MRI scans of monozygotic twins discordant for schizophrenia, what differences did they observe in almost all of the schizophrenic twins? (Study Figure 17.5 in your text. Suddath et al., 1990)

6. What changes in the brain were observed in adolescents with schizophrenia? (Rapoport et al., 1999)

7. Summarize evidence that the observed brain damage in schizophrenics may be caused by a virus.

    a. Compare the backgrounds of people most likely to develop schizophrenia and multiple sclerosis as well as the general course of both diseases. (Stevens, 1988)

    b. People born during the _____ months are more likely to develop schizophrenia later in life. The seasonality effect, seen most strongly in poor, urban locations, may result from seasonal variations in _____ factors or _____ or _____ agents in the air, food. or water. (Torrey et al., 1977; Machon et al., 1983)

    c. When is the developing brain most susceptible to damage?

d. Which offspring of Finnish mothers who contracted type A2 influenza while pregnant were most likely to develop schizophrenia later in life? (See Figure 17.6 in your text. Mednick et al., 1990)

8. What is a third possible cause of brain damage leading to the negative symptoms of schizophrenia? (Schwarzkopf et al., 1989)

17-12 Discuss research on the cognitive and environmental causes of schizophrenia.

Read pages 589-590 and answer the following questions.

1. Describe and explain how parental traits may be associated with a higher incidence of schizophrenia. Be sure to use the term *double-bind* in your answer. (Roff & Knight, 1981)

2 What did Lidz et al. (1965) conclude about the family atmosphere of 14 schizophrenic people?

3. a. Define *expressed emotion* in your own words and go on to explain how it may affect recovery from schizophrenia. (Brown et al., 1966; Brown, 1985)

   b. Describe evidence that suggests that the role of expressed emotion is common to all cultures? (Jenkins & Karno, 1992)

   c. List the two elements of expressed emotion.

      1.   2.

   d. Circle the culture in which expressed emotion tends to be higher.   industrialized   nonindustrialized

   e. Outline the reasons why this difference may occur

Read the interim summary on pages 595-596 of your text to reacquaint yourself with the material in this section.

17-13 Describe the symptoms of bipolar disorder and major depression and discuss research on their possible cognitive causes.

Read pages 590-593 and answer the following questions.

1. Briefly describe the most severe mood disorders: bipolar disorder and major depression.

2. Distinguish between major depression and two other forms of depression: dysthymic disorder and cyclothynic disorder.

3. a. Describe the thoughts and behaviour that people with bipolar disorder often experience during an episode of mania. (Davison & Neale, 1990)

   b. According to many therapists, how does mania appear to differ from happiness?

   c. In general, how long do these alternating episodes last?

4. a. List the five cardinal symptoms of depression identified by Beck (1967).

   b. Distinguish between major depression and grief.

   c. How may major depression affect people's thought processes?

5. Briefly explain how major depression affects a sufferer's interpersonal relationships and already negative outlook. (See Figure 17.7 in your text. Klerman & Weissman, 1986)

6. a. According to Beck (1967, 1991), what is the principal cause of depression? the cognitive triad?

   b. What is the utility of his approach?

7. a. Explain how a person's attributional style may predispose him or her to depression. (Abramson et al., 1978; Abramson et al., 1989)

   b. When is a person with a negative attributional style most likely to develop depression? (Abramson et al., 1995)

   c. Evidence indicates that a combination of a _____ _____ and _____ life events is predictive of depression.

   d. How may a negative attribution style also affect positive events?

17-14 Discuss research on the genetic and physiological causes of mood disorders.

Read pages 593-595 and answer the following questions.

1. Cite evidence that suggests mood disorders are heritable. (Rosenthal, 1970; Allen, 1976)

2. a.   What does the effectiveness of drug therapies suggest about the cause of mood disorders?

   b.   What neurotransmitters have been related to depression? How do levels of these neurotransmitters compare across people with and without the disorder?

   c.   Name the drug that is an effective treatment for bipolar disorder.

3. How does the reserpine, a drug sometimes used to treat high blood pressure, affect the brain? What side effect results and what does it suggest about the cause of major depression.

4. a.   How do researchers study the brain biochemistry of depressed people?

   b.   Compare the level of a compound produced when serotonin is broken down (5-HIAA) in the cerebrospinal fluid of depressed people who attempted suicide and normal people. (Träskmann et al., 1981)

   c.   What did an analysis of the urine of patients with mood disorders reveal? (Taube et al., 1978)

5. Describe research that suggests a biochemical imbalance may not be the first stage of depression. (Miller et al., 1977)

6. a.   Compare the sleep patterns of people suffering from a severe mood disorder and people suffering from the less severe dysthymic disorder.

   b.   How does the REM sleep cycle of depressed people differ from normal? (Kupfer, 1976)

   c.   If depressed people are deprived of REM sleep in the laboratory, how is depression affected? (Vogel et al., 1980)

d. Review how ECT and antidepressant drugs act to support the role of REM sleep in depression. (Scherschlicht et al., 1982)

7. a. Define *zeitgeber* in your own words and give an example of a physical and a social zeitgeber.

    b. What changes were observed in the biological or behavioural rhythms of depressed people who were recently widowed? (Flaherty et al., 1987)

    c. Summarize the hypothesis suggested by Ehlers et al. (1988) that accounts for both biological and environmental events that seem to trigger depression.

8. a. In what ways are the symptoms of depression and seasonal affective disorder similar? different?

    b. Explain the cause and describe the treatment for seasonal affective disorder. (Dalgleish et al., 1996; Lamberg, 1998; Lee & Chan, 1999)

    c. Describe observational and research data that suggests that some of the brain mechanisms involved in seasonal depression may also be involved in hibernation. (Rosenthal et al., 1986; Zvolsky et al., 1981)

9. a. What kind of sleep deprivation relieves depression immediately? produces long-lasting effects? (See Figure 17.8 in your text.)

    b. Study Figure 17.9 in your text and trace the pattern of mood changes reported by people who responded to sleep deprivation. (Wu & Bunney, 1990) How did a self-report of feelings of depression change after a night of total sleep deprivation? a night of normal sleep?

    c. Why, according to Wu and Bunney, may depression return when patients are permitted to sleep normally again?

    d. Although total sleep deprivation as a cure for depression is impractical, which people are most likely to respond positively to this treatment? (Reinick et al., 1990)

LESSON II SELF TEST

1. A common trait of a psychopath is
   a. truthfulness.
   b. lack of interest in sex.
   c. lack of guilt or remorse.
   d. social ineptitude.

2. Psychopathic subjects who were taught an avoidance task learned best when the aversive stimulus was
   a. an electric shock.
   b. the experimenter saying "wrong."
   c. loss of a quarter.
   d. disapproval from confederate subjects.

3. _____ drinkers begin drinking _____ in life and tend to _____.
   a. Binge; later; be anxiety-ridden
   b. Binge; later; have antisocial tendencies
   c. Steady; early; be anxiety-ridden
   d. Steady; later; have antisocial tendencies

4. Steady drinkers may have an _____ punishment mechanism and an _____ reinforcement mechanism.
   a. undersensitive; undersensitive
   b. oversensitive; undersensitive
   c. undersensitive; oversensitive
   d. oversensitive; oversensitive

5. The positive symptoms of schizophrenia are known by their
   a. absence of normal behaviour.
   b. presence.
   c. changing nature.
   d. unchanging nature.

6. When we say that schizophrenia is a heritable disease, we mean that
   a. a person who has inherited a "schizophrenia gene" will eventually develop the disease.
   b. a person inherits a tendency toward schizophrenia which may be triggered in certain environments.
   c. the likelihood of a person with a "schizophrenia gene" developing the disease is influenced solely by the biological family history.
   d. it is not possible to carry an unexpressed "schizophrenia gene."

7. Amphetamine and cocaine _____ symptoms of schizophrenia presumably because they _____ dopamine receptors.
   a. reduce; cause the stimulation of
   b. reduce; block
   c. cause; cause the stimulation of
   d. cause; block

8. Expressed emotion
   a. helps a person combat schizophrenia because it shows that family members care deeply about the person.
   b. interferes with recovery from schizophrenia.
   c. seems to be a culture-bound phenomenon.
   d. is highest in non-industrialized cultures.

9. Mania is
   a. characterized by wild, excited behaviour.
   b. indistinguishable from true happiness.
   c. seldom seen in women.
   d. usually a successful defense against depression.

10. The cerebrospinal fluid of depressed people contains significantly lower than normal levels of
    a. lithium carbonate.
    b. chlorpromazine.
    c. a compound produced by the breakdown of serotonin.
    d. a compound produced by the breakdown of norepinephrine.

Answers for Self Tests

Lesson I

1. d	Obj. 17-1	2. b	Obj. 17-2	3. c	Obj. 17-2	4. c	Obj. 17-3	5. d	Obj. 17-4
6. c	Obj. 17-4	7. b	Obj. 17-5	8. b	Obj. 17-5	9. b	Obj. 17-6	10. c	Obj. 17-6

Lesson II

1. c	Obj. 17-7	2. c	Obj. 17-7	3. a	Obj. 17-8	4. a	Obj. 17-8	5. b	Obj. 17-9
6. b	Obj. 17-10	7. c	Obj. 17-11	8. b	Obj. 17-12	9. a	Obj. 17-13	10. c	Obj. 17-14

CHAPTER 18

The Treatment of Mental Disorders

LESSON I

Read the interim summary on page 603 of your text to re-acquaint yourself with the material in this section.

18-1 Describe the early treatment of the mentally ill and outline the historical development of psychotherapy.

Read pages 600-603 and answer the following questions.

1. a. Summarize some of the earliest beliefs about the causes of mental illness and the first attempts at "treatment" beginning with *trephining*. (See Figure 18.1 in your text.)

    b. How did Johann Wier in the 16th century attempt to change prevailing attitudes toward the mentally ill?

    c. Describe how, despite changing attitudes, the mentally ill continued to be mistreated.

    d. Briefly describe Philippe Pinel's reforms and their effect, especially on reform in the United States, led by Dorothea Dix.

2. What treatment did Mesmer develop?

3. How did the apparently successful treatment of hysteria through hypnosis change the direction of Charcot's research?

4. How did Charcot influence Freud?

5. Briefly describe the eclectic approach to psychotherapy.

Read the interim summary on page 608 of your text to re-acquaint yourself with the material in the section.

18–2 Describe the treatment of mental disorders by means of traditional and modern psychoanalysis.

Read pages 603–605 and answer the following questions.

1. a. Define *insight psychotherapy* in your own words, paying special attention to the presumed cause and cure of mental conflicts.

   b. Give two examples of insight psychotherapies.

2. a. Define *psychoanalysis* in your own words.

   b. What is the purpose of therapy?

   c. What is the role of the psychoanalyst? the client?

   d. What may hamper clients from accurately interpreting the clues to their own conflicts?

3. Why did Freud use the technique of free association, and what two steps did he take to encourage clients?

4. Why is dream interpretation an important component of psychoanalysis? (Be sure to mention the manifest and latent content of dreams.)

5. When clients show resistance, how do they behave? What do therapists believe resistance indicates?

6. a. Explain the transference that develops between therapist and patient and why it is considered an essential step in therapy.

   b. Now explain countertransference and how a therapist may attempt to guard against its occurrence.

7. By what other name is psychoanalysis often known today?

8. Let's look at how psychoanalysis as conceived of by Freud has changed.

   a. What aspects of the unconscious are emphasized less today? more today?

   b. How has the range of experiences to be examined expanded?

   c. Explain how beliefs about the role and strength of the ego have changed.

   d. How has the notion about the length of analysis changed? (Binder, 1998)

   e. Briefly describe time-limited therapy including the number of sessions, its basis in Freudian theory, and its goals. (Strupp, 1993)

18-3 Discuss the treatment of mental disorders by means of client-centred and Gestalt therapies and evaluate the effectiveness of insight therapies.

Read pages 606-608 and answer the following questions.

1. State the aim and underlying assumptions of humanistic therapy and list two major forms.

   1.   2.

2. a. Why did Rogers develop client-centered therapy?

   b. Why is this an appropriate name?

   c. According to Rogers, psychological problems are caused by an _____ between what people are, their _____ _____, and what they would like to be, their _____ _____.

3. Summarize the role of the therapist in client-centered therapy.

   a. Describe how reflection is used and its importance in treatment.

   b. Why must a client-centred therapist be an empathetic person in order to be effective?

   c. Describe an atmosphere of unconditional positive regard and explain its importance in treatment.

   d. Unconditional positive regard does not necessarily mean acceptance of the patient's _____. The key is that the therapist has an abiding belief in the _____ _____ and _____ of the client.

4. a. Why did Perls (1969) develop Gestalt therapy?

   b. What two concepts are emphasized?

5. Summarize the role of the therapist in Gestalt therapy.

   a. How does the therapist assist the client to understand dreams, thought to be an important source of information?

   b. Describe the empty chair technique. Why does the therapist use this technique as well as encourage the client to talk to themselves or objects?

   c. When does the therapist challenge a client's statements?

6. Evaluate the effectiveness of insight psychotherapies.

   a. Outline the reasons why it is impossible to obtain a random sample of patients for evaluation of psychoanalysis.

   b. How did Rogers encourage evaluation of his own technique?

   c. How did Truax analyze Rogers's interactions with his clients and what did the analysis reveal about Rogers's responses? (Truax, 1966)

   d. What change did Rogers make as a result of Truax's findings?

   e. What conditions and what kind of patients respond best to insight psychotherapies?

Read the interim summary on page 617 of your text to re-acquaint yourself with the material in this section.

18-4 Describe the use of therapies based on classical conditioning: systematic desensitization, implosion therapy, and aversion therapy.

Read pages 608-610 and answer the following questions.

1. a. Insight therapist believe that maladaptive behaviour is a _____ of the psychological problem but behaviour therapists believe that maladaptive behaviour is the _____.

   b. The methods used by behaviour therapists are based on what kind of research?

c. Consider the example of the anxiety a person feels the first time he or she gets in a car after being in an accident. Identify the CS, UCS, CR, and UCR.

2. a. Define the goal of systematic desensitization in your own words.

b. Carefully describe the steps that are followed during the desensitization procedure. (See Table 18.1 in your text.)

c. Refer to the principles of classical conditioning to explain why each step in the procedure is essential. Cite research to support your answer. (Johnson & Sechrest, 1968)

d. How do these encounters differ for clients undergoing implosion therapy?

3. a. Define *aversion therapy* in your own words.

b. Describe how inappropriate behaviours can be treated using aversive classical conditioning, explain why such therapy must be voluntary, and evaluate its effectiveness. (Smith, Frawley, & Polissar, 1997)

18-5 Describe the use of therapies based on operant conditioning: token economies, modelling, assertiveness therapy, extinction, and punishment of maladaptive behaviours.

Read pages 610-614 and answer the following questions.

1. a. In general, how does behaviour modification therapy encourage desirable behaviours? discourage undesirable behaviours?

b. Suggest some of the problems for which behaviour modification is used.

2. a. Explain why a system of *token economies* was developed and how it operates in large institutions for the mentally ill. (See Figure 18.3 in your text.)

b. Give two reasons why token economies can be difficult to implement.

c. Review the overjustification effect discussed in Chapter 13, and explain how a token economy can decrease intrinsic motivation.

3. a. Summarize Bandura's (1971) description of a modelling session to help people overcome a severe fear of snakes.

    b. Explain some of the reasons why modelling is effective.

    c. How does successfully overcoming a phobia affect a person's self-confidence?

4. a. What kind of skills do clients learn during assertiveness therapy?

    b. When is it an appropriate choice?

    c. Briefly describe the important steps in the procedure.

    d. Outline a possible explanation of why assertiveness therapy is effective.

5. a. Once again, define *extinction* in your own words.

    b. Explain several difficulties with using extinction to eliminate maladaptive behaviour. Be sure to mention extinction burst in your answer.

6. a. Describe two situations that often undermine the effectiveness of punishment.

    b. Nevertheless, we continue to use punishment. Why?

7. a. Under what circumstances is punishment the most effective technique for eliminating undesirable behaviour? Cite research to support your answer. (Cowart & Whaley, 1971)

    b. According to Carr and Lovaas (1983), at what point during therapy is it appropriate to consider the use of aversive methods?

    c. Describe the use of covert sensitization. Be sure to explain the nature of the aversive stimulus in this type of therapy.

8. What difficulty with behaviour therapy was revealed by work with chronic alcoholics?

9. Outline some techniques behaviour therapists use to facilitate generalization of new behaviours to daily life.

   a. Why do behaviour therapists refrain from reinforcing every positive behavioural response?

   b. Describe the goals of self-observation in your own words.

   c. Describe how Drabman et al. (1973) taught a group of disruptive boys to evaluate their own behaviour. Explain why self-observation remained effective after the training sessions.

   d. Why are friends and family members often asked to participate in behaviour therapy?

18-6 Describe the use of cognitive-restructuring in cognitive behaviour therapy and evaluate behaviour and cognitive behaviour therapies.

Read pages 614-617 and answer the following questions.

1. Briefly compare these aspects of cognitive behaviour therapy and behaviour therapy.

   a. focus

   b. interest in past events

   c. presumed causes of behavioural changes

   d. methods (Be sure you mention *cognitive restructuring* in your answer.)

2. _____-_____ therapy, which was developed by Albert Ellis, asserts that psychological problems are the result of faulty _____ which must be exposed and challenged by the therapist.

3. Describe some of the irrational ideas that Ellis has identified that lead to inappropriate emotions.

4. Compare and contrast rational-emotive therapy and client-centered therapy, especially with respect to the role of the therapist.

5. What kind of emotional problems have been treated successfully and unsuccessfully using this approach? (Haaga & Davison, 1989)

6. What are some of the characteristics of people who are likely and unlikely to benefit from this kind of therapy?

7. What aspect of rational-emotive therapy has not been accepted by most psychotherapists?

8. a. Beck's (1967, 1997) therapy for depression rests on the belief that _____ _____ leads to _____ beliefs about the _____, the _____, and the _____—a cognitive triad. Faced with contradictory evidence, a depressed person often continues to interpret _____ news as _____.

   b. What is the role of the therapist in this kind of therapy?

9. a. What is the initial goal of stress inoculation training? (Meichenbaum, 1977, 1993)

   b. What is the next step?

10 .a. Why do some traditionally oriented psychotherapists object to behaviour therapy?

   b. Describe how bed-wetting was successfully treated without the occurrence of symptom substitution. (Baker, 1969)

   c. Describe a situation in which the use of behaviour therapy is inappropriate.

11. Explain why cognitive behaviour therapists concentrate on both cognitive and behavioural changes in their clients.

12. Although cognitive behaviour therapists and insight therapists stress the importance of unobservable thought processes, they differ in several important ways. State three of them.

   1.

   2.

   3.

13. What social influences work in favour of cognitive and cognitive-behavioural therapies? (Dobson & Khatri, 2000)

LESSON I SELF TEST

1. The idea that mental illness was no different from other physical diseases
   a. was one of the few advances made during the Middle Ages.
   b. gained widespread acceptance through the efforts of the Church.
   c. gradually brought an end to inhumane "treatments."
   d. was denounced by Johann Wier.

2. The early use of hypnosis to treat hysteria is attributed to
   a. Johann Wier
   b. Anton Mesmer
   c. Jean Charcot.
   d. Sigmund Freud.

3. Insight therapies are based on the assumption that insight
   a. leads to behavioural change.
   b. is less important than behavioural change.
   c. is a frightening realization that should only be attempted with an empathetic therapist.
   d. results from transferring emotional problems to the therapist.

4. The goal of client-centered therapy is to teach clients
   a. to reduce the incongruity between the real and ideal self.
   b. to rely on the empty chair technique to solve problems without help from the therapist.
   c. to understand the dynamics of transference and countertransference of maladaptive behaviour.
   d. to have unconditional positive regard for everyone.

5. Behaviour therapies are based on the assumption that
   a. symptom substitution is an important problem with insight therapy.
   b. people are basically good and problems are the result of faulty learning.

c. a sound scientific basis reduces the importance of the therapist.
   d. maladaptive behaviour is the psychological problem and not a reflection of it.

6. Systematic desensitization is an effective therapy for
   a. mentally ill people who do not readily communicate with others.
   b. specific phobias.
   c. generalized fears or anxieties.
   d. maladaptive behaviour that is harmful to the individual.

7. Punishment is not as good a treatment method as positive reinforcement because
   a. punishers are most effective in a professional setting and are less effective in a home setting.
   b. effective punishers are more difficult to develop than effective positive reinforcers.
   c. clients may develop resistance.
   d. clients may overgeneralize the punished response and avoid making a whole class of responses.

8. Self-observation is a technique to
   a. encourage unconditional positive regard.
   b. help patients recognize the first signs of symptom substitution.
   c. identify the sources of anxiety in daily life.
   d. help insure that positive behavioural changes generalize to real life situations.

9. Rational-emotive therapy asserts that
   a. an empathetic relationship between client and therapist is essential for treatment to be successful.
   b. self-blame is the beginning of accepting responsibility for personal failures.
   c. psychological problems are a result of a person's belief system.
   d. a directive, argumentative approach is counterproductive.

10. Symptom substitution
    a. is a hypothetical process for which there is little evidence.
    b. contributes to self-perpetuating emotional problems.
    c. that is recognized through self-observation has the best prognosis for change.
    d. is especially resistant to reinforcement and punishment as a means of eliminating maladaptive behaviour.

LESSON II

Read the interim summary on pages 625-626 of your text to re-acquaint yourself with the material in this section.

18-7 Outline some of the benefits of group psychotherapy, and describe and evaluate family and couples therapy.

Read pages 618-620 and answer the following questions.

1. a. Briefly describe the origins and structure of group psychotherapy.

   b. List four advantages of group sessions.

2. a. Explain why family therapy is often a good way to help solve the problems of an individual. (Cox & Paley, 1997; Lefley, 1998)

   b. What are some of the interactions a family therapist is careful to observe during a session?

   c. Describe how Minuchin (1974) organizes observed family relationships using the structural family therapy approach.

   d. What is the basis of the healthiest family interactions?

   e. List two kinds of alliances that are always regarded as unhealthy. (Foley, 1979)

      1.   2.

   f. What are some of the ways a therapist attempts to restructure unhealthy relationships?

3. What is the treatment strategy of behaviour therapists working with families?

4. What is one of the most important factors that affects the quality and durability of a couple's relationship?

5. In treating the problems of couples in a long-standing relationship, what may be some of the consequences of apparently successful treatments that therapists must anticipate?

18-8 Describe and evaluate treatment programs provided through community psychology.
Read pages 620-621 and answer the following questions.

1. a. Compare the way community psychologists and other therapists establish initial contacts with clients who may need assistance.

   b. Define *community psychology* in your own words.

   c. What is the purpose of a mental health center?

   d. What do the letters ACT stand for? Describe the ACT program, including the professionals involved, the care undertaken, and the goals.

   e. Describe the setting and goals of a half-way house.

2. Define *deinstitutionalization* in your own words.

3. a. What kind of skills did Gillham and her colleagues (1995) teach a group of school children at risk for depression?

   b. How successful was the training in reducing depression?

   c. What do the results suggest about the effectiveness of preventive psychology?

4. Explain the difference between primary and secondary prevention efforts. Give an original example of each kind of program.

5. What kinds of services are provided by community mental health centers?

6. Why may paraprofessionals employed in community mental health centers be especially effective models for clients?

18-9 Describe the role of cultural belief systems and indigenous healing therapies in the treatment of mental disorders and evaluate the effectiveness of psychotherapy.

Read pages 621-625 and answer the following questions.

1. When may it be appropriate to consider a treatment program for a mental disorder that combines Western and non-Western practices?

2. What is the name for non-Western approaches to medical problems?

3. List two similarities of all non-Western approaches.

   1.   2.

4. Now list two benefits of training mental health professionals in cultural belief systems.

   1.   2.

5. Why may a client respond better if the therapist is sensitive to his or her cultural beliefs?

6. Carefully explain these problems of evaluating the effectiveness of particular therapies and therapists.

   a. measurement

   b. ethics

   c. self-selection

   d. control group

7. Summarize Eysenck's (1952) conclusions concerning the effectiveness of psychotherapy and its implications for the field.

8. a. Define *meta-analysis* in your own words.

   b. Outline the findings of Smith et al. (1980) who used this technique to compare the effectiveness of several forms of treatment. (See Figure 18.4 in your text.)

   c. What are the results of more recent research on the effectiveness of different therapies? (Lambert &Bergin, 1994; Wampold et al., 1997)

9. Summarize a study to compare the effectiveness of two forms of psychotherapy with drug therapy for treating depression. (Elkin et al., 1985)

   a. Identify the two forms of psychotherapy and the drug that were compared.

   b. What steps were taken to insure that the therapeutic approaches were of the highest standard possible and that this standard was maintained throughout the study?

   c. Under what conditions did patients receive medication?

   d. How was the control group treated?

   e. In general, how did all patients including the control group respond to treatment? (Elkin et al., 1989; Hirshfeld, 1990)

   f. Which treatment(s) were effective for moderate depression? severe depression?

10. a. Summarize the responses to questions about the treatment of mental disorders that were part of a 1994 *Consumer Reports* subscriber survey.

    b. How was the effectiveness of psychotherapy affected by the

       1. length of treatment?

       2. form of therapy?

       3. addition of drugs?

c. According to Seligman, who later wrote a detailed report of this project, in what ways was this subscriber survey an innovative way of assessing the benefits of psychotherapy?

11. a. List the variables that Luborsky et al. (1971) investigated in their evaluation of psychotherapy.

   1.

   2.

   3.

   b. Next to each variable summarize the significant findings.

   c. Explain why it is encouraging to learn that experienced therapists are more effective.

12. What are two important factors in the patient–therapist relationship? (Bordin, 1994)

13. What is one of the most important traits of effective therapists?

14. Describe the procedure and results of research by Strupp and Hadley (1979) to identify the important factors in treating students with psychological difficulties.

15. What can we conclude about the effectiveness of psychotherapy for the treatment of mental disorders?

To review: Study Table 18.2 in your text.

Read the interim summary on page 631 of your text to re-acquaint yourself with the material in this section.

18-10 Describe and evaluate the treatment of mental disorders with antipsychotic, antidepressant and antimanic, and antianxiety drugs.

Read pages 627-629 and answer the following questions.

1. a. List three forms of biological treatment of mental illness.

   1.

   2.

   3.

   b. Now list the four classes of drugs used to treat mental disorders listed in Table 18.3 in your text.

   1.

   2.

   3.

   4.

2. a. Name the drug that reduces the positive symptoms of schizophrenia . (Lehmann &Ban, 1997; Shen & Giesler, 1998)

   b. Name the two prominent positive symptoms of schizophrenia that antipsychotic drugs alleviate and explain how these drugs are presumed to work.

   c. What is the location of the dopamine-secreting neurons thought to be involved in schizophrenia?

   d. What is the function of a second system of dopamine-secreting neurons?

   e. Describe a side effect that often occurs when a person begins taking an antipsychotic drug.

   f. Now describe the symptoms of tardive dyskinesia, a motor impairment that schizophrenics may develop after several years of treatment with antipsychotic drugs.(Cumming & Wirshing, 1989)

   g. What factors appear to contribute to the development of tardive dyskinesia and what is a temporary treatment? (Hughes & Pierattini, 1992; Yassa et al., 1990; Baldessarini & Tarsy, 1980)

   h. Describe the advantages of the new antipsychotic drug clozapine.

   i. What are the drawbacks of taking this drug?

3. a. _____ drugs are most effective for treating major depression and _____ drugs are most effective for treating bipolar disorders and mania.

   b. According to the most widely accepted theory, which neurotransmitters may be involved in depression and how do tricyclic drugs appear to affect them?

   c. Approximately what percentage of people suffering from depression are helped by the tricyclic drugs? (Hughes & Pierattini, 1992; Potter et al., 1995)

   d. What are some of the side-effects of the use of these drugs?

4. a. What does the acronym MAOI stand for and how do these drugs affect the brain?

   b. Which forms of depression respond well to MAOIs? (Hughes & Pierattini, 1992)

   c. What are some of the side-effects of their use?

5. a. How does fluoxetine (Prozac) affect the brain to relieve depression?

   b. What are some of the advantages of its use?

6. Briefly summarize some of the difficulties associated with the use of lithium carbonate: the physical side effects; the need to monitor dosage; and the complaints of patients.

7. a. What are some of the conditions for which antianxiety drugs are prescribed?

   b. Which antianxiety drugs are the most effective and most abused? (Julien, 1992)

   c. Carefully explain how the benzodiazepines may affect the brain.

   d. What initial belief about the benzodiazepines later proved false? (Lickey & Gordon, 1983)

   e. Why do some individuals find it difficult to stop taking this medication?

8. a. Identify some of the other anxiety disorders that respond to antidepressant drugs. (Klein et al., 1983)

   b. Carefully explain why antidepressant drugs are neither a cure nor a long-term solution to the treatment of antianxiety disorders.

18-11 Describe and evaluate the treatment of mental disorders with electroconvulsive therapy and psychosurgery.

Read pages 629-631 and answer the following questions.

1. Describe the preparation for and administration of electroconvulsive therapy (ECT). (See Figure 18.5 in your text.)

2. The _____, not the _____, produced by the brief surge of electricity, produces the therapeutic effect of ECT.

3. Briefly explain why ECT has acquired a bad reputation among some clinicians.

4. What change resulting from the seizure may account for the lifting of depression?

5. Describe the case of a middle-aged widow hospitalized for severe depression to illustrate the effects of ECT. (Fink, 1976)

    a. Why did the woman fail to show improvement during early treatment?

    b. When did she and her therapist notice a change in her mood?

    c. What does this case demonstrate about the effectiveness of ECT?

    d. List two situations in which ECT is the preferred treatment for severe depression.

       1.

       2.

    e. Describe a serious side effect of the excessive use of ECT reported by Lisanby et al., (2000) and explain the dilemma that it creates for patients and therapists.

    f. What precaution is now taken to reduce the occurrence of adverse side-effects?

    g. What does research suggest concerning ECT and brain damage? (Zachrisson et al., 2000)

    h. What are some intrapersonal consequences of the procedure? (Johnstone, 1999)

6. Define *psychosurgery* in your own words. Be sure to point out how it differs from other forms of brain surgery.

7. a. What were some of the serious side effects of early prefrontal lobotomies?

    b. Describe how this procedure was simplified, thus increasing the extent of its use.

    c. What development eventually led to the elimination of prefrontal lobotomies? (Valenstein, 1986)

8. a. A more refined form of psychosurgery continues to be performed. Name and describe this procedure.(Ballantine et al., 1987)

    b. For what condition is a cingulotomy an effective treatment? (Jenike, 1995)

c. Briefly summarize a long-term follow-up study of 18 people who underwent cingulotomies. Be sure to note their disorder, which more conservative treatments had failed to control, the results of the surgery and any side-effects. (Baer et al., 1995)

9. What improvement appears to follow cingulotomy? what impairments?

10. If psychosurgery is performed, it should only be as a _____ _____.

Read the interim summaries on pages 632 and 633-634 of your text to re-acquaint yourself with the material in this section.

18-12 Describe some ethical considerations in practising psychotherapy and discuss the strategies for selecting a therapist.

Read pages 632-633 and answer the following question.

1. Where are the ethical standards for psychologists set forth?

2. What do these standards state about sexual intimacy between the client and therapist? the confidentiality of information exchanged between the client and therapist?

3. a. What is the conflict for the therapist if he or she learns that the client is harming someone?

   b. How does the text suggest that the therapist deal with this situation?

5. a. What kind of resources are available to students who feel they need professional counselling? Table 18.4 in your text summarizes information on some common types of therapists.

   b. What steps should anyone seeking professional counselling take before beginning therapy?

   c. When deciding whether to leave therapy, what are some guidelines to follow?

LESSON II SELF TEST

1. What is the most important advantage of group therapy not found in individual therapy?
   a. All types of group therapy depend on interactions between participants, thus no one may remain silent.
   b. The obligation to maintain confidentiality is reduced because information is shared by all participants.
   c. Participants are often more motivated to strive to improve because lack of progress cannot be hidden from other group members.
   d. Participants gain insight into their own problems by listening to the experiences of others.

2. Family therapists believe that the healthiest family structure contains
   a. a child-oriented marriage.
   b. an alliance between one parent and one or more children.
   c. a three-generation household.
   d. a healthy relationship between husband and wife.

3. Community psychology
   a. focuses on crisis intervention rather than prevention programs.
   b. must limit treatment programs to group psychology because of almost constant underfunding.
   c. prefers to work with adults rather than children to minimize potential legal conflicts with the rights of parents.
   d. recognizes the importance of treating problems in their sociocultural context.

4. A comprehensive study using meta-analysis to compare the effectiveness of several kinds of treatment concluded that
   a. institutionalized patients who received no therapy showed almost as much improvement as patients who received treatment.
   b. behavioural and cognitive therapies were slightly more effective than the other methods.

   c. psychotherapy combined with drug therapy was more effective than either approach by itself in treating neuroses.
   d. the benefits of psychotherapy are permanent.

5. Several studies suggest that important characteristics of a successful therapist do not include the ability to
   a. create patient anxiety which motivates desire to improve.
   b. conclude treatment before patients form harmful dependent relationships with the therapist.
   c. form warm, understanding and empathetic relationship with their parents
   d. draw on years of experience and education

6. Tardive dyskinesia results because antipsychotic drugs
   a. cannot discriminate between dual systems of dopamine-secreting neurons in the brain.
   b. sometimes cause degeneration of dopamine-secreting neurons in the hypothalamus.
   c. are often discontinued by patients as soon as their symptoms decrease.
   d. interfere with REM sleep cycles.

7. Lithium carbonate is most effective in the treatment of
   a. bipolar disorder.
   b. obsessive compulsive disorder.
   c. schizophrenia.
   d. irregular heart beat.

8. An important objection to the use of electroconvulsive therapy is that
   a. there are concerns of memory loss.
   b. it is generally too slow-acting to be an effective treatment for depression.
   c. it is very difficult to evaluate the therapeutic effects of a treatment that produces permanent brain damage.
   d. even a few treatments blunt the effect of antidepressant drugs.

9. Cingulectomies
   a. are no longer performed because more refined techniques have been developed.
   b. are performed to remove diseased or damaged brain tissue.
   c. appear to be of most value in the treatment of severe compulsions.
   d. disconnect the two hemispheres of the brain.

10. Ethical standards for psychologists
   a. are specific to the kind of therapy the therapist practices.
   b. are mutually developed and agreed to by both client and therapist during a treatment program.
   c. are more stringent for individual therapy and less stringent for group therapy.
   d. have been established by the Canadian Code of Ethics for Psychologists.

Answers to Self Tests

Lesson I
1. c	Obj. 18-1	2. c	Obj. 18-1	3. a	Obj. 18-2	4. a	Obj. 18-3	5. d	Obj. 18-4
6. b	Obj. 18-4	7. d	Obj. 18-5	8. d	Obj. 18-5	9. c	Obj. 18-6	10. a	Obj. 18-6

Lesson II
1. d	Obj. 18-7	2. d	Obj. 18-7	3. d	Obj. 18-8	4. b	Obj. 18-9	5. a	Obj. 18-9
6. a	Obj. 18-10	7. a	Obj. 18-10	8. a	Obj. 18-11	9. c	Obj. 18-11	10. d	Obj. 18-12

1.1	psychology	1.10	developmental psychology
1.2	causal event	1.11	social psychology
1.3	physiological psychology	1.12	personality psychology
1.4	psychophysiology	1.13	cross-cultural psychology
1.5	comparative psychology	1.14	clinical psychology
1.6	behaviour analysis	1.15	clinical neuropsychologist
1.7	behaviour genetics	1.16	health psychologist
1.8	cognitive psychology	1.17	school psychologist
1.9	experimental neuropsychology	1.18	consumer psychologist

1.10 The branch of psychology that studies the changes in behavioural, perceptual, and cognitive capacities of organisms as a function of age and experience.	**1.1** The scientific study of the causes of behaviour; also, the application of the findings of psychological research to the solution of problems.
1.11 The branch of psychology devoted to the study of the effects people have on each other's behaviour.	**1.2** An event that causes another event to occur.
1.12 The branch of psychology that attempts to categorize and understand the causes of individual differences in patterns of behaviour.	**1.3** The branch of psychology that studies the physiological basis of behaviour.
1.13 The branch of psychology that studies the effects of culture on behaviour.	**1.4** The measurement of physiological responses, such as blood pressure and heart rate, to infer changes in internal states, such as emotions.
1.14 The branch of psychology devoted to the investigation and treatment of abnormal behaviour and mental disorders.	**1.5** A branch of psychology that studies the behaviours of a variety of organisms, in an attempt to understand the adaptive and functional significance of the behaviours and their relation to evolution
1.15 A psychologist who specializes in the identification and treatment of the behavioural consequences of nervous system disorders and injuries.	**1.6** A branch of psychology that studies the effect of the environment on behaviour—primarily the effects of the consequences of behaviours on the behaviours themselves.
1.16 A psychologist who works to promote behaviours and lifestyles that improve and maintain health and prevent illness.	**1.7** The branch of psychology that studies the role of genetics in behaviour.
1.17 A psychologist who deals with the behavioural problems of students at school.	**1.8** The branch of psychology that studies complex behaviours and mental processes such as perception, attention, learning and memory, verbal behaviour, concept formation, and problem solving.
1.18 A psychologist who helps organizations that manufacture products or that buy products or services.	**1.9** The branch of psychology that attempts to understand human brain functions by studying patients whose brains have been damaged through accident or disease.

1.19	community psychologist	1.28	doctrine of specific nerve energies
1.20	organizational psychologist	1.29	experimental ablation
1.21	engineering psychologist	1.30	psychophysics
1.22	animism	1.31	structuralism
1.23	reflex	1.32	introspection
1.24	dualism	1.33	functionalism
1.25	model	1.34	behaviourism
1.26	empiricism	1.35	law of effect
1.27	materialism	1.36	Gestalt psychology

1.28 Johannes Miller's observation that different nerve fibres convey specific information from one part of the body to the brain or from the brain to one part of the body.	**1.19** A psychologist who works for the welfare of individuals in the social system, attempting to improve the system rather than treating people as problems.
1.29 The removal or destruction of a portion of the brain of an experimental animal for the purpose of studying the functions of that region.	**1.20** A psychologist who works to increase the efficiency and effectiveness of organizations.
1.30 The branch of psychology that measures the quantitative relation between physical stimuli and perceptual experience.	**1.21** A psychologist who studies the ways that people and machines work together and helps design machines that are safer and easier to operate.
1.31 Wundt's system of experimental psychology; it emphasized introspective analysis of sensation and perception.	**1.22** The belief that all animals and all moving objects possess spirits providing their motive force.
1.32 Literally, "looking within," in an attempt to describe one's own memories, perceptions, cognitive processes, or motivations.	**1.23** An automatic response to a stimulus, such as the blink reflex to the sudden approach of an object toward the eyes.
1.33 The strategy of understanding a species' structural or behavioural features by attempting to establish their usefulness with respect to survival and reproductive success.	**1.24** The philosophical belief that humans consist of physical bodies and nonmaterial minds or souls.
1.34 A movement in psychology that asserts that the only proper subject matter for scientific study in psychology is observable behaviour.	**1.25** A relatively simple system that works on known principles and is able to do at least some of the things that a more complex system can do.
1.35 Thorndike's observation that stimuli that occur as a consequence of a response can increase or decrease the likelihood of making that response again.	**1.26** The philosophical view that all knowledge is obtained through the senses.
1.36 A movement in psychology that emphasized that cognitive processes could be understood by studying their organization, not their elements.	**1.27** A philosophical belief that reality can be known only through an understanding of the physical world, of which the mind is a part.

1.37	humanistic psychology	2.8	variable
1.38	information processing	2.9	manipulation
2.1	naturalistic observations	2.10	experimental group
2.2	correlational study	2.11	control group
2.3	experiment	2.12	independent variable
2.4	scientific method	2.13	dependent variable
2.5	replication	2.14	nominal fallacy
2.6	hypothesis	2.15	operational definition
2.7	theory	2.16	validity

2.8 A measure capable of assuming any of several values.	**1.37** An approach to the study of human behaviour that emphasizes human experience, choice and creativity, self-realization, and positive growth.
2.9 Setting the value of an independent variable in an experiment to see whether the value of the dependent variable is affected.	**1.38** An approach used by cognitive psychologists to explain the workings of the brain; information received through the senses is processed by systems of neurons in the brain.
2.10 A group of subjects in an experiment, the members of which are exposed to a particular value of the independent variable, which has been manipulated by the experimenter.	**2.1** The observation of the behaviour of people or other animals in their natural environments.
2.11 A comparison group used in an experiment, the members of which are exposed to the naturally occurring or zero value of the independent variable.	**2.2** The observation of two or more variables in the behaviour or other characteristics of people or other animals.
2.12 The variable that is manipulated in an experiment as a means of determining cause-and-effect relations. Manipulation of an independent variable demonstrates whether it affects the value of the dependent variable.	**2.3** A study in which the experimenter changes the value of an independent variable and observes whether the manipulation affects the value of a dependent variable. Only experiments can confirm the existence of cause-and-effect relations among variables.
2.13 The event whose value is measured in an experiment. Manipulation of independent variables demonstrates whether they affect the value of dependent variables.	**2.4** A set of rules that govern the collection and analysis of data gained through observational studies or experiments.
2.14 The false belief that one has explained the causes of a phenomenon by identifying and naming it; for example, believing that one has explained lazy behaviour by attributing it to "laziness."	**2.5** Repetition of an experiment or observational study to see whether previous results will be obtained.
2.15 The definition of a variable in terms of the operations the experimenter performs to measure or manipulate it.	**2.6** A statement, usually designed to be tested by an experiment, that tentatively expresses a cause-and-effect relationship between variables.
2.16 The degree to which the operational definition of a variable accurately reflects the variable it is designed to measure or manipulate.	**2.7** A set of statements designed to explain a set of phenomena; more encompassing than a hypothesis.

2.17	confounding of variables		2.26	sample
2.18	counterbalancing		2.27	generalization
2.19	reliability		2.28	informed consent
2.20	interrater reliability		2.29	confidentiality
2.21	random assignment		2.30	debriefing
2.22	placebo		2.31	cross-cultural psychology
2.23	single-blind study		2.32	descriptive statistics
2.24	double-blind study		2.33	measure of central tendency
2.25	matching		2.34	mean

2.26 A selection of items from a larger population—for example, a group of subjects selected to participate in an experiment.	**2.17** An inadvertent alteration of more than one variable during an experiment. The results of an experiment involving confounded variables permit no valid conclusions about cause and effect.
2.27 The conclusion that the results obtained from a sample apply also to the population from which the sample was taken.	**2.18** A systematic variation of conditions in an experiment, such as the order of presentation of stimuli, so that different subjects encounter them in different orders; prevents confounding of independent variables with time-dependent processes such as habituation or fatigue.
2.28 Agreement to participate as a subject in an experiment after being informed about the nature of the research and any possible adverse effects,	**2.19** The repeatability of a measurement; the likelihood that if the measurement was made again it would yield the same value.
2.29 Privacy of subjects and nondisclosure of their participation in a research project.	**2.20** The degree to which two or more independent observers agree in their ratings of another organism's behaviour.
2.30 Full disclosure to research participants of the true nature and purpose of a research project after its completion.	**2.21** An assignment of subjects to the various groups of an experiment by random means, thereby ensuring comparable groups.
2.31 A branch of psychology that studies the effects of culture on behaviour.	**2.22** An inert substance that cannot be distinguished from a real medication by the patient or subject: used as the control substance in a single-blind or double-blind experiment.
2.32 Mathematical procedures for organizing collections of data, such as determining the mean, the median, the range, the variance, and the correlation coefficient.	**2.23** An experiment in which the experimenter but not the subject knows the value of the independent variable.
2.33 A statistical measure used to characterize the value of items in a sample of numbers.	**2.24** An experiment in which neither the subjects nor the experimenter knows the value of the independent variable.
2.34 A measure of central tendency; the sum of a group of values divided by their number; the arithmetical average.	**2.25** A systematic selection of subjects in groups in an experiment or (more often) a correlational study to ensure that the mean values of important subject variables of the groups are similar.

2.35	median	3.2	adaptive significance
2.36	measure of variability	3.3	ultimate causes
2.37	range	3.4	proximate causes
2.38	standard deviation	3.5	evolutionary psychology
2.39	scatterplot	3.6	culture
2.40	correlation coefficient	3.7	artificial selection
2.41	statistical significance	3.8	natural selection
2.42	inferential statistics	3.9	reproductive success
3.1	biological evolution	3.10	variation

3.2 The effectiveness of behaviour in aiding organisms in adjusting to changing environmental conditions	**2.35** A measure of central tendency; the midpoint of a group of values arranged numerically.
3.3 Evolutionary conditions that have slowly shaped the behaviour of a species over generations.	**2.36** A statistical measure used to characterize the dispersion in values of items in a sample of numbers.
3.4 Immediate environmental events and conditions that affect behaviour.	**2.37** The difference between the highest score and the lowest score of a sample.
3.5 The branch of psychology that studies the ways in which an organism's evolutionary history contributes to the development of behavioural patterns and cognitive strategies related to reproduction and survival during its lifetime.	**2.38** A statistic that expresses the variability of a measurement; square root of the sum of the squared deviations from the mean.
3.6 The sum of socially-transmitted knowledge, customs, and behaviour patterns common to a particular group of people.	**2.39** A graph of items that have two values; one value is plotted against the horizontal axis and the other against the vertical axis.
3.7 A procedure in which animals are deliberately mated to produce offspring that possess particularly desirable characteristics.	**2.40** A measurement of the degree to which two variables are related.
3.8 The consequence of the fact that organisms reproduce differentially, which is caused by differences among in their characteristics. Within any given population, some animals—the survivors—will produce more offspring than other animals.	**2.41** The likelihood that an observed relation or difference between two variables is not due to chance factors.
3.9 The number of viable offspring an individual produces relative to the number of viable offspring produced by other members of the same species.	**2.42** Mathematical procedures for determining whether relations or differences between samples are statistically significant.
3.10 The differences found across individuals of any given species in terms of their genetic, biological (size, strength, physiology), and psychological characteristics (intelligence, sociability, behaviour).	**3.1** Changes in the genetic and physical characteristics of a population or group of organisms over time.

3.11	genotype	3.20	DNA
3.12	phenotype	3.21	enzymes
3.13	competition	3.22	chromosomes
3.14	bipedalism	3.23	sex chromosomes
3.15	encephalization	3.24	meiosis
3.16	cultural evolution	3.25	alleles
3.17	genetics	3.26	dominant allele
3.18	heredity	3.27	recessive allele
3.19	genes	3.28	mutations

3.20 Deoxyribonucleic acid, the structure of chromosomes. DNA structure resembles that of a twisted ladder. Strands of sugar and phosphates are connected by rungs made from adenine and thymine and guanine and cytosine.	3.11 An organism's genetic makeup.
3.21 Proteins that regulate the structure of bodily cells and the processes occurring within those cells.	3.12 The outward expression of an organism's genotype; an organism's physical appearance and behaviour.
3.22 Rodlike structures in the nuclei of living cells that contain genes.	3.13 A striving or wing with others who share the same ecological niche for food, mates, and territory.
3.23 The chromosomes that contain the instructional code for the development of male or female sex characteristics.	3.14 The ability to move about the environment on two feet.
3.24 The form of cell division by which new sperm and ova are formed. The chromosomes within the cell are randomly rearranged so that new sperm and ova contain 23 individual chromosomes, or half of that found in other cells of the body.	3.15 Increases in brain size.
3.25 Alternative forms of the same gene.	3.16 The adaptive changes of cultures in response to recurrent environmental changes over time. Cultural evolution is possible only because humans have been genetically endowed with a capacity for learning and language.
3.26 The form of the gene that controls the expression of a trait. When a gene pair contains two dominant alleles or when it contains both a dominant and recessive allele, the trait regulated by the dominant gene will be expressed.	3.17 The study of the genetic makeup of organisms and how it influences their physical and behavioural characteristics.
3.27 The form of the gene that does not influence the expression of a trait unless it is paired with another recessive allele.	3.18 The sum of the traits and tendencies inherited from a person's parents and other biological ancestors.
3.28 Accidental alterations in the DNA code within a single gene. Mutations can either be spontaneous and occur naturally or be the result of environmental factors such as exposure to high-energy radiation.	3.19 Small units of chromosomes that direct the synthesis of proteins and enzymes.

3.29	chromosomal aberration	3.38	An artificially constructed genetic sequence inserted into a gene to inactivate it.
3.30	Down syndrome	3.39	A known DNA sequence that occurs at a particular place in the chromosome.
3.31	Huntington's chorea	3.40	concordance research
3.32	phenylketonuria	3.41	sociobiology
3.33	genetic counselling	3.42	reproductive strategies
3.34	heritability	3.43	monogamy
3.35	behaviour genetics	3.44	polygyny
3.36	A trait showing a classical dominant, recessive, or sex-linked pattern of inheritance. Mendelian traits are usually dichotomous and are controlled by a single locus.	3.45	polyandry
3.37	A trait which does not show the inheritance pattern described by Mendel. Nonmendelian traits are usually polygenic and show continuous variation in the phenotype.	3.46	polygynandry

3.38 An articially constructed genetic sequence inserted into a gen to inactivate it.	**3.29** The rearrangement of genes within cells or a change in the total number of chromosomes.
3.39 A known DNA sequence that occurs at a particular place in the chromosome.	**3.30** A genetic disorder caused by a chromosomal aberration resulting in an extra 21st chromosome. People with Down syndrome are generally short with broad skulls and round faces, and suffer impairments in physical, psychomotor, and cognitive development.
3.40 Research that studies the degree of similarity in traits expressed between twins. Twins are said to be concordant for a trait if either both or neither twin expresses it and discordant if only one twin expresses it.	**3.31** A genetic disorder caused by a dominant lethal gene in which a person experiences slow but progressive mental and physical deterioration.
3.41 The study of the biological bases of social behaviour.	**3.32** A genetic disorder caused by a pair of homozygous recessive genes and characterized by the inability to break down phenylalanine, an amino acid found in many high protein foods. The resulting high blood levels of phenylalanine cause mental retardation.
3.42 Different systems of mating and rearing offspring. These include monogamy, polygny, polyandry, and polygamy.	**3.33** A form of counselling in which people receive information regarding their family history of genetic disorders and the likelihood that they or their children may have a genetic disorder.
3.43 The mating of one female and one male.	**3.34** The amount of variability in a given trait in a given population at a given time due to genetic factors.
3.44 The mating of one male with more than one female.	**3.35** The study of genetic influences on behaviour, largely through research involving artificial selection procedures and investigations into the similarities and differences between twins.
3.45 The mating of one female with more than one male.	**3.36** A trait showing a classical dominant, recessive, or sex-linked pattern of inheritance. Mendelian traits are usually dichotomous and are controlled by a single locus.
3.46 The mating of several females with several males.	**3.37** A trait which does not show the inheritance pattern described by Mendel. Nonmendelian traits are usually polygenic and show continuou variation in the phenotype.

3.47	parental investment	4.3	nerve
3.48	sexual selection	4.4	peripheral nervous system
3.49	altruism	4.5	brain stem
3.50	inclusive fitness	4.6	cerebral hemisphere
3.51	kin selection	4.7	cerebellum
3.52	reciprocal altruism	4.8	vertebra
3.53	ethnocentrism	4.9	meninges
4.1	central nervous system	4.10	cerebrospinal fluid (CSF)
4.2	spinal cord	4.11	cerebral cortex

4.3 A bundle of nerve fibres that transmit information between the central nervous system and the body's sense organs, muscles, and glands.	3.47 The resources including time, physical effort, and risks to life that a parent spends in procreation and in the feeding, nurturing, and protecting of the resulting offspring
4.4 The cranial and spinal nerves; that part of the nervous system peripheral to the brain and spinal cord.	3.48 Selection for traits specific to gender, such as body size or particular patterns of behaviour.
4.5 The "stem" of the brain, including the medulla, pons, and midbrain.	3.49 The unselfish concern of one individual for the welfare of another.
4.6 The largest part of the brain; covered by the cerebral cortex and containing parts of the brain that evolved most recently.	3.50 The reproductive success of those who share common genes.
4.7 A pair of hemispheres resembling the cerebral hemispheres but much smaller and lying beneath and in back of them; controls posture and movements, especially rapid ones.	3.51 A type of selection that altruistic acts aimed at individuals who share some of the altruist's genes, such as parents, siblings, grandparents, grandchildren, and under certain conditions, distant relatives.
4.8 One of the bones that encase the spinal cord and constitute the vertebral column.	3.52 Altruism in which people behave altruistically toward one another because they, are confident that such acts will be reciprocated toward either them or their kin.
4.9 The three-layered set of membranes that enclose the brain and spinal cord.	3.53 The idea that one's own cultural, national, racial, or religious group is superior to or more deserving than others.
4.10 The liquid in which the brain and spinal cord float; provides a shock-absorbing cushion.	4.1 The brain and the spinal cord.
4.11 The outer layer of the cerebral hemispheres of the brain, approximately 3 mm thick.	4.2 A long, thin collection of nerve cells attached to the base of the brain and running the length of the spinal column.

4.12	gray matter	4.21	terminal button
4.13	white matter	4.22	transmitter substance
4.14	spinal nerve	4.23	myelin sheath
4.15	cranial nerve	4.24	action potential
4.16	neuron	4.25	ion
4.17	glial cell	4.26	ion channel
4.18	soma	4.27	ion transporter
4.19	dendrite	4.28	synapse
4.20	axon	4.29	presynaptic neuron

4.21 The rounded swelling at the end of the axon of a neuron; releases transmitter substance.	4.12 The portions of the central nervous system that are abundant in cell bodies of neurons rather than axons.
4.22 A chemical released by the terminal buttons that causes the postsynaptic neuron to be excited or inhibited.	4.13 The portions of the central nervous system that are abundant in axons rather than cell bodies of neurons. The colour derives from the presence of the axons' myelin sheaths.
4.23 The insulating material that encases most large axons.	4.14 A bundle of nerve fibres attached to the spinal cord; conveys sensory information from the body and carries messages to muscles and glands.
4.24 A brief electrochemical event that is carried by an axon from the soma of the neuron to its terminal buttons; causes the release of a transmitter substance.	4.15 A bundle of nerve fibres attached to the base of the brain, conveying sensory information from the face and head and carrying messages to muscles and glands.
4.25 A positively or negatively charged particle; produced when many substances dissolve in water.	4.16 A nerve cell; consists of a cell body with dendrites and an axon whose branches end in terminal buttons that synapse with muscle fibres, gland cells, or other neurons.
4.26 A special protein molecule located in the membrane of a cell; controls the entry or exit of particular ions.	4.17 A cell of the central nervous system that provides support for neurons and supplies them with some essential chemicals.
4.27 A special protein molecule located in the membrane of a cell; actively transports ions into or out of the cell.	4.18 A cell body; the largest part of a neuron.
4.28 The junction between the terminal button of one neuron and the membrane of a muscle fibre, a gland, or another neuron.	4.19 A treelike part of a neuron on which the terminal buttons of other neurons form synapses.
4.29 A neuron whose terminal buttons form synapses with and excite or inhibit another neuron.	4.20 A long, thin part of a neuron attached to the soma; divides into a few or many branches, ending in terminal buttons.

4.30	postsynaptic neuron	4.39	brain plasticity
4.31	motor neuron	4.40	CT scanner
4.32	synaptic cleft	4.41	brain lesion
4.33	receptor molecule	4.42	stereotaxic apparatus
4.34	reuptake	4.43	primary visual cortex
4.35	sensory neuron	4.44	primary auditory cortex
4.36	interneuron	4.45	primary somatosensory cortex
4.37	neuromodulator	4.46	contralateral
4.38	opioid	4.47	primary motor cortex

4.39 Structural change in the brain resulting from experience.	4.30 A neuron with which the terminal buttons of another neuron form synapses and that is excited or inhibited by that neuron.
4.40 A device that uses a special X-ray machine and a computer to produce images of the brain that appear as slices taken parallel to the top of the skull.	4.31 A neuron whose terminal buttons form synapses with muscle fibres. When an action potential travels down its axon, the associated muscle fibres will twitch.
4.41 Damage to a particular region of the brain.	4.32 A fluid-filled gap between the presynaptic and postsynaptic membranes; the terminal button releases transmitter substance into this space.
4.42 A device used to insert an electrode into a particular part of the brain for the purpose of recording electrical activity, stimulating the brain electrically, or producing localized damage.	4.33 A special protein molecule located in the membrane of the postsynaptic neuron that responds to molecules of the transmitter substance. Receptors such as those that respond to opiates are sometimes found elsewhere on the surface of neurons.
4.43 The region of the cerebral cortex that receives information directly from the visual system; located in the occipital lobes.	4.34 The process by which a terminal button retrieves the molecules of transmitter substance that it has just released; terminates the effect of the transmitter substance on the receptors of the postsynaptic neuron.
4.44 The region of the cerebral cortex that receives information directly from the auditory system; located in the temporal lobes.	4.35 A neuron that detects changes in the external or internal environment and sends information about these changes to the central nervous system.
4.45 The region of the cerebral cortex that receives information directly from the somatosensory system (touch, pressure, vibration, pain, and temperature); located in the front part of the parietal lobes.	4.36 A neuron located entirely within the central nervous system.
4.46 Residing in the side of the body opposite the reference point.	4.37 A substance secreted in the brain that modulates the activity of neurons that contain the appropriate receptor molecules.
4.47 The region of the cerebral cortex that directly controls the movements of the body; located in the back part of the frontal lobes.	4.38 A neuromodulator whose action is mimicked by a natural or synthetic opiate, such as opium, morphine, or heroin.

4.48	anterior/posterior	4.57	visual agnosia
4.49	frontal lobe	4.58	homeostasis
4.50	parietal lobe	4.59	species-typical behaviour
4.51	temporal lobe	4.60	medulla
4.52	occipital lobe	4.61	pons
4.53	sensory association cortex	4.62	midbrain
4.54	prefrontal cortex	4.63	thalamus
4.55	motor association cortex	4.64	hypothalamus
4.56	corpus callosum	4.65	pituitary gland

4.57 The inability of a person who is not blind to recognize the identity or use of an object by means of vision; usually caused by damage to the brain.	4.48 Toward the front/back.
4.58 The process by which important physiological characteristics (such as body temperature and blood pressure) are regulated so that they remain at their optimum level.	4.49 The front portion of the cerebral cortex, including Broca's speech area and the motor cortex; damage impairs movement, planning, and flexibility in behavioural strategies.
4.59 A behaviour seen in all or most members of a species, such as nest building, special food-getting behaviours, or reproductive behaviours.	4.50 The region of the cerebral cortex behind the frontal lobe and above the temporal lobe; contains the somatosensory cortex; is involved in spatial perception and memory.
4.60 The part of the brain stem closest to the spinal cord; controls vital functions such as heart rate and blood pressure.	4.51 The portion of the cerebral cortex below the frontal and parietal lobes and containing the auditory cortex.
4.61 The part of the brain stem just anterior to the medulla; involved in control of sleep.	4.52 The rearmost portion of the cerebral cortex; contains the primary visual cortex.
4.62 The part of the brain stem just anterior to the pons; involved in control of fighting and sexual behaviour and in decreased sensitivity to pain during these behaviours.	4.53 Those regions of cerebral cortex that receive information from the primary sensory areas.
4.63 A region of the brain near the center of the cerebral hemispheres. All sensory information, except smell, is sent to the thalamus and then relayed to the cerebral cortex.	4.54 The anterior part of the frontal lobe; contains the motor association cortex.
4.64 A region of the brain located just above the pituitary gland; controls the autonomic nervous system and many behaviours related to regulation and survival, such as eating, drinking, fighting, shivering, and sweating.	4.55 Those regions of cerebral cortex that control the primary motor cortex; involved in planning and executing behaviours.
4.65 An endocrine gland attached to the hypothalamus at the base of the brain.	4.56 A large bundle of axons ("white matter") that connects the cortex of the two cerebral hemispheres.

4.66	endocrine gland	4.75	hippocampus
4.67	hormone	4.76	barbiturate
4.68	target cell	4.77	antianxiety drug
4.69	autonomic nervous system (ANS)	4.78	benzodiazepine
4.70	sympathetic branch	4.79	tolerance
4.71	parasympathetic branch	4.80	withdrawal symptom
4.72	limbic system	5.1	learning
4.73	limbic cortex	5.2	performance
4.74	amygdala	5.3	orienting response

4.75 A part of the limbic system of the brain, located in the temporal lobe; plays important roles in learning.	4.66 A gland that secretes a hormone.
4.76 A drug that causes sedation: one of several derivatives of barbituric acid.	4.67 A chemical substance secreted by an endocrine gland that has physiological effects on target cells in other organs.
4.77 A "tranquilizer," which reduces anxiety. The most common include chlordiazepoxide (Librium) and diazepam (Valium).	4.68 A cell whose physiological processes are affected by a particular hormone; contains special receptor molecules that respond to the presence of the hormone.
4.78 A class of drug having anxiolytic ("tranquilizing") effects; examples are Librium and Valium.	4.69 The portion of the peripheral nervous system that controls the functions of the glands and internal organs.
4.79 The decreased sensitivity to a drug resulting from its continued use.	4.70 The portion of the autonomic nervous system that activates functions that accompany arousal and expenditure of energy.
4.80 An effect produced by discontinuance of use of a drug after a period of continued use; generally opposite to the drug's primary effects.	4.71 The portion of the autonomic nervous system that activates functions that occur during a relaxed state.
5.1 An adaptive process in which the tendency to perform a particular behaviour is changed by experience.	4.72 A set of interconnected structures of the brain important in emotional and species-typical behaviour; includes the amygdala, hippocampus, and limbic cortex.
5.2 The behavioural change produced by the internal changes brought about by learning.	4.73 The cerebral cortex located around the edge of the cerebral hemisphere where they join with the brain stem; part of the limbic system.
5.3 Any response by which an organism directs appropriate sensory organs (eyes, ears, nose) toward the source of a novel stimulus.	4.74 A part of the limbic system of the brain located deep in the temporal lobe; damage causes changes in emotional and aggressive behaviour.

5.4	habituation	5.13	generalization
5.5	classical conditioning	5.14	discrimination
5.6	unconditional stimulus (UCS)	5.15	phobia
5.7	unconditional response (UCR)	5.16	operant conditioning
5.8	conditional stimulus (CS)	5.17	law of effect
5.9	conditional response (CR)	5.18	operant chamber
5.10	acquisition	5.19	cumulative recorder
5.11	extinction	5.20	discriminative stimulus
5.12	spontaneous recovery	5.21	three-term contingency

5.13 In classical conditioning, CRs elicited by stimuli that resemble the CS used in training.	5.4 The simplest form of learning; learning not to respond to an unimportant event that occurs repeatedly.
5.14 In classical conditioning, the appearance of a CR when one stimulus is presented (the CS+) but not another (the CS-).	5.5 The process by which a response normally elicited by one stimulus (the UCS) comes to be controlled by another stimulus (the CS) as well.
5.15 Unreasonable fear of specific objects or situations, such as insects, animals, or enclosed spaces, learned through classical conditioning.	5.6 In classical conditioning, a stimulus, such as food, that naturally elicits a reflexive response, such as salivation.
5.16 A form of learning in which behaviour is affected by its consequences. Favorable consequences strengthen the behaviour and unfavorable consequences weaken the behaviour.	5.7 In classical conditioning, a response, such as salivation, that is naturally elicited by the UCS.
5.17 Thorndike's idea that the consequences of a behaviour determine whether that behaviour is likely to be repeated.	5.8 In classical conditioning, a stimulus which, because of its repeated association with the UCS, eventually elicits a CR.
5.18 An apparatus in which an animal's behaviour can be easily observed, manipulated, and automatically recorded.	5.9 In classical conditioning, the response elicited by the CS.
5.19 A mechanical device connected to an operant chamber for the purpose of recording operant responses as they occur in time.	5.10 In classical conditioning, the time during which a CR first appears and increases in frequency.
5.20 In operant conditioning, the stimulus that sets the occasion for responding because, in the past, a behaviour has produced certain consequences in the presence of that stimulus.	5.11 The elimination of a response that occurs when the CS is repeatedly presented without being followed by the UCS (classical conditioning) or when the response is not followed by the reinforcer (instrumental conditioning).
5.21 The relation among discriminative stimuli, behaviour, and the consequences of that behaviour. A motivated organism emits a specific response in presence of a discriminative stimulus because in the past, that response was reinforced only when the discriminative stimulus is present.	5.12 After an interval of time, the reappearance of a response that had previously been extinguished.

5.22	positive reinforcement	5.31	fixed-interval schedule
5.23	negative reinforcement	5.32	variable-interval schedule
5.24	punishment	5.33	generalization
5.25	response cost	5.34	discrimination
5.26	extinction	5.35	primary reinforcer
5.27	shaping	5.36	primary punisher
5.28	intermittent reinforcement	5.37	conditioned (or secondary) reinforcer (or punisher)
5.29	fixed-ratio schedule	5.38	superstitious behaviour
5.30	variable-ratio schedule	5.39	escape response

5.31 A schedule of reinforcement in which the first response that is made after a fixed interval of time since the previous reinforcement (or the start of the session) is reinforced.	5.22 A consequence that increases the frequency of a response that is regularly and reliably followed by an appetitive stimulus.
5.32 A schedule of reinforcement similar to a fixed-interval schedule but characterized by a variable time requirement with a particular mean.	5.23 A consequence that increases the frequency of a response that is regularly and reliably followed by the termination of an aversive stimulus.
5.33 In operant conditioning, the occurrence of responding when a stimulus similar (but not identical) to the discriminative stimulus is present.	5.24 A consequence that decreases the frequency of a response that is regularly and reliably followed by an aversive stimulus.
5.34 In operant conditioning, responding only when a specific discriminative stimulus is present but not when similar stimuli are present.	5.25 A consequence that decreases the frequency of response that is regularly and reliably followed by the termination of an appetitive stimulus.
5.35 A biologically significant appetitive stimulus, such as food or water.	5.26 In operant conditioning, the decrease in responding that occurs when responding is no longer reinforced.
5.36 A biologically significant aversive stimuli, such as pain.	5.27 The reinforcement of behaviour that successively approximates the desired response until that response is fully acquired.
5.37 A stimulus that acquires its reinforcing (or punishing) properties through association with a primary reinforcer (or punisher). Sometimes referred to as a secondary reinforcer (or punisher).	5.28 The occasional reinforcement of a particular behaviour; produces responding that is more resistant to extinction.
5.38 A behaviour that occurs in response to the regular, noncontingent occurrence of an appetitive stimulus to a motivated organism; appears to cause a certain event, but in reality does not.	5.29 A schedule of reinforcement in which reinforcement occurs only after a fixed number of responses have been made since the previous reinforcement (or the start of the session).
5.39 An operant response acquired through negative reinforcement that terminates an aversive stimulus.	5.30 A schedule of reinforcement similar to a fixed-ratio schedule but characterized by a variable response requirement with a particular mean.

5.40	avoidance response	6.7	psychophysics
5.41	conditioned flavour-aversion learning	6.8	just-noticeable difference (jnd)
5.42	behavioural pharmacology	6.9	Weber faction
6.1	sensation	6.10	threshold
6.2	perception	6.11	difference threshold
6.3	transduction	6.12	absolute threshold
6.4	receptor cell	6.13	signal detection theory
6.5	anatomical coding	6.14	receiver operating characteristic curve (ROC curve)
6.6	temporal coding	6.15	subliminal perception

6.7 A branch of psychology that measures the quantitative relation between physical stimuli and perceptual experience.	5.40 An operant response acquired through negative reinforcement that prevents an aversive stimulus from occurring.
6.8 The smallest difference between two similar stimuli that can be distinguished. Also called *difference threshold*.	5.41 A type of learning in which a substance is avoided because its flavour has been associated with illness.
6.9 The ratio between a just-noticeable difference and the magnitude of a stimulus; reasonably constant over the middle range of most stimulus intensities.	5.42 The study of how drugs influence behaviour; combines the principles of operant conditioning with the principles of drug action.
6.10 The point at which a stimulus, or a change in the value of a stimulus, can just be detected.	6.1 The detection of the elementary properties of a stimulus.
6.11 An alternate name for just noticeable difference.	6.2 The detection of the more complex properties of a stimulus, including its location and nature; involves learning.
6.12 The minimum value of a stimulus that can be detected.	6.3 The conversion of physical stimuli into changes in the activity of receptor cells of sensory organs.
6.13 A mathematical theory of the detection of stimuli, which involves discriminating a signal from the noise in which it is embedded, and which takes into account the subjects' willingness to report detecting the signal.	6.4 A neuron that directly responds to a physical stimulus, such as light, vibrations, or aromatic molecules.
6.14 A graph of hits and false alarms of subjects under different motivational conditions; indicates people's ability to detect a particular stimulus.	6.5 A means of representing information by the nervous system; different features are coded by the activity, of different neurons.
6.15 The perception of a stimulus, as indicated by a change in behaviour, at an intensity insufficient to produce a conscious sensation.	6.6 A means of representing information by the nervous system; different features are coded by the pattern of activity of neurons.

6.16	wavelength	6.25	bipolar cell
6.17	cornea	6.26	ganglion cell
6.18	sclera	6.27	rod
6.19	iris	6.28	cone
6.20	lens	6.29	fovea
6.21	accommodation	6.30	photopigment
6.22	retina	6.31	rhodopsin
6.23	photoreceptor	6.32	dark adaptation
6.24	optic disk	6.33	conjugate movement

6.25 A neuron in the retina that receives information from photoreceptors and passes it on to the ganglion cells, from which axons proceed through the optic nerves to the brain.	**6.16** The distance between adjacent waves of radiant energy; in vision most closely associated with the perceptual dimension of hue.
6.26 A neuron in the retina that receives information from photoreceptors by means of bipolar cells, and from which axons proceed through the optic nerves to the brain.	**6.17** The transparent tissue covering the front of the eye.
6.27 A photoreceptor that is very sensitive to light but cannot detect changes in hue.	**6.18** The tough outer layer of the eye; the "white" of the eye.
6.28 One of the photoreceptors in the retina; responsible for acute daytime vision and for colour perception.	**6.19** The pigmented muscle of the eye that controls the size of the pupil.
6.29 A small pit near the center of the retina containing densely packed cones; responsible for the most acute and detailed vision.	**6.20** The transparent organ situated behind the iris of the eye; helps focus an image on the retina.
6.30 A complex molecule found in photoreceptors; when struck by light, it bleaches and stimulates the membrane of the photoreceptor in which it resides.	**6.21** Changes in the thickness of the lens of the eye that focus images of near or distant objects on the retina.
6.31 The photopigment contained by rods.	**6.22** The tissue at the back inside surface of the eye that contains the photoreceptors and associated neurons.
6.32 The process by which the eye becomes capable of distinguishing dimly illuminated objects after going from a bright area to a dark one.	**6.23** A receptive cell for vision in the retina; a rod or a cone.
6.33 The cooperative movement of the eyes, which ensures that the image of an object falls on identical portions of both retinas.	**6.24** A circular structure located at the exit point from the retina of the axons of the ganglion cells that form the optic nerve.

6.34	saccadic movement	6.43	protanopia
6.35	pursuit movement	6.44	deuteranopia
6.36	hue	6.45	tritanopia
6.37	brightness	6.46	hertz (Hz)
6.38	saturation	6.47	ossicle
6.39	colour mixing	6.48	cochlea
6.40	trichromatic theory	6.49	oval window
6.41	opponent process	6.50	basilar membrane
6.42	negative afterimage	6.51	round window

6.43 A form of hereditary anomalous colour vision; caused by defective "red" cones in the retina.	**6.34** The rapid movement of the eyes that is used in scanning a visual scene, as opposed to the smooth pursuit movements used to follow a moving object.
6.44 A form of hereditary anomalous colour vision; caused by defective "green" cones in the retina.	**6.35** The movement that the eyes make to maintain an image of a moving object upon the fovea.
6.45 A form of hereditary anomalous colour vision; caused by a lack of "blue" cones in the retina.	**6.36** A perceptual dimension of colour, most closely related to the wavelength of a pure light.
6.46 The primary measure of the frequency of vibration of sound waves; cycles per second.	**6.37** A perceptual dimension of colour, most closely related to the intensity, or degree of radiant energy emitted by a visual stimulus.
6.47 One of the three bones of the middle ear (the *hammer, anvil,* and *stirrup*) that transmit acoustical vibrations from the eardrum to the membrane behind the oval window of the cochlea.	**6.38** A perceptual dimension of colour, most closely associated with purity of a colour
6.48 The snail-shaped chamber set in bone in the inner ear, where audition takes place.	**6.39** The perception of two or more lights of different wavelengths seen together as light of an intermediate wavelength.
6.49 An opening in the bone surrounding the cochlea. The stirrup presses against a membrane behind this opening and transmits sound vibrations into the fluid within the cochlea.	**6.40** The theory that colour vision is accomplished by three types of photoreceptors, each of which is maximally sensitive to a different wavelength of light.
6.50 A membrane that divides the cochlea of the inner ear into two compartments. The receptive organ for audition resides here.	**6.41** The representation of colours by the rate of firing of two types of neurons: red/green and yellow/blue.
6.51 An opening in the bone surrounding the cochlea. Movements of the membrane behind this opening permit vibrations to be transmitted through the oval window into the cochlea.	**6.42** The image seen after a portion of the retina is exposed to an intense visual stimulus; a negative afterimage consists of colours complementary to those of the physical stimulus.

6.52	auditory hair cell	6.61	taste bud
6.53	cilium	6.62	olfaction
6.54	tectorial membrane	6.63	olfactory mucosa
6.55	overtone	6.64	olfactory bulbs
6.56	fundamental frequency	6.65	somatosense
6.57	timbre	6.66	free nerve ending
6.58	chemosense	6.67	Pacinian corpuscle
6.59	gustation	6.68	two-point discrimination threshold
6.60	papilla	6.69	phantom limb

6.61 A small organ on the tongue that contains a group of gustatory receptor cells.	6.52 The sensory neuron of the auditory system; located on the basilar membrane.
6.62 The sense of smell.	6.53 A hairlike appendage of a cell; involved in movement or in transducing sensory information. They are found on the receptors in the auditory and vestibular system.
6.63 The mucous membrane lining the top of the nasal sinuses; contains the cilia of the olfactory receptors.	6.54 A membrane located above the basilar membrane; serves as a shelf against which the cilia of the auditory hair cells move.
6.64 Stalk-like structures located at the base of the brain that contain neural circuits that perform the first analysis of olfactory information.	6.55 The frequencies of complex tones that occur at multiples of the fundamental frequency.
6.65 Bodily sensations; sensitivity to such stimuli as touch, pain, and temperature.	6.56 The lowest, and usually most intense, frequency of a complex sound; most often perceived as the sound's basic pitch.
6.66 An unencapsulated (naked) dendrite of somatosensory neurons.	6.57 A perceptual dimension of sound, determined by the complexity of the sound—or example, as shown by a mathematical analysis of the sound wave.
6.67 A specialized encapsulated somatosensory nerve ending, which detects mechanical stimuli, especially vibrations.	6.58 One of the two sense modalities (gustation and olfaction) that detect the presence of particular molecules present in the environment.
6.68 The minimum distance between two small points that can be detected as separate stimuli when pressed against a particular region of the skin.	6.59 The sense of taste.
6.69 Sensations that appear to originate in a limb that has been amputated.	6.60 A small bump on the tongue that contains a group of taste buds.

6.70	muscle spindle	7.6	prosopagnosia
6.71	vestibular apparatus	7.7	figure
6.72	semicircular canal	7.8	ground
6.73	vestibular sac	7.9	Gestalt psychology
7.1	perception	7.10	law of proximity
7.2	receptive field	7.11	law of similarity
7.3	achromatopsia	7.12	good continuation
7.4	Balint's syndrome	7.13	law of closure
7.5	visual agnosia	7.14	law of common fate

7.6 A form of visual agnosia characterized by difficulty in the recognition of people's faces; caused by damage to the visual association cortex.	6.70 A muscle fibre that functions as a stretch receptor, arranged parallel to the muscle fibres responsible for contraction of the muscle, thus detecting muscle length.
7.7 A visual stimulus that is perceived as a self-contained object.	6.71 The receptive organs of the inner ear that contribute to balance and perception of head movement.
7.8 A visual stimulus that is perceived as a formless background against which objects are seen.	6.72 One of a set of three receptor organs in the inner ear that respond to rotational movements of the head.
7.9 A branch of psychology that asserts that the perception of objects is produced by particular configurations of the elements of stimuli.	6.73 One of a set of two receptor organs in the inner ear that detect changes in the tilt of the head.
7.10 A Gestalt law of organization; elements located closest to each other are perceived as belonging to the same figure.	7.1 A rapid, automatic, unconscious process by which we recognize what is represented by the information provided by our sense organs.
7.11 A Gestalt law of organization; similar elements are perceived as belonging to the same figure.	7.2 That portion of the visual field in which the presentation of visual stimuli will produce an alteration in the firing rate of a particular neuron.
7.12 A Gestalt law of organization; given two or more interpretations of elements that form the outline of the figure, the simplest interpretation will be preferred.	7.3 The inability to discriminate among different hues; caused by damage to the visual association cortex.
7.13 A Gestalt law of organization; elements missing from the outline of a figure are "filled in" by the visual system.	7.4 A syndrome caused by bilateral damage to the parieto-occipital region of the brain; includes difficulty in perceiving the location of objects and reaching for them under visual guidance.
7.14 A Gestalt law of organization; elements that move together give rise to the perception of a particular figure.	7.5 The inability of a person who is not blind to recognize the identity of an object visually; caused by damage to the visual association cortex.

7.15	template	7.24	top-down processing
7.16	prototype	7.25	convergence
7.17	distinctive feature	7.26	retinal disparity
7.18	geon	7.27	stereopsis
7.19	artificial intelligence	7.28	interposition
7.20	parallel processor	7.29	linear perspective
7.21	neural network	7.30	texture
7.22	tachistoscope	7.31	haze
7.23	bottom-up processing	7.32	shading

7.24 A perception based on information provided by the context in which a particular stimulus is encountered.	7.15 A hypothetical pattern that resides in the nervous system and is used to perceive objects or shapes by a process of comparison.
7.25 The result of conjugate eye movements whereby the fixation point for each eye is identical; feedback from these movements provides information about the distance of objects from the viewer.	7.16 A hypothetical idealized pattern that resides in the nervous system and is used to perceive objects or shapes by a process of comparison; recognition can occur even when an exact match is not found.
7.26 The fact that points on objects located at different distances from the observer will fall on slightly different locations on the two retinas; provides the basis for stereopsis, one of the forms of depth perception.	7.17 A physical characteristic of an object that helps distinguish it from other objects.
7.27 A form of depth perception based on retinal disparity.	7.18 According to Biederman, an elementary shape that can serve as a prototype in recognizing objects; a given object can consist of one or more individual geons.
7.28 A monocular cue of depth perception; an object that partially occludes another object is perceived as closer.	7.19 A field of study in which computer programs are designed to simulate human cognitive abilities with the expectation that the endeavor will help the investigator understand the mechanisms that underlie these abilities.
7.29 A monocular cue of depth perception; the arrangement or drawing of objects on a flat surface such that parallel lines receding from the viewer are seen to converge at a point on the horizon.	7.20 A computing device that can perform several operations simultaneously.
7.30 A monocular cue of depth perception; the fineness of detail present in the surface of objects or in the ground or floor of a scene.	7.21 A model of the nervous system based on interconnected networks of elements that have some of the properties of neurons.
7.31 A monocular cue of depth perception; objects that are less distinct in their outline and texture are seen as farther from the viewer.	7.22 A device that can present visual stimuli for controlled (usually very brief) durations of time.
7.32 A monocular cue of depth perception; determines whether portions of the surface of an object are perceived as concave or convex.	7.23 A perception based on successive analyses of the details of the stimuli that are present.

7.33	elevation	8.2	encoding
7.34	motion parallax	8.3	storage
7.35	linguistic relativity	8.4	retrieval
7.36	brightness constancy	8.5	sensory memory
7.37	form constancy	8.6	short-term memory
7.38	unconscious inference	8.7	long-term memory
7.39	backward masking	8.8	iconic memory
7.40	phi phenomenon	8.9	echoic memory
8.1	memory	8.10	working memory

8.2 The process by which sensory information is converted into a form that can be used by the brain's memory system	**7.33** A monocular cue of depth perception; objects nearer the horizon are seen as farther from the viewer.
8.3 The process of maintaining information in memory.	**7.34** A cue of depth perception. As we pass by a scene, objects closer to us pass in front of objects farther away.
8.4 The active processes of locating and using stored information.	**7.35** The hypothesis that the language a person speaks is related to his or her thoughts and perceptions.
8.5 Memory, in which representations of the physical features of a stimulus are stored for very brief durations.	**7.36** The tendency to perceive objects as having constant brightness even when they are observed under varying levels of illumination.
8.6 An immediate memory for stimuli that have just been perceived. It is limited in terms of both capacity (7 ± 2 chunks of information) and duration.	**7.37** The tendency to perceive objects as having a constant form, even when they are rotated or their distance from the observer changes.
8.7 Memory in which information is represented on a permanent or near-permanent basis.	**7.38** A mental computation of which we are unaware that plays a role in perception.
8.8 A form of sensory memory that holds a brief visual image of a scene that has just been perceived.	**7.39** The ability of a stimulus to interfere with the perception of a stimulus presented just before it.
8.9 A form of sensory memory for sounds that have just been perceived.	**7.40** The perception of movement caused by the turning on of two or more lights, one at a time, in sequence; often used on theatre marquees; responsible for the apparent movement of images in movies and television.
8.10 Another name for short-term memory	**8.1** The cognitive processes of encoding, storing, and retrieving information.

8.11	primacy effect	8.20	elaborative rehearsal
8.12	recency effect	8.21	shallow processing
8.13	chunking	8.22	deep processing
8.14	phonological short-term memory	8.23	effortful processing
8.15	subvocal articulation	8.24	automatic processing
8.16	conduction aphasia	8.25	encoding specificity
8.17	consolidation	8.26	mnemonic system
8.18	retrograde amnesia	8.27	method of loci
8.19	maintenance rehearsal	8.28	peg word method

8.20 The processing of information on a meaningful level, such as forming associations, attending to the meaning of the material, thinking about it, and so on.	**8.11** The tendency to remember initial information. In the memorization of a list of words, the primacy effect is evidenced by better recall of the words early in the list.
8.21 The analysis of the superficial characteristics of a stimulus, such as its size or shape.	**8.12** The tendency to recall later information. In the memorization of a list of words, the recency effect is evidenced by better recall of the last words in the list.
8.22 The analysis of the complex characteristics of a stimulus, such as its meaning or its relationship to other stimuli.	**8.13** A process by which information is simplified by rules that make it easier to remember. For example, the string of letters TWAABCFBI are easier to remember if a person learns the rule that organizes them into smaller" "chunks": TWA, ABC, and FBI.
8.23 Practicing or rehearsing information through either shallow or deep processing.	**8.14** Short-term memory for verbal information.
8.24 The formation of memories of events and experiences with little or no attention or effort.	**8.15** An unvoiced speech utterance.
8.25 The principle that how we encode information determines our ability to retrieve it later.	**8.16** An inability, to remember words that are heard, although they usually can be understood and responded to appropriately. This disability is caused by damage to connections between Wernicke's and Broca's areas.
8.26 A special technique or strategy consciously employed in an attempt to improve memory.	**8.17** The process by which information in short-term memory is transferred to long-term memory, presumably because of physical changes that occur in neurons in the brain.
8.27 A mnemonic system in which items to be remembered are mentally associated with specific physical locations or landmarks.	**8.18** The loss of the ability to retrieve memories of one's past, particularly memories episodic or autobiographical events.
8.28 A mnemonic system in which items to be remembered are associated with a set of mental pegs that one already has in memory, such as key words of a rhyme.	**8.19** The rote repetition of information; repeating a given item over and over again.

8.29	narrative	8.38	retroactive interference
8.30	episodic memory	8.39	proactive interference
8.31	semantic memory	9.1	selective attention
8.32	explicit memory	9.2	dichotic listening
8.33	implicit memory	9.3	shadowing
8.34	anterograde amnesia	9.4	inhibition of return
8.35	hippocampus	9.5	isolation aphasia
8.36	tip-of-the-tongue experience	9.6	visual agnosia
8.37	retrieval cue	9.7	split-brain operation

8.38 Interference in recall that occurs when recently learned information disrupts our ability to remember older information.	8.29 A mnemonic system in which items to be remembered are linked together by a story.
8.39 Interference in recall that occurs when previously learned information disrupts our ability to remember newer information.	8.30 A type of long-term memory that serves as a record of our life's experiences.
9.1 The process that controls our awareness of, and readiness to respond to, particular categories of stimuli or stimuli in a particular location.	8.31 A type of long-term memory that contains data, facts, and other information, including vocabulary.
9.2 A task that requires a person to attend to one of two different messages being presented simultaneously, one to each ear, through headphones.	8.32 Memory that can be described verbally and of which a person is therefore aware.
9.3 The act of continuously repeating verbal material as soon as it is heard.	8.33 Memory that cannot be described verbally and of which a person is therefore not aware.
9.4 A reduced tendency to perceive a target when the target's presentation is consistent with a noninformative cue. Usually, inhibition of return is tested with respect to spatial location and is present when the target is presented several hundred milliseconds after the cue.	8.34 A disorder caused by brain damage that disrupts a person's ability to form new long-term memories of events that occur after the time of the brain damage.
9.5 A language disturbance that includes an inability to comprehend speech or to produce meaningful speech without affecting the ability to repeat speech and to learn new sequences of words; caused by damage that isolates the brain's speech mechanisms from other parts of the brain.	8.35 A structure in the limbic system, located deep in the temporal lobe, which plays an important role in memory.
9.6 The inability of a person who is not blind to recognize the identity of an object visually; caused by damage to the visual association cortex.	8.36 An occasional problem with retrieval of information that we are sure we know but cannot immediately remember.
9.7 A surgical procedure that severs the corpus callosum, thus abolishing the direct connections between the cortex of the two cerebral hemispheres.	8.37 A contextual variable, such as a physical object or verbal stimulus, which improves the ability to recall information from memory.

9.8	posthypnotic suggestibility	9.17	theta activity
9.9	posthypnotic amnesia	9.18	delta activity
9.10	polygraph	9.19	slow-wave sleep
9.11	electroencephalogram (EEG)	9.20	rapid eye movement (REM) sleep
9.12	electromyogram (EMG)	9.21	circadian rhythm
9.13	electrocardiogram (EKG)	9.22	basic rest-activity cycle (BRAC)
9.14	electro-oculogram (EOG)	9.23	preoptic area
9.15	beta activity	10.1	psycholinguistics
9.16	alpha activity	10.2	phoneme

9.17 EEG activity of 3.5-7.5 Hz; occurs during the transition between sleep and wakefulness.	9.8 The tendency of a person to perform a behaviour suggested by the hypnotist some time after the person has left the hypnotic state.
9.18 The rhythmical activity of the electroencephalogram; having a frequency of less than 3.5 Hz, indicating deep (slow-wave) sleep.	9.9 A failure to remember what occurred during hypnosis; induced by suggestions made during hypnosis.
9.19 Sleep other than REM sleep, characterized by regular, slow waves on the electroencephalograph.	9.10 An instrument that records changes in physiological processes such as brain activity, heart rate, and breathing.
9.20 A period of sleep during which dreaming, rapid eye movements, and muscular paralysis occur and the EEG shows beta activity.	9.11 The measurement and graphical presentation of the electrical activity of the brain, recorded by means of electrodes attached to the scalp.
9.21 A daily rhythmical change in behaviour or physiological process.	9.12 The measurement and graphical presentation of the electrical activity of muscles, recorded by means of electrodes attached to the skin above them.
9.22 A 90-minute cycle (in humans) of waxing and waning alertness controlled by a biological clock in the pons; during sleep, it controls cycles of REM sleep and slow-wave sleep.	9.13 The measurement and graphical presentation of the electrical activity of the heart, recorded by means of electrodes attached to the skin.
9.23 A region at the base of the brain just in front of the hypothalamus; contains neurons that appear to control the occurrence of slow-wave sleep.	9.14 The measurement and graphical presentation of the electrical activity caused by movements of the eye, recorded by means of electrodes attached to the skin adjacent to the eye.
10.1 The branch of psychology devoted to the study of verbal behaviour.	9.15 The irregular, high-frequency activity of the electroencephalogram, usually indicating a state of alertness or arousal.
10.2 The minimum unit of sound that conveys meaning in a particular language, such as /p/.	9.16 Rhythmical, medium-frequency activity of the electroencephalogram, usually indicating a state of quiet relaxation.

10.3	voice-onset time		10.12	script
10.4	syntactical rule		10.13	Broca's aphasia
10.5	function word		10.14	agrammatism
10.6	content word		10.15	Wernicke's area
10.7	affix		10.16	Wernicke's aphasia
10.8	semantics		10.17	pure word deafness
10.9	prosody		10.18	isolation aphasia
10.10	deep structure		10.19	eye tracker
10.11	surface structure		10.20	fixation

10.12 The characteristics (events, rules, and so on) that are typical of a particular situation; assists the comprehension of verbal discourse.	**10.3** The delay between the initial sound of a voiced consonant (such as the puffing sound of the phoneme /p/) and the onset of vibration of the vocal cords.
10.13 Severe difficulty in articulating words, especially function words, caused by damage that includes Broca's area, a region of the frontal cortex on the left (speech-dominant) side of the brain.	**10.4** A grammatical rule of a particular language for combining words to form phrases, clauses, and sentences.
10.14 A language disturbance; difficulty in the production and comprehension of grammatical features, such as proper use of function words, word endings, and word order. Often seen in cases of Broca's aphasia.	**10.5** A preposition, article, or other word that conveys little of the meaning of a sentence but is important in specifying its grammatical structure. See also *content word*.
10.15 A region of auditory association cortex located in the upper part of the left temporal lobe; involved in the recognition of spoken words.	**10.6** A noun, verb, adjective, or adverb that conveys meaning. See also *function word*.
10.16 A disorder caused by damage to the left temporal and parietal cortex, including Wernicke's area; characterized by deficits in the perception of speech and by the production of fluent but rather meaningless speech.	**10.7** A sound or group of letters that is added to the beginning of a word (prefix) or its end (suffix).
10.17 The ability to hear, to speak, and (usually) to write, without being able to comprehend the meaning of speech; caused by bilateral temporal lobe damage.	**10.8** The meanings and the study of the meanings represented by words.
10.18 A language disturbance that includes an inability to comprehend speech or to produce meaningful speech accompanied by the ability to repeat speech and to learn new sequences of words; caused by brain damage to the left temporal/parietal cortex that spans Wernicke's area.	**10.9** The use of changes in intonation and emphasis to convey meaning in speech besides that specified by the particular words; an important means of communication of emotion.
10.19 A device that measures the location of a person's gaze while he or she observes a visual display.	**10.10** The essential meaning of a sentence, without regard to the grammatical features (surface structure) of the sentence that are needed to express it in words. See also *surface structure*.
10.20 A brief interval between saccadic eye movements during which the eye does not move; visual information is gathered during this time.	**10.11** The grammatical features of a sentence. See also *deep structure*.

10.21	phonetic reading	10.30	overextension
10.22	whole-word reading	10.31	underextension
10.23	surface dyslexia	10.32	language universal
10.24	phonological dyslexia	11.1	intelligence
10.25	direct dyslexia	11.2	differential approach
10.26	semantic priming	11.3	developmental approach
10.27	protoword	11.4	information-processing approach
10.28	child-directed speech	11.5	g factor
10.29	inflection	11.6	s factor

10.30 The use of a word to denote a larger class of items than is appropriate, for example, referring to the moon as a *ball*.	**10.21** Reading by decoding the phonetic significance of letter strings; "sound reading."
10.31 The use of a word to denote a smaller class of items than is appropriate, for example, referring only to one particular animal as a *dog*.	**10.22** Reading by recognizing a word as a whole; "sight reading."
10.32 A characteristic feature found in all natural languages.	**10.23** A reading disorder in which people can read words phonetically but have difficulty reading irregularly spelled words by the whole-word method.
11.1 A person's ability to learn and remember information, to recognize concepts and their relations, and to apply the information to their own behaviour in an adaptive way.	**10.24** A reading disorder in which people can read familiar words but have difficulty reading unfamiliar words or pronounceable nonwords because they cannot sound out words.
11.2 An approach to the study of intelligence that tries to devise tests that identify and measure individual differences in people's knowledge and abilities to solve problems.	**10.25** A language disorder caused by brain damage in which people can read words aloud without understanding them.
11.3 An approach to the study of intelligence that studies the way infants and children learn to perceive, manipulate, and think about the world.	**10.26** A facilitating effect on the recognition of words having meanings related to a word that was presented previously.
11.4 An approach to the study of intelligence based on research methods that cognitive psychologists developed to study the types of skills people use to think and solve problems.	**10.27** A unique string of phonemes that an infant invents and uses as a word.
11.5 According to Spearman, a factor of intelligence that is common to all intellectual tasks; includes apprehension of experience, eduction of relations, and eduction of correlates.	**10.28** The speech of an adult directed toward a child; differs in important features from adult-directed speech and tends to facilitate learning of language by children.
11.6 According to Spearman, a factor of intelligence that is specific to a particular task.	**10.29** A change in the form of a word (usually by adding a suffix) to denote a grammatical feature such as tense or number.

11.7	factor analysis	11.16	Stanford-Binet Scale
11.8	successful intelligence	11.17	intelligence quotient (IQ)
11.9	analytic intelligence	11.18	ratio IQ
11.10	creative intelligence	11.19	deviation IQ
11.11	practical intelligence	11.20	Wechsler Adult Intelligence Scale (WAIS)
11.12	syllogism	11.21	Wechsler Intelligence Scale for Children (WISC)
11.13	Binet-Simon Scale	11.22	criterion
11.14	norm	11.23	mental retardation
11.15	mental age	11.24	heritability

11.16 An intelligence test that consists of various tasks grouped according to mental age; provides the standard measure of the intelligence quotient.	**11.7** A statistical procedure that identifies common factors among groups of tests.
11.17 A simplified single measure of general intelligence; by definition, the ratio of a person's mental age to his or her chronological age, multiplied by 100; often derived by other formulas.	**11.8** According to Sternberg, the ability to effectively analyze and manage personal strengths and weaknesses.
11.18 A formula for computing the intelligence quotient; mental age divided by chronological age, multiplied by 100.	**11.9** According to Sternberg, the mental mechanisms people use to plan and execute tasks; includes metacomponents, performance components, and knowledge acquisition components.
11.19 A procedure for computing the intelligence quotient; compares a child's score with those received by other children of the same chronological age.	**11.10** According to Sternberg, the ability to deal effectively with novel situations and to automatically solve problems that have been encountered previously.
11.20 An intelligence test for adults devised by David Wechsler; contains eleven subtests divided into the categories of verbal and performance.	**11.11** According to Sternberg, intelligence that reflects the behaviours that were subject to natural selection; adaption-fitting oneself into one's environment by developing useful skills and behaviours; selection-finding one's own niche in the environment; and shaping-changing the environment.
11.21 An intelligence test for children devised by David Wechsler; similar in form to the Wechsler Adult Intelligence Scale.	**11.12** A logical construction that contains a major premise, a minor premise, and a conclusion. The major and minor premises are assumed to be true, and the truth of the conclusion is to be evaluated by deductive reasoning.
11.22 An independent measure of a variable being assessed. For example, university grades are the criterion measure for scores on the Scholastic Aptitude Test.	**11.13** An intelligence test developed by Binet and Simon in 1905; the precursor of the Stanford-Binet Scale.
11.23 Mental development that is substantially below normal; often caused by some form of brain damage or abnormal brain development.	**11.14** Data concerning comparison groups that permit the score of an individual to be assessed relative to his or her peers.
11.24 The degree to which the variability of a particular trait in a particular population of organisms is a result of genetic differences among those organisms.	**11.15** A measure of a person's intellectual development; the level of intellectual development that could be expected for an average child of a particular age.

11.25	fetal alcohol syndrome	11.34	mental model
11.26	concept	11.35	inductive reasoning
11.27	formal concept	11.36	confirmation bias
11.28	natural concept	11.37	algorithm
11.29	exemplar	11.38	heuristics
11.30	basic-level concept	11.39	means-ends analysis
11.31	superordinate concept	12.1	prenatal period
11.32	subordinate concept	12.2	zygote stage
11.33	deductive reasoning	12.3	embryo stage

11.34 A mental construction based on physical reality that is used to solve problems of logical deduction.	11.25 A disorder that adversely affects an offspring's brain development that is caused by the mother's alcohol intake during pregnancy.
11.35 Inferring general principles or rules from specific facts.	11.26 A category of objects or situations that share some common attributes.
11.36 A tendency to seek evidence that might confirm a hypothesis rather than evidence that might disconfirm it; a logical error.	11.27 A category of objects or situations defined by listing their common essential characteristics, as dictionary definitions do.
11.37 A procedure that consists of a series of steps that will solve a specific type of problem.	11.28 A category, of objects or situations based on people's perceptions and interactions with things in the world; based on exemplars.
11.38 A general rule that guides decision making.	11.29 A memory of particular examples of objects or situations that are used as the basis of classifying objects or situations into concepts.
11.39 A general heuristic method of problem solving that involves looking for differences between the current state and the goal state and seeking ways to reduce the differences.	11.30 A concept that makes important distinctions between different categories.
12.1 The nine months between conception and birth. This period is divided into three developmental stages: the zygote, the embryo, and the fetal stages.	11.31 A concept that refers to collections of basic-level concepts.
12.2 The first stage of prenatal development, during which the zygote divides many times and the internal organs begin to form.	11.32 A concept that refers to types of items within a basic-level category.
12.3 The second stage of prenatal development beginning 2 weeks and ending about 8 weeks after conception, during which the heart begins to beat, the brain starts to function, and most of the major body structures begin to form.	11.33 Inferring specific instances from general principles or rules.

12.4	teratogens	12.13	sensorimotor period
12.5	androgens	12.14	object permanence
12.6	fetal stage	12.15	deferred imitation
12.7	maturation	12.16	preoperational period
12.8	critical period	12.17	conservation
12.9	cognitive structures	12.18	egocentrism
12.10	schemata	12.19	period of concrete operations
12.11	assimilation	12.20	period of formal operations
12.12	accommodation	12.21	mental space (M-Space)

12.13 The first period in Piaget's theory of cognitive development, from birth to 2 years. Marked by an orderly progression of increasingly complex cognitive development: reflexes, permanence, appreciation of causality, imitation, and symbolic thinking.	**12.4** Drugs or other substances that can cause birth defects.
12.14 The idea that objects do not disappear when they are out of sight.	**12.5** The primary class of sex hormones in males. The most important androgen is testosterone.
12.15 A child's ability to imitate the actions he or she has observed others perform. Piaget believed deferred imitation to result from the child's increasing ability to form mental representations of behaviour performed by others.	**12.6** The third and final stage of prenatal development, which lasts for about 7 months, beginning with the appearance of bone tissue and ending with birth.
12.16 The second of Piaget's periods, which represents a 4- to 5-year transitional period between first being able to think symbolically and then being able to think logically. During this stage, children become increasingly capable of speaking meaningful sentences.	**12.7** Any relatively stable change in thought, behaviour, or physical growth that is due to the aging process and not to experience.
12.17 Understanding that specific properties of objects (height, weight, volume, length) remain the same despite apparent changes in the shape or arrangement of those objects.	**12.8** A specific time in development during which certain experiences must occur for normal development to occur.
12.18 Self-centeredness; preoperational children can see the world only from their own perspective.	**12.9** According to Piaget, mental representations or rules, such as schemata or concepts, that are used for understanding and dealing with the world and for thinking about and solving problems.
12.19 The third period in Piaget's theory of cognitive development, during which children come to understand the conservation principle and other concepts, such as categorization.	**12.10** Mental representations or sets of rules that define a particular category of behaviour. Schemata include rules that help us to understand current and future experiences.
12.20 The fourth period in Piaget's theory of cognitive development, during which individuals first become capable of more formal kinds of abstract thinking and hypothetical reasoning.	**12.11** The process by which new information about the world is modified to fit existing schemata.
12.21 A hypothetical construct in Case's model of cognitive development similar to working memory, whose primary function is to process information from the external world.	**12.12** The process by which existing schemata are modified or changed by new experiences.

12.22	attachment	12.31	gender role
12.23	stranger anxiety	12.32	gender stereotypes
12.24	separation anxiety	12.33	moral realism
12.25	Strange Situation	12.34	morality of cooperation
12.26	secure attachment	12.35	preconventional level
12.27	resistant attachment	12.36	conventional level
12.28	avoidant attachment	12.37	postconventional level
12.29	disoriented attachment	12.38	puberty
12.30	gender identity	12.39	Alzheimer's disease

12.31 Cultural expectations about the ways in which men and women should think and behave.	12.22 A social and emotional bond between infant and caregiver that spans both time and space.
12.32 Beliefs about differences in the behaviours, abilities, and personality traits of males and females.	12.23 The wariness and fearful responses, such as crying and clinging to their caregivers, that infants exhibit in the presence of strangers.
12.33 The first stage of Piaget's model of moral development, which includes egocentrism and blind adherence to rules.	12.24 A set of fearful responses, such as crying, arousal, and clinging to the caregiver, that infants exhibit when the caregiver attempts to leave the infant.
12.34 The second stage of Piaget's model of moral development, which involves the recognition of rules as social conventions.	12.25 A test of attachment in which an infant is exposed to different stimuli that may be distressful.
12.35 Kohlberg's first level of moral development, which bases moral behaviour on external sanctions, such as authority and punishment.	12.26 A kind of attachment in which infants use their mothers as a base for exploring a new environment. They will venture out from their mothers to explore a Strange Situation but return periodically.
12.36 Kohlberg's second level of moral development, in which people realize that society has instituted moral rules to maintain order and to serve the best interests of its citizenry.	12.27 A kind of attachment in which infants show mixed reactions to their mothers. They may approach their mothers upon their return but, at the same time, continue to cry or even push their mothers away.
12.37 Kohlberg's third and final level of moral development, in which people come to understand that moral rules include principles that apply across all situations and societies.	12.28 A kind of attachment in which infants avoid or ignore their mothers and often do not cuddle when held.
12.38 The period during which the reproductive systems mature, marking the beginning of the transition from childhood to adulthood.	12.29 A kind of attachment in which infants behave in a confused and contradictory ways toward their mother.
12.39 A fatal degenerative disease in which neurons of the brain progressively die, causing loss of memory and other cognitive processes.	12.30 One's private sense of being male or female.

13.1	motivation	13.10	drive
13.2	regulatory behaviour	13.11	optimum-level hypothesis
13.3	homeostasis	13.12	perseverance
13.4	system variable	13.13	overjustification hypothesis
13.5	set point	13.14	learned helplessness
13.6	detector	13.15	glycogen
13.7	correctional mechanism	13.16	glucostatic hypothesis
13.8	negative feedback	13.17	anorexia nervosa
13.9	drive reduction hypothesis	13.18	bulimia nervosa

13.10 A condition, often caused by physiological changes or homeostatic disequilibrium, that energizes an organism's behaviour.	**13.1** A general term for a group of phenomena that affect the nature, strength, or persistence of an individual's behaviour.
13.11 The hypothesis that organisms will perform behaviour that restores the level of arousal to an optimum level.	**13.2** A behaviour that tends to bring physiological conditions back to normal, thus restoring the condition of homeostasis.
13.12 The tendency to continue to perform a behaviour even when it is not being reinforced.	**13.3** The process by which important physiological characteristics (such as body temperature and blood pressure) are regulated so that they remain at their optimum level.
13.13 The superfluous application of entrinsic rewards to intrinsically motivated behaviour will undermine intrinsic motivation.	**13.4** The variable controlled by a regulatory mechanism; for example, temperature in a heating system.
13.14 A response to exposure to an inescapable aversive stimulus, characterized by reduced ability to learn a solvable avoidance task; thought to play a role in the development of some psychological disturbances.	**13.5** The optimum value of the system variable in a regulatory mechanism. The set point for human body temperature, recorded orally, is approximately 98.6°F.
13.15 An insoluble carbohydrate that can be synthesized from glucose or converted to it; used to store nutrients.	**13.6** In a regulatory process, a mechanism that signals when the system variable deviates from its set point.
13.16 The hypothesis that hunger is caused by a low level or availability of glucose, a condition that is monitored by specialized sensory neurons.	**13.7** In a regulatory process, the mechanism that is capable of restoring the system variable to the set point.
13.17 An eating disorder characterized by attempts to lose weight, sometimes to the point of starvation.	**13.8** A process whereby the effect produced by an action serves to diminish or terminate that action. Regulatory systems are characterized by negative feedback loops.
13.18 A loss of control over food intake characterized by gorging binges followed by self-induced vomiting or use of laxatives; also accompanied by feelings of guilt and depression.	**13.9** The hypothesis that a drive (resulting from physiological need or deprivation) produces an unpleasant state that causes an organism to engage in motivated behaviours. Reduction of drive is assumed to be reinforcing.

13.19	organizational effect	13.28	masking
13.20	activational effect	13.29	modulation
13.21	estrous cycle	13.30	simulation
13.22	intraspecific aggression	13.31	display rule
13.23	threat gesture	13.32	leakage
13.24	appeasement gesture	13.33	James-Lange theory
13.25	emotion	14.1	personality
13.26	conditioned emotional response	14.2	personality types
13.27	orbitofrontal cortex	14.3	personality trait

13.28 Attempting to hide the expression of an emotion.	13.19 An effect of a hormone that usually occurs during prenatal development and produces permanent changes that alter the subsequent development of the organism. An example is androgenization.
13.29 An attempt to exaggerate or minimize the expression of an emotion.	13.20 The effect of a hormone on a physiological system that has already developed. If the effect involves the brain, it can influence behaviour. An example is facilitation of sexual arousal and performance.
13.30 An attempt to express an emotion that one does not actually feel.	13.21 The ovulatory cycle in mammals other than primates; the sequence of physical and hormonal changes that accompany the ripening and disintegration of ova.
13.31 A culturally determined rule that prescribes the expression of emotions in particular situations.	13.22 The attack by one animal upon another member of its species.
13.32 A sign of expression of an emotion that is being masked.	13.23 A stereotyped gesture that signifies that one animal is likely to attack another member of the species.
13.33 A theory of emotion that suggests that behaviours and physiological responses are directly elicited by situations and that feelings of emotions are produced by feedback from these behaviours and responses.	13.24 A stereotyped gesture made by a submissive animal in response to a threat gesture by a dominant animal; tends to inhibit an attack.
14.1 A particular pattern of behaviour and thinking prevailing across time and situations that differentiates one person from another.	13.25 A relatively brief display of a feeling made in response to environmental events having motivational significance or to memories of such events.
14.2 Different categories into which personality characteristics can be assigned based on factors such as developmental experiences or physical characteristics.	13.26 A classically conditioned response produced by a stimulus that evokes an emotional response—in most cases, including behavioural and physiological components.
14.3 An enduring personal characteristic that reveals itself in a particular pattern of behaviour in a variety of situations.	13.27 A region of the prefrontal cortex that plays an important role in translating judgments about events into appropriate actions and emotional responses.

14.4	extroversion	14.13	expectancy
14.5	introversion	14.14	observational learning
14.6	neuroticism	14.15	reciprocal determinism
14.7	emotional stability	14.16	self-efficacy
14.8	psychoticism	14.17	person variables
14.9	self-control	14.18	locus of control
14.10	five-factor model	14.19	psychodynamic
14.11	Neuroticism, Extraversion, and Openness	14.20	unconscious
14.12	social learning theory	14.21	id

14.13 The belief that a certain consequence will follow a certain action.	14.4 The tendency to seek the company of other people, to be lively, and to engage in conversation and other social behaviours with them.
14.14 Learning through observing the kinds of consequences others (called *models*) experience as a result of their behaviour.	14.5 The tendency to avoid the company of other people, especially large groups of people; shyness.
14.15 The idea that behaviour, environment, and person variables, such as perception, interact to determine personality.	14.6 The tendency to be anxious, worried, and full of guilt.
14.16 The expectation of success; the belief in one's own competencies.	14.7 The tendency to be relaxed and at peace with oneself.
14.17 Individual differences in cognition, which, according to Mischel, include competencies, encoding strategies and personal constructs, expectancies, subjective values, and self-regulatory systems and plans.	14.8 The tendency to be aggressive, egocentric, and antisocial.
14.18 An individual's beliefs that the consequences of his or her actions are controlled by internal person variables or by external environmental variables.	14.9 The tendency to be kind, considerate, and obedient of laws and rules.
14.19 A term used to describe the Freudian notion that the mind is in a state of conflict among instincts, reasons, and conscience.	14.10 A theory stating that personality is composed of five primary dimensions: neuroticism, extraversion, openness, agreeableness, and conscientiousness. This theory was developed using factor analyses of ratings of the words people use to describe personality characteristics.
14.20 The inaccessible part of the mind.	14.11 The instrument used to measure the elements described in the five-factor model (neuroticism, extraversion, openness, agreeableness, and conscientiousness).
14.21 The unconscious reservoir of libido; the psychic energy that fuels instincts and psychic processes.	14.12 The idea that both consequences of behaviour and the individual's beliefs about those consequences determine personality.

14.22	libido		14.31	free association
14.23	pleasure principle		14.32	defence mechanisms
14.24	ego		14.33	repression
14.25	reality principle		14.34	reaction formation
14.26	superego		14.35	projection
14.27	conscience		14.36	sublimation
14.28	ego-ideal		14.37	rationalization
14.29	manifest content		14.38	conversion
14.30	latent content		14.39	fixation

14.31 A method of Freudian analysis in which an individual is asked to relax, clear his or her mind of current thoughts, and then report all thoughts, images, perceptions, and feelings that come to mind.	14.22 An insistent, instinctual force that is unresponsive to the demands of reality; the primary source of motivation.
14.32 Mental systems that become active whenever unconscious instinctual drives of the id come into conflict with internalized prohibitions of the superego.	14.23 The rule that the id obeys: Obtain immediate gratification, whatever form it may take.
14.33 The mental force responsible for actively keeping memories, most of which are potentially threatening or anxiety-provoking, from being consciously discovered.	14.24 The self. The ego also serves as the general manager of personality, making decisions regarding the pleasures that will be pursued at the id's request and the moral dictates of the superego that will be followed.
14.34 A defence mechanism that involves behaving in a way that is the opposite of how one really feels because the true feelings produce anxiety.	14.25 The tendency to satisfy, the id's demands realistically, which almost always involves compromising the demands of the id and superego.
14.35 A defence mechanism in which one's unacceptable behaviours or thoughts are attributed to someone else.	14.26 The repository of an individual's moral values, divided into the conscience—the internalization of a society's rules and regulations—and the ego-ideal the internalization of one's goals.
14.36 A defence mechanism that involves redirecting pleasure-seeking or aggressive instincts toward socially acceptable goals.	14.27 The internalization of the rules and restrictions of society; it determines which behaviours are permissible and punishes wrongdoing with feelings of guilt.
14.37 A defence mechanism that justifies an unacceptable action with a more acceptable, but false, excuse.	14.28 The internalization of what a person would like to be—his or her goals and ambitions.
14.38 A defence mechanism that involves converting an intrapsychic conflict into a physical form, such as blindness, deafness, paralysis, or numbness.	14.29 The apparent story line of a dream.
14.39 An unconscious obsession with an erogenous zone resulting from failure to resolve the crisis associated with the corresponding stage of psychosexual development.	14.30 The hidden message of a dream, produced by the unconscious.

14.40	oral stage	14.49	humanistic approach
14.41	anal stage	14.50	self-actualization
14.42	phallic stage	14.51	conditions of worth
14.43	latency period	14.52	unconditional positive regard
14.44	genital stage	14.53	objective personality test
14.45	collective unconscious	14.54	Minnesota Multiphasic Personality
14.46	archetypes	14.55	projective test
14.47	striving for superiority	14.56	Rorschach Inkblot Test
14.48	basic orientations	14.57	Thematic Apperception Test (TAT)

14.49 An approach to the study of personality in which the emphasis is placed on the positive, fulfilling aspects of life.	**14.40** The first of Freud's psychosexual stage, during which the mouth is the major erogenous zone—the major source of physical pleasure. Early in this stage, the mouth is used for sucking; later in the stage it is used for biting and chewing.
14.50 The realization of one's true intellectual and emotional potential.	**14.41** The second of Freud's psychosexual stages, during which the primary, erogenous zone is the anal region. During this time, children take pleasure in retaining or expelling feces.
14.51 Conditions that others place on us for receiving their positive regard.	**14.42** The third of Freud's psychosexual stage, during which the primary erogenous zone is the genital area. During this time, children become attached to the opposite-sex parent.
14.52 Unconditional love and acceptance of an individual by another person.	**14.43** The period between the phallic stage and the genital stage during which there are no unconscious sexual urges or intrapsychic conflicts.
14.53 A test for measuring personality that can be scored objectively, such as a multiple-choice or true/false test.	**14.44** The final of Freud's psychosexual stages, during which the adolescent develops adult sexual desires.
14.54 An objective test originally designed to distinguish individuals with different psychological problems from normal individuals. It has since become popular as a means of attempting to identify personality characteristics of people in many everyday settings.	**14.45** According to Jung, the part of the unconscious that contains memories and ideas inherited from our ancestors over the course of evolution.
14.55 An unstructured personality measure in which a person is shown a series of ambiguous stimuli, such as pictures, inkblots, or incomplete drawings. The person is asked to describe what he or she "sees" in each stimulus or to create stories that reflect the theme of the drawing or picture.	**14.46** Universal thought forms and patterns that Jung believed resided in the collective unconscious.
14.56 A projective test in which a person is shown a series of sym-metrical inkblots and asked to describe what he or she thinks they represent.	**14.47** The motivation to seek superiority. Adler argued that striving for superiority is born from our need to compensate for our inferiorities.
14.57 A projective test in which a person is shown a series of ambiguous pictures that involve people. The person is asked to make up a story about what the people are doing or thinking. The person's responses are believed to reflect aspects of his or her personality.	**14.48** Horney's sets of personality characteristics that correspond to the strategies of moving toward others, moving against others, and moving away from others.

15.1	social psychology	15.10	attribution
15.2	social cognition	15.11	external factors
15.3	impression formation	15.12	internal factors
15.4	schema	15.13	consensual behaviour
15.5	central traits	5.14	distinctiveness
15.6	primary effect	15.14	consistency
15.7	self-concept	15.16	fundamental attribution error
15.8	self	15.17	belief in a just world
15.9	self-schema	15.18	actor-observer effect

15.10 The process by which people infer the causes of other people's behaviour.	**15.1** The branch of psychology that studies our social nature—how the actual, imagined, or implied presence of others influences our thoughts, feelings, and behaviours.
15.11 People, events, and other stimuli in an individual's environment that can affect his or her thoughts, feelings, attitudes, and behaviours.	**15.2** The processes involved in perceiving, interpreting, and acting on social information.
15.12 An individual's traits, needs, and intentions, which can affect his or her thoughts, feelings, attitudes, and behaviours.	**15.3** The way in which we form impressions of others and attribute specific characteristics and traits to them.
15.13 Behaviour that is shared by many people; behaviour that is similar from one person to the next. To the extent that people engage in the same behaviour, their behaviour is consensual.	**15.4** A mental framework or body of knowledge that organizes and synthesizes information about a person, place, or thing.
15.14 The extent to which a person engages in a particular behaviour in one situation but not in others.	**15.5** Personality attributes that seem to be the most typical of a particular individual.
15.15 The extent to which a person's behaviour is consistent across time.	**15.6** The tendency to form impressions of people based on the first information received about them.
15.16 The tendency to overestimate the significance of dispositional factors and underestimate the significance of situational factors in explaining other people's behaviour.	**15.7** Self-identity. One's knowledge, feelings, and ideas about oneself.
15.17 The belief that people get what they deserve in life; a fundamental attribution error.	**15.8** A person's distinct individuality.
15.18 The tendency to attribute one's own behaviour to situational factors but others' behaviour to dispositional factors.	**15.9** A mental framework that represents and synthesizes information about oneself; a cognitive structure that organizes the knowledge, feelings, and ideas that constitute the self-concept.

15.19	self-serving bias	15.28	compliance
15.20	false consensus	15.29	self-perception theory
15.21	representativeness heuristic	15.30	prejudice
15.22	base-rate fallacy	15.31	stereotype
15.23	availability heuristic	15.32	discrimination
15.24	attitude	15.33	illusory correlation
15.25	mere exposure effect	15.34	illusion of out-group homogeneity
15.26	elaboration likelihood model	15.35	stereotype self-fulfilling prophecy
15.27	cognitive dissonance theory	15.36	group

15.28 Engaging in a particular behaviour at another person's request.	**15.19** The tendency to attribute our accomplishments and successes to internal causes and our failures and mistakes to external causes.
15.29 The theory that we come to understand our attitudes and emotions by observing our own behaviour and the circumstances under which it occurs.	**15.20** The tendency of a person to perceive his or her own response as representative of a general consensus.
15.30 An attitude or evaluation, usually negative, toward a group of people defined by their racial, ethnic, or religious heritage or by their gender, occupation, sexual orientation, level of education, place of residence, or membership in a particular group.	**15.21** A general rule for decision making through which people classify a person, place, or thing into the category to which it appears to be the most similar.
15.31 An overgeneralized and false belief about the characteristics of members of a particular group.	**15.22** The failure to consider the likelihood that a person, place, or thing is a member of a particular category.
15.32 The differential treatment of people based on their membership in a particular group.	**15.23** A general rule for decision making through which a person judges the likelihood or importance of an event by the ease with which examples of that event come to mind.
15.33 An apparent correlation between two distinctive elements that does not actually exist.	**15.24** An evaluation of persons, places, and things.
15.34 A belief that members of groups to which one does not belong are very similar to one another.	**15.25** The formation of a positive attitude toward a person, place, or thing based solely on repeated exposure to that person, place, or thing.
15.35 A stereotype-based expectancy that causes a person to act in a manner consistent with the stereotype.	**15.26** A model that explains the effectiveness of persuasion. The *central route* requires a person to think critically about an argument and the *peripheral route* entails the association of the argument with a positive stimulus.
15.36 A collection of individuals who generally have common interests and goals.	**15.27** The theory that changes in attitudes can be motivated by an unpleasant state of tension caused by a disparity between a person's beliefs or attitudes and behaviour, especially beliefs or attitudes that are related to the person's self-esteem.

15.37	social norms		15.46	liking
15.38	conformity		15.47	loving
15.39	bystander intervention		15.48	passionate love/romantic love
15.40	diffusion of responsibility		15.49	companionate love
15.41	social facilitation		16.1	cultural evolution
15.42	social loafing		16.2	life-style
15.43	group polarization		16.3	coronary heart disease (CHD)
15.44	groupthink		16.4	cancer
15.45	interpersonal attraction		16.5	serum cholesterol

15.46 A feeling of personal regard, intimacy, and esteem toward another person.	15.37 Informal rules defining the expected and appropriate behaviour in specific situations.
15.47 A combination of liking and a deep sense of attachment to, intimacy with, and caring for another person.	15.38 The adoption of attitudes and behaviours shared by a particular group of people.
15.48 An emotional, intense desire for sexual union with another person.	15.39 The intervention of a person in a situation that appears to require his or her aid.
15.49 Love that is characterized by a deep, enduring affection and caring for another person, accompanied by a strong desire to maintain the relationship.	15.40 An explanation of the failure of bystander intervention stating that when several bystanders are present, *no one* person assumes responsibility for helping.
16.1 The adaptive change of a culture to recurrent environmental pressures.	15.41 The enhancement of task performance caused by the mere presence of others.
16.2 The aggregate behaviour of a person; the way a person leads his or her life.	15.42 The decreased effort put forth by individuals when performing a task with other people.
16.3 The narrowing of blood vessels that supply nutrients to the heart.	15.43 The tendency for the initial decision of a group to become exaggerated during the discussion preceding a decision.
16.4 A malignant, uncontrolled growth of cells that destroys surrounding tissue.	15.44 The tendency to avoid dissent in the attempt to achieve group consensus in the course of decision making.
16.5 A fatlike chemical found in the blood. One form (LDL) promotes the formation of atherosclerotic plaques. Another form (HDL) may protect against coronary heart disease.	15.45 People's tendency to approach each other and to evaluate each other positively.

16.6	aerobic exercises	16.15	cognitive appraisal
16.7	alcoholism	16.16	type A pattern
16.8	self-control	16.17	type B pattern
16.9	health psychology	16.18	posttraumatic stress disorder
16.10	stress	16.19	psychoneuroimmunology
16.11	stressors	16.20	immune system
16.12	general adaptation syndrome (GAS)	16.21	antigen
16.13	fight-or-flight response	16.22	antibodies
16.14	glucocorticoid	16.23	B lymphocytes

16.15 One's perception of a stressful situation.	16.6 Physical activity that expends considerable energy, increases blood flow and respiration and thereby stimulates and strengthens the heart and lungs and increase the body's efficient use of oxygen.
16.16 A behaviour pattern characterized by high levels of competitiveness and hostility, impatience, and an intense disposition; supposedly associated with an increased risk of CHD.	16.7 An addiction to ethanol, which is the psychoactive agent in alcohol.
16.17 A behaviour pattern characterized by lower levels of competitiveness and hostility, patience, and an easygoing disposition; supposedly associated with a decreased risk of CHD.	16.8 Behaviour that produces the larger, longer-term reward when people are faced with the choice between it and the smaller, short-term reward.
16.18 An anxiety disorder in which the individual has feelings of social withdrawal accompanied by untypically low levels of emotion caused by prolonged exposure to a stressor, such as a catastrophe.	16.9 The branch of psychology involved in the promotion and maintenance of sound health practices.
16.19 Study of the interactions between the immune system and behaviour as mediated by the nervous system.	16.10 A pattern of physiological, behavioural, and cognitive responses to stimuli that are perceived as endangering one's well-being.
16.20 A network of organs and cells that protects the body from invading bacteria, viruses, and other foreign substances.	16.11 Stimuli that are perceived as endangering one's well-being.
16.21 The unique proteins found on the surface of bacteria; these proteins are what enable the immune system to recognize the bacteria as foreign substances.	16.12 The model proposed by Selye to describe the body's adaptation to chronic exposure to severe stressors. The body passes through an orderly sequence of three physiological stages: alarm, resistance, and exhaustion.
16.22 Proteins in the immune system that recognize antigens and help kill invading microorganisms.	16.13 Physiological reactions that help ready us to fight or to flee a dangerous situation.
16.23 Cells that develop in bone marrow and release immunoglobulins to defend the body against antigens.	16.14 A chemical, such as cortisol, that influences the metabolism of glucose, the main energy source of the body.

16.24	immunoglobulins	16.33	stress inoculation training
16.25	T lymphocytes	17.1	diathesis-stress model
16.26	autoimmune diseases	17.2	Diagnostic and Statistical Manual IV
16.27	type C personality	17.3	clinical judgments
16.28	coping strategy	17.4	actuarial judgments
16.29	problem-focused coping	17.5	anxiety
16.30	emotion-focused coping	17.6	panic
16.31	cognitive reappraisal	17.7	panic disorder
16.32	progressive relaxation technique	17.8	anticipatory anxiety

16.33 The stress management program developed by Meichenbaum for teaching people to develop coping skills that increase their resistance to the negative effects of stress.	**16.24** The antibodies that are released by B lymphocytes.
17.1 A causal account of mental disorders based on the idea that mental disorders develop when a person possesses a predisposition for a disorder, acquired through genetics and early learning experiences, and faces stressors that exceed his or her abilities to cope with them.	**16.25** Cells that develop in the thymus gland that produce antibodies, which defend the body against fungi, viruses, and multicellular parasites.
17.2 A widely used manual for classifying psychological disorders.	**16.26** Diseases such as rheumatoid arthritis, diabetes, lupus, and multiple sclerosis, in which the immune system attacks and destroys some of the body's own tissue.
17.3 Diagnoses of mental disorders or predictions of future behaviour based largely on experts' experience and knowledge.	**16.27** A behaviour pattern characterized by cooperativeness, unassertiveness, patience, suppression of negative emotions, and acceptance of external authority; supposedly associated with an increased likelihood of cancer.
17.4 Diagnoses of mental disorders or predictions of future behaviour based on numerical formulas derived from analyses of prior outcomes.	**16.28** A plan of action that a person follows to reduce the perceived level of stress, either in anticipation of a stressor or in response to its occurrence.
17.5 A sense of apprehension or doom that is accompanied by many physiological reactions, such as accelerated heart rate, sweaty palms, and tightness in the stomach.	**16.29** Any coping behaviour that is directed at reducing or eliminating a stressor.
17.6 A feeling of fear mixed with hopelessness or helplessness.	**16.30** Any coping behaviour that is directed toward changing one's own emotional reaction to a stressor.
17.7 Unpredictable attacks of acute anxiety that are accompanied by high levels of physiological arousal and that last from a few seconds to a few hours.	**16.31** Any coping strategy in which one alters one's perception of the threat posed by a stressor to reduce stress.
17.8 A fear of having a panic attack; may lead to the development of agoraphobia.	**16.32** A relaxation technique involving three steps: (1) recognizing the body's signals that indicate the presence of stress; (2) using those signals as a cue to begin relaxing; and (3) relaxing groups of muscles, beginning with those in the head and neck and then those in the arms and legs.

17.9	phobic disorder	17.18	somatization disorder
17.10	agoraphobia	17.19	hypochondriasis
17.11	social phobia	17.20	conversion disorder
17.12	specific phobia	17.21	dissociative disorders
17.13	obsessive-compulsive disorder	17.22	dissociative amnesia
17.14	obsession	17.23	dissociative fugue
17.15	compulsion	17.24	dissociative identity disorder
17.16	Tourette's syndrome	17.25	culture-bound syndromes
17.17	somatoform disorder	17.26	antisocial personality disorder

17.18 A class of somatoform disorder, occurring mostly among women, that involves complaints of wide-ranging physical ailments for which there is no apparent biological cause.	**17.9** An unrealistic, excessive fear of a specific class of stimuli that interferes with normal activities. The object of the anxiety is readily identifiable: It may be a snake, an insect, the out-of-doors, or closed spaces.
17.19 A somatoform disorder involving persistent and excessive worry about developing a serious illness. People with this disorder often misinterpret the appearance of normal physical aches and pains.	**17.10** A mental disorder characterized by fear of and avoidance of being alone in public places; this disorder is often accompanied by panic attacks.
17.20 A somatoform disorder involving the actual loss of bodily function, such as blindness, paralysis, and numbness, due to excessive anxiety.	**17.11** A mental disorder characterized by an excessive and irrational fear of situations in which the person is observed by others.
17.21 A class of disorders in which anxiety is reduced by a sudden disruption in consciousness, which in turn produces changes in one's sense of identity.	**17.12** An excessive and irrational fear of specific things, such as snakes, darkness, or heights.
17.22 A dissociative disorder characterized by the inability to remember important events or personal information.	**17.13** Recurrent, unwanted thoughts or ideas and compelling urges to engage in repetitive ritual-like behaviour.
17.23 Amnesia with no apparent organic cause accompanied by adoption of a new identity and relocation.	**17.14** An involuntary recurring thought, idea, or image.
17.24 A rarely seen dissociative disorder in which two or more distinct personalities exist within the same person; each personality dominates in turn.	**17.15** An irresistible impulse to repeat some action over and over even though it serves no useful purpose.
17.25 Highly unusual mental disorders, similar in nature to non-psychotic mental disorders, that appear to be specific to only one or a few cultures.	**17.16** A neurological disorder characterized by tics and involuntary utterances, some of which may involve obscenities and the repetition of others' utterances.
17.26 A disorder characterized by a failure to conform to of decency; repeated lying and stealing; a failure to sustain lasting, loving relationships; low tolerance of boredom; and a complete lack of guilt.	**17.17** A mental disorder involving a bodily or physical problem for which there is no physiological basis.

17.27	psychoactive substance use disorders	17.36	undifferentiated schizophrenia
17.28	schizophrenia	17.37	catatonic schizophrenia
17.29	positive symptoms	17.38	paranoid schizophrenia
17.30	thought disorder	17.39	disorganized schizophrenia
17.31	delusions of persecution	17.40	reactive schizophrenia
17.32	delusions of grandeur	17.41	process schizophrenia
17.33	delusions of control	17.42	dopamine hypothesis
17.34	hallucinations	17.43	double-bind
17.35	negative symptoms	17.44	expressed emotion

17.36 A type of schizophrenia characterized by fragments of the symptoms of different types of schizophrenia.	17.27 Disorders are characterized by addiction to drugs or by abuse of drugs.
17.37 A form of schizophrenia characterized primarily by various motor disturbances, including catatonic postures and waxy flexibility.	17.28 A serious mental disorder characterized by thought disturbances, hallucinations, anxiety, emotional withdrawal, and delusions.
17.38 A form of schizophrenia in which the person suffers from delusions of persecution, grandeur, or control.	17.29 Symptoms of schizophrenia that may include thought disorder, hallucinations, or delusions.
17.39 A type of schizophrenia characterized primarily by disturbances of thought and a flattened or silly affect.	17.30 A pattern of disorganized, illogical, and irrational thought that often accompanies schizophrenia.
17.40 According to Bleuler, a form of schizophrenia characterized by rapid onset and brief duration; he assumed the cause was stressful life situations.	17.31 The false belief that other people are plotting against one; symptom of schizophrenia.
17.41 According to Bleuler, a form of schizophrenia characterized by a gradual onset and a poor prognosis.	17.32 The false belief that one is famous, powerful, or important.
17.42 The hypothesis that the positive symptoms of schizophrenia are caused by overactivity of synapses in the brain that use dopamine.	17.33 The false belief that one's thoughts and actions are being controlled by other people or forces.
17.43 The conflict caused for a child when he or she is given inconsistent messages or cues from a parent.	17.34 Perceptual experiences that occur in the absence of external stimulation of the corresponding sensory organ.
17.44 Expressions of criticism, hostility, and emotional overinvolvement by family members toward a person with schizophrenia.	17.35 Symptoms of schizophrenia that may include the absence of normal behaviour, flattened emotion, poverty of speech, lack of initiative and persistence, and social withdrawal.

17.45	mood disorder	18.4	free association
17.46	bipolar disorder	18.5	resistance
17.47	major depression	18.6	transference
17.48	mania	18.7	countertransference
17.49	zeitgeber	18.8	humanistic therapy
17.50	seasonal affective disorder	18.9	client-centred therapy
18.1	trephining	18.10	incongruence
18.2	eclectic approach	18.11	unconditional positive regard
18.3	psychoanalysis	18.12	Gestalt therapy

18.4 A psychoanalytic procedure in which the client is encouraged to speak freely, without censoring possibly embarrassing or socially unacceptable thoughts or ideas.	17.45 A disorder characterized by significant shifts or disturbances in mood that affect normal perception, thought, and behaviour. Mood disorders may be characterized by deep, foreboding depression, or a combination of the depression and euphoria.
18.5 A development during therapy in which the client becomes defensive, unconsciously attempting to halt further insight by censoring his or her true feelings.	17.46 Alternating states of depression and mania separated by periods of relatively norma affect.
18.6 The process by which a client begins to project powerful attitudes and emotions onto the therapist.	17.47 Persistent and severe feelings of sadness and worthlessness accompanied by changes in appetite, sleeping, and behaviour.
18.7 The process by which the therapist projects his or her emotions onto the client.	17.48 Excessive emotional arousal and wild, exuberant, unrealistic activity.
18.8 A form of therapy focusing on the person's unique potential for personal growth and self-actualization.	17.49 Any stimulus, such as light, that synchronizes daily biological rhythms.
18.9 A form of therapy in which the client is allowed to decide what to talk about without strong direction and judgment from the therapist.	17.50 A mood disorder characterized by depression, lethargy, sleep disturbances, and craving for carbohydrates. This disorder generally occurs during the winter, when the amount of daylight, relative to the other seasons, is low. This disorder can be treated with exposure to bright lights.
18.10 A discrepancy between a client's real and ideal selves.	18.1 A surgical procedure in which a hole is made in the skull of a living person
18.11 According to Rogers, the therapeutic expression that a client's worth as a human being is not dependent on anything that he or she does, says, feels, or thinks.	18.2 A form of therapy in which the therapist uses whatever method he or she feels will work best for a particular client at a particular time.
18.12 A form of therapy emphasizing the unity of mind and body by teaching the client to "get in touch" with unconscious bodily sensations and emotional feelings.	18.3 A form of therapy aimed at providing the client insight into his or her unconscious motivations and impulses.

18.13	systematic desensitization	18.22	group psychotherapy
18.14	implosion therapy	18.23	structural family therapy
18.15	aversion therapy	18.24	community psychology
18.16	behaviour modification	18.25	deinstitutionalization
18.17	token economy	18.26	preventive psychology
18.18	covert sensitization	18.27	indigenous healing
18.19	cognitive-behaviour theory	18.28	meta-analysis
18.20	cognitive restructuring	18.29	pharmacotherapy
18.21	rational-emotive therapy	18.30	antipsychotic drugs

18.22 Therapy in which two or more clients meet simultaneously with a therapist, discussing problems within a supportive and understanding environment.	18.13 A method of treatment in which the client is trained to relax in the presence of increasingly fearful stimuli.
18.23 A form of family therapy in which the maladaptive relationships among family members is inferred from their behaviour and attempts are made to restructure these behaviours into more adaptive ones.	18.14 A form of therapy that attempts to rid people of fears by arousing them intensely until their responses diminish through habituation and learn that nothing bad happens.
18.24 A form of treatment and education whose goal is to address psychological problems through an assessment of the sociocultural context in which they develop.	18.15 A form of treatment in which the client is trained to respond negatively to a neutral stimulus that has been paired with an aversive stimulus.
18.25 The process of returning previously hospitalized patients to their communities for treatment of psychological problems and mental disorders.	18.16 Behaviour therapy based on the principles of operant conditioning.
18.26 Any attempt to forestall the development of psychological problems by altering the sociocultural variables predictive of psychological distress.	18.17 A program often used in institutions in which a person's adaptive behaviour is reinforced with tokens that are exchangeable for desirable goods or special privileges.
18.27 Non-Western, culture-bound approaches to the treatment of psychological and medical problems.	18.18 A method used by behaviour therapists in which a client imagines the aversive consequences of his or her inappropriate behaviour.
18.28 A statistical procedure by which the results of many studies are combined to estimate the magnitude of a particular effect.	18.19 A treatment method that focuses on altering the client's thoughts, beliefs, and perceptions.
18.29 The treatment of psychological problems with chemical agents.	18.20 The process of replacing the client's maladaptive thoughts with more constructive ways of thinking.
18.30 Drugs used to treat psychotic disorders such as schizophrenia.	18.21 Therapy based on the belief that psychological problems are caused not by upsetting events but by how people think about them.

18.31	tardive dyskinesia	18.35	electroconvulsive therapy (ECT)
18.32	antidepressant drugs	18.36	psychosurgery
18.33	antimanic drugs	18.37	cingulotomy
18.34	antianxiety drugs		

18.35 Treatment of severe depression that involves passing small amounts of electric current through the brain to produce seizure activity.	18.31 A serious movement disorder that can occur when a person has been treated with antipsychotic drugs for an extended period.
18.36 Surgical destruction of brain tissue in the absence of any evidence of disease or damage in an attempt to treat mental disturbances.	18.32 Drugs used to treat depression.
18.37 Surgical destruction of the cingulum bundle, which connects the prefrontal cortex with the limbic system; helps to reduce intense anxiety, and the symptoms of obsessive-compulsive disorder.	18.33 Drugs used to treat bipolar disorder and mania.
	18.34 Drugs used to treat anxiety-related disorders.

NOTES

NOTES

NOTES

NOTES

NOTES

NOTES